The New Work of Educational Leaders

The New Work
of
Educational Leaders

Changing Leadership Practice
in an Era of School Reform

Peter Gronn

P·C·P

Paul Chapman
Publishing

First published 2003

Paul Chapman Publishing
A SAGE Publications Company
6 Bonhill Street
London EC2A 4PU

SAGE Publications Inc
2455 Teller Road
Thousand Oaks, California 91320

SAGE Publications India Pvt Ltd
32, M-Block Market
Greater Kailash - I
New Delhi 110 048

Library of Congress Control Number: 2002106579

A catalogue record for this book is available from the British Library

ISBN 0 7619 4748 5
ISBN 0 7619 4749 3 (pbk)

Typeset by C&M Digitals (P) Ltd., Chennai, India
Printed in India at Gopsons Papers Ltd., Noida

Contents

Figures and Tables

Author Details

Peter Gronn is a member of the Faculty of Education, Monash University, Australia. He has researched, taught and published extensively on aspects of school, educational and organisational leadership. His teaching and research interests include leadership, administration and management generally, and leadership and management in a variety of educational settings (especially schools), school reform and restructuring; history of schooling and education, organisation theory, organisational behaviour, and biographical and naturalistic research methods.

Acknowledgements

This book would not have become a reality without the encouragement and support of my family, in particular my wife, Barbara. As always, my greatest debt is to her, for which I extend to her many thanks. I am also grateful to the numerous research students and colleagues who have stimulated my thinking. I also wish to thank Dr Felicity Rawlings for her helpful comments on parts of the manuscript.

The poem on page 60 is reprinted by permission of PFD on behalf of Roger McGough © Roger McGough.

Abbreviations

CC	curriculum committee
CCSSO	Council of Chief State School Officers
CEO	chief executive officer
COO	chief operating officer
CPEA	Cooperative Program in Educational Administration
CSCW	computer-supported co-operative work
DEET	Department of Education, Employment and Training
DGM	district general manager
EIPP	evidence-informed policy and practice
ETWR	experienced teacher with responsibility
ETS	Educational Testing Service
GM	general manager
HEADLAMP	Headteacher Leadership and Management Programme
ISLLC	Interstate School Leaders Licensure Consortium
LAC	local administration committee
LASG	Latin American study group
LPSH	Leadership Programme for Serving Headteachers
MBA	Master of Business Administration
MoE	Ministry of Education
NCSL	National College for School Leadership
NPBEA	National Policy Board for Educational Administration
NPM	new public management
NPQH	National Professional Qualification for Headship
OCB	organisational citizenship behaviour
OFSTED	Office for Standards in Education
PD	personal development
PSSP	Professional Standards for School Principals
SCRELM	Standing Conference on Research in Educational Leadership and Management
SLLA	School Leaders Licensure Assessment
SMT	senior management team
TTA	Teacher Training Agency
UCEA	University Council for Educational Administration

Introduction

This book was originally intended as the sequel to my earlier publication *The Making of Educational Leaders* (Gronn, 1999b). There I outlined a four-stage leadership career framework and I discussed in detail the first two stages: the initial formation of leaders, and the subsequent accession of those leaders to locations of influence in schools and educational organisations generally. The focus here, by contrast, is on the third of the four stages, incumbency, and what it means to be an educational leader in the new millennium.

The gap in time between the publication of this book and its predecessor has been fortuitous, because three important emerging trends, which are likely to shape the practice of school leadership for the foreseeable future, have come into even sharper focus. The first factor is systemic in origin and part of the wider framework of school policy. It is the increasing reliance by school-system employing authorities on an entirely new means of producing and replenishing cohorts of school leaders. I have labelled this emerging mode of leader formation designer-leadership or, analogous to other design systems, the method of producing leaders according to design specifications. The second is a structural factor which is also externally induced but institutional in its manifestation. This is the increasing reliance of school personnel on qualitatively different modes of work performance. These modes represent a loosening of previously tightly defined and interpreted individual role boundaries, and the exploitation of informal workplace interdependencies in accomplishing tasks. I refer to this phenomenon as distributed practice. The third factor is cultural, and manifests itself both institutionally and systemically. It emanates from a reappraisal and redefinition of those traditional employee commitments which comprise part of what it means to be a good organisational citizen. This factor signals a potential legitimation problem for education systems, and it might loosely be termed an emerging culture of disengagement or abstention in respect of leadership roles. It is manifest most glaringly in the increasing inability of school systems, globally, to recruit senior school-level administrators.

Taken together, the themes of design, distribution and disengagement constitute the three main components of a definitional or architectural framework for school leadership in the sense that, for the foreseeable future, they can be expected to shape much of the new work of educational leaders. 'New', because these factors will provide qualitatively different points of reference for understanding professional practice, compared with the traditional sets of assumptions that have informed the work of previous generations of school leaders. Not only will these factors help determine school leadership practice but, as I hope to show in more detail in Part 1, there are tensions between them. Here is a simple illustration of the point. Grace (1995) has drawn attention to the phenomenon of UK principals' work intensification under conditions of local school management. A consequence of intensification, he notes (Grace, 1995, p. 203), is that 'the culture of individual school leadership, as practised by the headteacher, is breaking'. It is partly these intensified pressures, I suggest in Chapter 2, which have resulted in a reliance on distributed forms of work practice in schools. Yet, at the very time that work demands are intensifying, and distributed practices appear to be becoming the norm, governments are adopting leadership accountability measures that bear little connection with distributed practice and are likely to exacerbate intensification. Standardisers, such as the National College for School Leadership (NCSL), as I show in Chapter 1, are invoking a hero paradigm in their leadership designs. A slightly more technical way of putting this is to say that they are relying on neo-trait theories of leadership. Trait theories fell into disrepute amongst commentators during the 1950s but, since the mid-1980s, they have undergone a huge revival. The effect of heroic individualism, however, is to raise the bar of individual school leader performance even higher than it is currently positioned and, as I point out in Chapter 3, it risks making school leader roles even less attractive as career options for teachers. Moreover, such a regime of heightened performance expectations provides those teachers who may be uncertain about the future direction of their careers with additional grounds for disengaging and abstaining from becoming leaders.

Designer-leadership was an idea implicit in the early discussion of leader formation systems in *The Making of Educational Leaders* but it has since become a defining theme for leadership. The significance, but also the flaw, of the idea of leadership by design, as I shall try to show, is captured in Wenger's (1999, p. 229) remark that 'one can design roles, but one cannot design the identities that will be constructed through those roles'. What this statement means is that there are limits to the capacity of a training regime to tightly and precisely mould the consciousness and future behaviour of its products, quite apart from any ethical concerns about the desirability of doing so. On the other hand, while designer-leadership seems to represent a substantial break with the past, one should always tread warily, as historians would readily attest, when asserting the emergence of qualitative breaks, turning points or watersheds in explanations of the development of social systems and institutions. With the resort to leadership by design, however, in the guise of regimes of assessment, accreditation and, in a couple of instances, licensure standards for school leaders, some education systems appear to be changing their leadership development and succession planning trajectories. But what is meant by this idea of trajectories?

From the perspective of social structure, a trajectory represents a relatively stable and enduring period of regular action and activity, or 'an overarching social process that has the character of coercing processes within it, and of preventing those processes from creating combinations that disrupt it' (Abbott, 1997, p. 93). The pre-specified roles to which Wenger draws attention are the products of such institutionalised trajectories. Yet, just as identities differ from roles, so too do personal experiences of trajectories differ. From the point of view of the individual, trajectories are 'interlocked and interdependent sequences of events in different areas of life' (Abbott, 1997, p. 88). But whichever the level – individual or social structural – trajectories are separated by periods of transition or radical shifts known as turning points. Structurally, however, unless we are concerned with events as extreme as revolutions, transition points rarely amount to abrupt breaks in policy or practice. With these thoughts in mind, the leadership of schools appears to be experiencing one such transition which, if I am right, is likely to spawn an entirely new set of master narratives as the justification for school leadership, in the form of nationally defined design specifications for leaders.

Two common points of reference in the social sciences for positioning one's research and writing are the analytical levels of focus known as the macro and the micro. Partly in reaction to what was referred to in derogatory tones in some quarters as 'grand theory', the 1970s and early 1980s witnessed a hefty swing towards micro-level focused research. This 'turn', as it is sometimes known, was evident in the popularity of methodologies and theoretical approaches such as life history, ethnomethodology, conversational analysis, hermeneutics, interpretivism, case study and so on. More recently, rather than juxtaposing these two levels as alternative analytical standpoints, commentators have been calling for an explicit recognition of their interplay in the construction of interaction orders (e.g., Mouzelis, 1991), while others of a critical realist persuasion (e.g., Archer, 1995; Sayer, 1992; 2000) have been arguing for causal accounts of institutionalised action which acknowledge the dynamic interplay of structure, culture and agency.

The structure and argument of this book is intended to be in keeping with these trends. In Archer's terms, the significance of the architectural factors considered in Part 1 is that they impose constraints on both individual and concertive agency. But, while the reality of their contextual imposition cannot be ignored by the particular situated actors, at the same time such constraints on practice are unlikely to be experienced as insuperable. For a start, their impact will vary from school context to school context, for reasons of differences in the amount and quality of pre-existing resources, differences in personnel composition, and differences in the make-up and social capital of the communities served by schools. The impact of design, distribution and disengagement trajectories in particular policy contexts is also likely to vary because of the differing personal dispositions and capacities of the actors. While some organisation members will no doubt feel powerless in the face of what they perceive to be overwhelming external constraints, others, in the pursuit of their interests, will display a flair for ingenuity, improvising, making do or, in the microcosmic circumstances of their practice, devising what Suchman (1995) has termed 'workarounds'. Thus, at the same time as practice may be constrained, it is to some degree enabled and new options for practice are opened up and exploited.

It is the possibility of this dynamism which I have sought to capture in Part 2, and which, in an attempt to bridge the micro and the macro, I have labelled 'the ecology of leadership'. In Chapters 4–7 I have synthesised research into the practice of leadership. I focus on the micro-level details of practice as these articulate with the three identified effects of macro-level policies, because the micro is the point at which policy-required roles and subjectively defined professional identities meet. Here, structure is realised through the acts of agents and, recursively, agents have an impact on structure through their words, deeds and emotions. For these reasons, practice represents an accomplishment, the outcome of both the intentions of agents and the unintended consequences of their actions.

In Chapter 4, I consider a number of problems and possibilities in a tradition of field research intended by its proponents to answer a question, roughly worded as: 'What do managers (and leaders) do?' Beginning in the early 1950s, the findings of this work accumulated in a number of countries over the next four decades or so. There were some landmark studies within this tradition, one of which, Mintzberg's (1973) *The Nature of Managerial Work*, has had (and continues to have) a significant impact on research into educational administration and leadership. There were other studies which, in retrospect, as I shall show, merited considerably more attention than they received (e.g., Sayles, 1964). Broadly, this body of work emphasised the tracking or shadowing of senior and mid-level organisational personnel in an attempt to pinpoint the rhythm and flow of their work patterns and routines. Its appeal and promise was that it offered both descriptions and analyses of role performance, rather than the kind of normative theoretical fare which comprises the substance of much leadership and management theory. Unfortunately, this 'work activity' school, as Mintzberg labelled it, failed to live up to its promise. But as I point out, the emerging field of workplace studies has begun to revitalise field research into leadership practices in a way which accommodates the distributed realities of work.

One of the consistent findings in these investigations into the work of leaders and managers has been their strong reliance on talk. As I was able show in two pioneering studies which helped to develop this area of research in education and beyond (Gronn, 1983; 1985), 'talk is the work'. Subsequently, others (e.g., Boden, 1995) have built on and extended this line of research in other realms of management. Managerial and leadership talk plays an important structuring role. That is, the significance of talk in the structure–agency interplay is that, while providing evidence of social and institutional structure, and being the vehicle for its realisation in practice, talk is simultaneously a means for the potential modification of structure. This claim is consistent with the popular emphasis amongst social theorists, in particular discourse analysts, on 'social construction', except that I eschew the tendency, criticised by Sayer (2000, p. 91), for some social constructionists to maintain that the objects of social reality are solely the artefacts of our discursive practices.

Apart from conversations, the most prevalent manifestation of leadership and management talk occurs in meetings. As Van Vree (1999, p. 278) notes in his historical study of the development of the meeting genre and meeting manners, contemporary organisation members 'seem to be socially fated to meet and to meet again with the same colleagues on set places and at set times to perform similar acts every time'. The two most prominent arenas in which leaders meet to talk are committees and teams, respectively the subjects of Chapters 5 and 6. As mechanisms for work co-ordination and concertive action, committees and teams are vehicles for distributed work practice, although only teams have been theorised from this perspective. The literature on committees, especially, and, to a lesser extent, teams, combines what commentators refer to as 'tool' and 'topic' material. That is, each of these meeting forms has generated its own 'how to' or advice and improvement publications, on the one hand, and a set of research findings into the constituent properties of each form, which is substantially larger and more recent for teams than for committees, on the other. Chapters 5 and 6 discuss this 'topic', rather than 'tool', literature.

In Chapter 7, I review work on a relatively new dimension of school leadership and managerial practice: emotions. Beatty (2000, p. 333) notes that the emotional effects of leaders' actions 'remain under-explored' and that 'the emotional processes of the leader her/himself remain virtually unchartered territory'. While this observation may be an accurate one for the specific domain of school leadership, it applies less to leadership generally where the passions aroused by charismatic leaders, for example, have been well rehearsed and documented for some time. Further, negotiation of the emotional division of labour between the three hospital executives who formed a role constellation was central to the early work of Hodgson, Levinson and Zaleznik (1965). There is also, of course, extensive writing on feelings and organisational pathologies within some post-Freudian schools of psychoanalysis, and a growing body of material on humour in management. The principal insights from these areas are synthesised in this chapter.

In Chapter 8, I conclude by outlining the rudiments of a grammar of leadership. Here, the theme of work intensification, which recurs throughout the discussion, is focused on the idea of leadership as 'greedy work'. The concept of greedy work builds on Coser's (1974) early study of greedy institutions and is used to characterise the heightened demands and expectations placed on institutional-level leaders. In the late 1980s, Stewart (1989) proposed a particularly helpful and influential template for future research into the work of managers, which is broadly in keeping with the tradition of research considered in Chapter 4. Subsequent developments, such as Archer's (1995) attempt to systematise the duality of agency and structure, and the recent emergence of activity theory (see Engeström, 1999; Engeström and Middleton, 1998), have brought to bear some useful analytical tools for extending Stewart's suggestions to the realm of educational leadership. My argument in Chapter 2 (and again in Chapter 8) will be that the appropriate point of anchorage and departure for understanding the dynamics of leadership has to be the changing division of labour. This stipulation has great significance for the study of leadership where the convention is for commentators to *pre*scribe or take for granted a division of labour (i.e., 'leader' and 'followers'), rather than to *de*scribe actual, contextualised divisions of labour. Sayles's (1964) focus on the idea of the division of labour was one of the great virtues of his pioneering field studies of managers, an emphasis which, curiously, was completely ignored by later writers, but which is the main reason for my earlier assertion that his analysis deserved better recognition. Sayles is the sole writer in management and leadership, in my view, who has accorded the division of labour the pride of place it warrants.

My final point concerns terminology. There has always been, and continues to be, constant confusion in discussions of leadership regarding its connection with management. Briefly, as I have endeavoured to make clear in a number of my recent writings, I regard management as work activity encompassed by the duties and responsibilities of organisation managers as determined by the terms and conditions of their employment contracts. Leadership, on the other hand, while it may be part of what managers do, is by no means the whole of it. Nor do managers have a monopoly on leadership, which I take to be a lay label of convenience encompassing emergent actions (verbal, physical, reputed or imagined) that influence the deeds and thoughts of colleagues, for leadership is something which is open to any organisation member. Thus, leaders may be managers and managers may be leaders, but whereas management has a legal contractual basis, the basis of leadership is cognitive and grounded in the mental attributions of workplace peers (for a more detailed discussion of these points see Gronn, 2002b). Despite the force of these distinctions, the reality is that it is well nigh impossible to quarantine discussions of leadership and management from each other, principally because so many practitioners expect their managers to lead. With these points in mind, in my discussion of the work of leadership commentators I adhere mostly to the authors' original usage of terms and clarify, when necessary, whether and in what ways their work applies to both the domains of leadership and management. On the other hand, given the depth and extent of the expectations of leadership held for managers, I sometimes slip into using a compound noun 'leader-managers'.

PART 1

THE ARCHITECTURE OF LEADERSHIP

---

1   Designing Leaders[1]

Since their establishment, public school systems have experienced periodic pressures for reform in numerous countries. The latest wave of reform during the last two decades, particularly in the USA, UK, Canada, Australia and New Zealand, has emphasised the need for school restructuring along with a renewed focus on teaching and learning. For many current reformers, the key ingredient in the success of restructured schools is leadership, in particular the leadership of principals. From the inception of mass schooling in the late nineteenth century, the provision and replenishment of cohorts of principals and other school leaders has been accorded a high policy priority by governments and public school authorities. Unlike previous eras, however, the current reform period has yielded a qualitatively different approach to the formation of school leaders. This new view of leader formation, which is the subject of this chapter, may be termed the production of leaders by design or the idea of designer-leadership.

Central to the notion of designer-leadership is the determination of sets of standards and competencies for the preparation and development of educational administrators, both as a precursor to the certification of prospective principals and others as suitable or fit for employment, or for the purposes of contractual renewal and the professional upgrading of incumbent school administrators. The creation of designer-leaders forms part of the ideology of the new managerialism, known as the new public management (NPM) (Hood, 1995), which now legitimates the overwhelming bulk of global public school sector reform. Moreover, the adoption of standards as a model for the accreditation of an individual's fitness for school administration parallels a similar movement from the late 1980s for the definition and implementation of standards for classroom teachers. If the solution proffered by the British Prime Minister, Tony Blair, for the attainment of a world-competitive British economy, following the accession to office of the Labour government in May 1997, was said to be 'Education, education, education ...', then 'Standards, standards, standards ...' is fast becoming the mantra of school reformers. As Elmore (2000, p. 12), suggests, for example, 'standards-based reform has a deceptively simple logic: schools, and school systems, should be held accountable for their contributions to student learning'.

At the heart of the discourse of the new managerialism is an apparatus of governance comprising indirect steering rather than direct supervision, in which control of employees is achieved through a policy regime and a culture of performativity. Previous direct modes of control of employee performance through traditional, interventionist bureaucratic line management approaches have been superseded by quasi-autonomous, self-managing institutions subject to discursive disciplinary and surveillance rubrics of quality assurance and performance targeting. Standards for school leaders are central to the notion of performativity. As such they embody detailed expectations of preferred (as opposed to best) practice, yet they differ from traditional scientific management understandings of effort norms, for (as I show) they are grounded in a discourse of desirability rather than a Taylorite calculus for the measurement of bodily exertion. On the other hand, the significance of standards is that they provide new modalities of regulation and control (Anderson, 2001, p. 203). In this sense, they are vehicles for the steerers of systems to micro-manage the day-to-day work of institutional personnel by seeking to ensure adherence and conformity to officially sanctioned codes of conduct (Ball, 1998).

In this chapter, I consider a range of problems and possibilities inherent in the adoption of standards-based preparation for school leaders. The discussion has four aims. First, with a view to clarifying the distinctiveness of standards-driven preparation, as part of a broad developmental survey, it compares the attributes of this most recent approach to school leader formation with its historical precursors – namely, an initial historical reliance on the vagaries of individual character and virtue, and their subsequent abandonment in favour of formally codified professional knowledge. Second, it compares the various approaches currently being taken to standards determination in a number of educational systems, in particular the UK and the USA, where adherence to the idea of designer-leadership is strongest, and also Australia. Here it will be shown how the evidentiary sources from both the agencies responsible for, and the interests which seek to promote, standards-driven preparation programmes, reveal two contrasting approaches: a profession-driven view of leadership standards in the USA, and a national government-driven approach in the UK. Third, I analyse a number of problems with the heroic leader paradigm which is embedded in the discourse underpinning the machinery of standards and capabilities, and I review a range of empirical data on standards implementation. Fourth, I conclude with a discussion of a number of general issues associated with the global implications of the move to standards-based administrator preparation. These concern aspects of leadership development and succession planning, in particular the unintended consequences of the introduction of standards for leadership careers and the recruitment of school leaders, the subject of Chapter 3.

Standards and the Regulation of Conduct

We inhabit a world of standards. Standards are a type of social technology which comprises a discursive apparatus of codified, abstract rules or norms. Standards give voice to intentionality in that they purport to govern and legitimate modes of human conduct, and the production of material objects. Leaving aside material objects, commentators normally see the governance of standards-mediated conduct as encompassing the domains of morality and epistemology, and possibly aesthetics (Bowker and Star, 2000, p. 148). With regard to the morality of conduct, Baer (1987, p. 533) notes that standards articulate 'a profession's view on the appropriate distribution of societal resources under its "authority" and the values underlying their allocation'. Yet, while such moral authority may be generated by a particular professional group, it may equally be imposed on a profession by an external agency (e.g., government), as with teachers and administrators in the recent past in the UK. In regard to the second dimension, standards-based knowledge, Baer (1987, p. 533) defines this as 'formalized and codified decision rules that join professional knowledge to action', with the main consequence of the act of codification being that 'expert knowledge is "stored" in the standard and not in any person' (Jacobsson, 2000, p. 45).

The production of standards creates an intimate relationship between standards and standardisers. Standardisers are sets of agents, representing key political and professional interests, who are authorised to define and apply standards. Standardisers define standards for a range of economic and cultural activities associated with the production, distribution, exchange and consumption of valued goods and services. A key feature of standards production is that there is an inherent bias in the act of standard-setting. When standardisers define standards, they decide, in effect, which components of activities shall be visible and which shall be invisible. Their criteria for distinguishing between these visible and invisible dimensions may be explicit and publicly accessible, or implicit and tacit. A significant effect of making some dimensions visible is to create a public agenda of admissibility. Thus, 'every standard and each category valorizes some point of view and silences another' (Bowker and Star, 2000, p. 156).

Three particular features of the relationship between standards of admissible conduct and practices in the workplace are worthy of comment. First, the link between standards and contexts of work is a paradoxical one. Ostensibly, the rhetoric of standards is separated from work practice by virtue of its decontexualised character. That is, standards are not generally derived from, nor grounded in, what counts as acceptable conduct that is idiosyncratic or peculiar to particular locales of work (e.g., Mrs Smith's Year 7 at High School X), because standards are meant to be immune from the exigencies of localism. An important exception to this first point, as will be seen later on, is Louden and Wildy's (1999a, pp. 417, 418) vignette-based approach to the development of standards for Western Australian school principals, which is 'grounded in the context it describes' and which also reflects 'the common-sense knowledge of principals'. At the same time as standards are divorced from contexts, however, they bear an intimate relation to them. This is because the precepts which they embody are intended to secure relationships of conformity in every set of circumstances which is deemed to fall within the remit or brief of a particular standard.

A second general effect of the introduction of standards to spheres of activity is to standardise experience within those activity realms by eliminating variations in the conduct of practice. The result is that standards can be characterised as solutions in search of problems, in that they prescribe anticipated, legitimated and programmed responses to societal and organisational possibilities yet to be realised. As solutions to problems, standards embody a number of presumptions. One is a presumption of superiority, in that persons other than practitioners (i.e., standardisers) are deemed, or deem themselves, to know better or to know best. Another is that uniformity of conduct is considered preferable to differences and variations in performance. The third feature of standards is that they become a source of predation for a whole range of interests. This consequence occurs because the introduction of standards creates a regime of compliance and an industry of verification. Compliance and verification turn on the issue of correspondence, or the extent of the conformity between workplace operations and the standardised stipulations which they are supposed to mirror. Compliance with standards and verification of compliance give rise to the monitoring of conduct. The result is an incipient game of infinite regress in which groups of experts (governed by their own sets of standards?) are constantly checking up on other groups of experts who are required to provide 'auditable accounts' (Power, 2001, p. 10).

In some respects, standard-setting and standardisation can be seen as the final pieces in the mosaic of the new managerialism (e.g., significant downsizing of the public sector; the privatisation of public instrumentalities; the contracting out of service delivery; the introduction of outcome-based performance targeting and appraisal). Much of the groundwork for control by standards had already been laid in the post-Keynesian political climate of the 1980s. In this decade, a variety of salaried professionals (e.g., nurses, teachers, social workers, university academics and civil servants) were ferociously derided by Hayekian, neo-liberal governments for their alleged 'provider capture' of the Welfare State (Perkin, 1990, pp. 483–95). Much earlier, the playwright, George Bernard Shaw, had chided the professions generally with his witty aphorism that they were 'conspiracies against the laity', but the claim that the interests of client and beneficiary groups had been betrayed signalled an abandonment of public trust. As a means of bringing these allegedly recalcitrant occupational groups to heel, in order to make them responsive to client interests, and to discipline their work performance in the pursuit of advantageous national positioning for a competitive knowledge economy, standards regimes proved irresistible to governments.

Standards and the Design of Leaders

This repositioning of interests along market lines, with a view to privileging the demand side rather than the supply side of the relationship, represents a form of customising the production and delivery of services. A corresponding mode of customisation also applies to the production of school leaders. In school and educational leadership, the adoption of standards is the most recent of three broad historical solutions to the enduring problem of leadership succession faced by societies, systems and institutions. This is the problem of how to produce individuals fit for leadership roles and to guarantee the production of successive requisite cohorts of institutional-level leaders. 'Fitness' here entails some form of evidence of capacity to fulfil role responsibilities and duties. The process of determining such fitness is known as leader formation. Judgements about fitness for office have generally encompassed the search for evidence of either or both a particular candidate's presumed suitability and eligibility. In some cases, the criteria for selection on each of these grounds have been explicitly defined, whereas in others they have been left implicit.

Over (roughly) the last two centuries, three historically sequential sets of ruling assumptions concerning fitness for leadership have underwritten the preparation and development of educational leaders. These are the norms of ascription, merit and customisation. In nineteenth-century England and Europe, and their colonial offshoots, ascriptive leadership was broadly coterminous with the prototype of the gentleman. The principal claim here was that key individuals (overwhelmingly high-status males) were somehow *naturally* endowed or fitted for leadership. With industrialisation, the expansion of higher education and the emergence of an urban middle class, ascriptive assumptions in these societies began to yield to (although they were not entirely replaced by) demands for evidence of merit and achievement. Increasingly, fitness for leadership came to mean being *formally* fitted. But in the new millennium, a number of governments, employing authorities and professional associations are claiming that the credentialism afforded by the assimilation of esoteric knowledge no longer provides sufficient evidence of capacity to lead communities of learners. Instead, these agencies are customising their requirements by accrediting individuals according to standards-determined profiles of preferred leader types. Hence the characterisation of this approach as designer-leadership. With the adoption of standards regimes, leaders may be said to be *suitably* fitted. These three leader formation modes are considered in turn.[2]

Ascription: Naturally Fitted Leaders

In the European version of ascription, the male offspring of a socially exclusive stratum were selected and segregated at a young age for later elite roles (Armstrong, 1973, p. 20). The selection criteria included heredity, family status and an aristocratic outlook. The quintessence of European ascriptive leadership formation was the English public boarding school which was prominent in the late Victorian and Edwardian eras. The classical, Platonic assumptions which legitimated this schooling informed the world views of the English policy-making and opinion-forming elites, including those within state secondary schooling until the comprehensivisation of the mid-1960s (McCulloch, 1991). Moreover, in the 1980s, the persistence of gentlemanly power assumptions and their alleged negative cultural influence on Britain's underperforming economy prompted one leading Conservative cabinet minister to promote a new entrepreneurial Britain as an antidote to the so-called 'British disease' (Annan, 1988).

The English public schools were Anglican, fee-paying and boarding, and competed with one another at games. They stood for ideals of religion, character, culture, team games and service. Their male pupils experienced institutionalised paternalism in the boarding houses, occasional inspiring and intellectually challenging teaching in the sixth form, and were prepared for public life through membership of societies and clubs (e.g., debating). A gentlemanly disposition, the outcome of the translation of these ideals into practice, comprised a combination of godliness and good learning. Other components of this ascriptive infrastructure included an upbringing comprising a *ménage à trois* of parents, children and nannies, followed by preparatory schooling at age eight before entry to a boarding school. The hegemony of the classics was the hallmark of the public schools, a situation reflecting the perpetuation of an aristocratic style in the moulding of character, which was cemented by subsequent attendance at the universities of Oxford and Cambridge.

In the early nineteenth century, compared to their brothers, English gentlewomen were educated in the 'accomplishments': dexterity in music, languages, dancing and drawing etc. These activities provided desired models of female elegance, grace, style and moral rectitude. Critics dismissed the accomplishments as, at best, education for subordination or, at worst, servility. Eventually, for middle- and upper middle-class girls, the accomplishments were replaced by education at public boarding and day schools. Reformers emphasised public duty and middle-class family values, 'a curious amalgam that bore slight resemblance to either the boys' school or the Victorian family, in spite of the ideological borrowings from both' (Vicinus, 1985, p. 164). Until well into the twentieth century, the opportunities for public leadership roles for educated English women were confined to high-minded, practical, good works in such spheres as philanthropy, voluntary work (e.g., in settlement houses), religion and charity (e.g., church communities, temperance reform), and to employment in the helping professions (e.g., nursing, school teaching and social work).

Achievement: Formally Fitted Leaders

Recognition of ability as the basis of leadership capacity paralleled a wider acceptance of meritocracy in the nineteenth and twentieth centuries, and the rise of the professions in modernising societies (Perkin, 1990). The assumption was that leadership could be learnt, which signalled the eclipse of being 'born to the purple', the idea that a privileged class or stratum with an inborn instinct to rule should monopolise leadership. Instead of personal attributes, birth and heritage, appeal was made by rising occupational strata, such as salaried managers (Burnham, 1962, pp. 78–93), to impersonal evidence of requisite individual capacity. In this way, knowledge and ability substituted for pedigree, and higher education became an instrument for preparing managers and leaders. There were three important aspects of this development. First, an enduring tension emerged in university-based programmes between the advancement of knowledge and the application of knowledge. The former idea fostered the proliferation of graduate schools, and the latter the expansion of training outside the university sector. Second, university-based programmes, symbolised by the Master of Business Administration (MBA), diversified rapidly. Third, degree programmes became stratified into pecking orders of preferred career routes to elite roles. Corporate and public sector managerial strata had emerged in all of the major industrial nations by the mid-twentieth century, but diverse cultural assumptions about higher education, entrepreneurialism, the role of managers, and links between management and higher education ensured that different national approaches to management preparation developed in the USA, France, Germany and England (Locke, 1984).

A parallel process of knowledge codification and diffusion occurred in educational administration. In the USA, the professionalisation of school administration began during the Progressive Era (Tyack and Hansot, 1982). In this period, the nineteenth-century idea of an aristocracy of character was supplanted by leadership expertise based on specialised training and appointment by merit. Moreover, there was a clear division of labour between a teaching service dominated by women and an overwhelmingly male administrative superintendency (Blount, 1998, p. 54). Part of the initial early twentieth century burst of professionalisation in the USA entailed the incorporation of business ideas of efficiency into the schools (Callahan, 1962), an influence which persisted until after the Second World War when administrator training and preparation became infused with behavioural science (Cooper and Boyd, 1987, p. 11). By the late 1940s, the Cooperative Program in Educational Administration (CPEA) had begun in five universities. The CPEA leaders aimed at improving university preparation programmes through a Theory Movement (as it became known) intended to link prospective administrators with social science theory. The new movement reshaped the field for about three decades (Culbertson, 1988, pp. 15–17).

In Australia, a robust climate of voluntarism proved antithetical to credentialism, and character-based and self-made traditions of administrative practice prevailed until well into the twentieth century. State education authorities did not require formal licensure for school administrators. Apart from the Diploma of Educational Administration at the University of New England, which commenced in 1959 (Cunningham and Radford, 1963, p. 20), there were few university programmes in educational administration until the 1970s. A popular choice for Australian students' postgraduate study was the University of Alberta, Canada. Others went to the USA. Upon return home, these graduates, who were often state officials, introduced North American ideas into in-service education programmes for administrators. An important state-sponsored initiative was the Institute of Educational Administration in Victoria (1976–93) which provided training for principals (Moyle and Andrews, 1987). Specialist masters coursework degrees in educational administration and leadership are now offered by most Australian universities.

By the late 1980s, more than 400 graduate preparation programmes were recognised by state authorities in the USA for mandatory licensure requirements. Forty-five states in 1993 required a Masters degree for a principal's licence (McCarthy, 1998, p. 120). But so modest was the pedagogical variation between the programmes that they had converged around a national norm described by Cooper and Boyd (1987, p. 3) as 'the One Best Model': 'state controlled, closed to nonteachers, mandatory for all those entering the profession, university based, credit driven, and certification bound'. By the mid- to late-1980s, the Theory Movement had run its race. Stimulated by damning national reports on the failure of US schools and a welter of academic criticism (Cooper and Boyd, 1987, pp. 12–15), a new reform movement gathered pace. Reformers now aimed at a concerted national, rather than sectoral, educational approach. To that end, the National Policy Board for Educational Administration (NPBEA), comprising representatives of the peak professional bodies for administrators in education, was established in January 1988. In the next decade, the NPBEA pushed hard to secure the adoption of national standards of effective leadership practice and assessment of practice. According to its Executive Secretary, the NPBEA's initiatives 'stemmed from the conviction that the theory-based movement launched in the 1950s was threadbare and approaching obsolescence, and that it required a major makeover to accommodate contemporary requirements' (Thompson, 1999, p. 111).

Customisation: Suitably Fitted Leaders

Customised leader formation is a substantial, paradigmatic break with precedent. Inherent in customisation, is the idea of a good, service or product being tailor-made to replicate a pre-specified model. Universities and other providers now operate in a buyer's, rather than a seller's, market. Customised leader formation is still taking shape, but two core elements can be distinguished. The first is the determination of national or system-wide standards of effective leadership and the second is accredited diagnostic assessment of the performance potential of individuals against sets of standards.

Standards: UK   In 1997, the Teacher Training Agency (TTA), the government authority responsible for the determination of standards, released *National Standards for Headteachers*. A key driver behind the adoption of standards was the 'close correlation between the quality of teaching and the achievement of pupils and between the quality of leadership and the quality of teaching' (Teacher Training Agency, 1998, p. 1). *National Standards* comprises a series of criteria set out under five headings concerned with the core purpose, key outcomes, professional knowledge and understanding, skills and attributes, and five key areas of headship (strategy, teaching and learning, staff, deployment of resources and accountability).

The TTA devised a training and development strategy for school heads comprising three programmes, for which the newly founded NCSL is now responsible. These are the Headteacher Leadership and Management Programme (HEADLAMP) for the induction of newly appointed heads (1995); the National Professional Qualification for Headship (NPQH) for aspiring heads (1996); the Leadership Programme for Serving Headteachers (LPSH) for heads in post (1998). The NPQH is a mandatory requirement for first-time heads which consists of a series of evaluation stages entailing individual needs assessment and assessment of candidates for headship against the *National Standards*. Originally a three-year programme, NPQH was reduced in 2000 to one year, including a residential period at the NCSL. By early 2001, more than 7,000 candidates had registered. For HEADLAMP, heads are granted up to £2,500 with which they may purchase training within two years of their appointment. By mid-1998, nearly 5,000 heads had undertaken training with over 300 registered (mainly tertiary and private) providers. In contrast, only seven national providers (a mix of university and private consortia) deliver the LPSH, a programme for heads in post for three or more years. The LPSH offers initial evaluation against the *National Standards*, and subsequent training and professional development. There is a strong emphasis on information and communications technology, and heads are linked to a Partner in Leadership, a senior figure in their local business community.

Standards: USA   In contrast to government-mandated national standards in the UK, US reform of administrator preparation over the last decade or so proceeded via a number of simultaneous initiatives undertaken by a broad coalition of stakeholders anchored on the NPBEA. These activities have proceeded at two levels: generically, in relation to standards for school leaders and the accreditation of preparation programmes, and specifically in relation to the licensure assessment of school principals.

Three key initiatives have given the reform movement its momentum. First, following consultation, NPBEA-sponsored recommendations to strengthen existing university programmes were implemented by the network of universities comprising the University Council for Educational Administration (UCEA). Second, some NPBEA affiliates, supported by philanthropic foundation funds, began redefining the knowledge base of the principalship. Third, in 1994, common standards for the state licensure of school administrators were developed through a working partnership of the NPBEA and the Council of Chief State School Officers (CCSSO). The fruit of this relationship was the Interstate School Leaders Licensure Consortium (ISLLC), now comprising 30 states (Murphy, Yff and Shipman, 2000, p. 18), which produced the document *Standards for School Leaders* in 1996 (McCarthy, 1998, pp. 122–3; Murphy, 1998, pp. 367–8).

Standards for School Leaders enshrines the same kind of presumed causal linkage between leadership effectiveness and student learning as in the UK, which is evident in the stem phrase which introduces each standard: 'A school administrator is an educational leader who promotes the success of all students by …'. But in contrast with the UK, the ISLLC standards apply to the incumbents of all formal roles, rather than solely to heads or principals, despite the fact that for much of the 1980s school reform was 'synonymous with reform of the principalship' (Murphy, 1990, p. 237). Moreover, the drafters of the document have opted for parsimony in devising only six standards rather than 'a forest' of 'long hierarchical lists' (Louden and Wildy, 1999b, p. 102). These six include vision, school culture, organisation management, stakeholder relations, ethics and external contexts. Within each standard are clustered a number of indicators under three headings: knowledge, dispositions and performances. By late-2000, 35 states had distributed *Standards for School Leaders* (Interstate School Leaders Licensure Consortium, 1996), with eight states adopting *Standards in toto* and a further nine devising standards consistent with and/or incorporating elements of those of the ISLLC (Murphy, Yff and Shipman, 2000, p. 35).

But the creation of standards 'is only half the battle' (Latham and Pearlman, 1999, p. 246). Given that the states' influence on professional preparation in the USA has been indirect and confined to licensing individual principals, 'rather than by imposing mandates directly on the universities' (McCarthy, 1998, p. 120), the ISLLC has recently tackled licensure assessment. In 1996, five ISLLC states and the District of Columbia contracted the Educational Testing Service (ETS) to draft a new licensure assessment for principals, based on *Standards for School Leaders*. The ETS produced the School Leaders Licensure Assessment (SLLA) which, by early-2000, had been adopted by six states. Finally, the NPBEA wants universities to restructure, and seek accreditation for, their Masters programs in conformity with the ISLLC standards and the curriculum guidelines introduced in 1997 by the National Council for the Accreditation of Teacher Education for accrediting educational leadership programmes (Thompson, 1999, pp. 104–6).

The Language of Standards

There are three noteworthy features of both the UK and US standards frameworks. First, each set of standards accords overwhelming discursive prominence to leadership, rather than to management or administration. Second, the particular version of leadership which is privileged tends to be individualistic and transformational, and is focused principally on the deeds of senior hierarchical role incumbents – i.e., a hero paradigm. Third, the normative emphasis on superleadership in the standards is significantly at odds with current organisational practice. These points are considered in turn.

Symbolic Power of Leadership

School reformers and standards proponents tend to define principals as leaders rather than as managers. Their assumption is that leadership, rather than management, is the vehicle for structural change, and that principal leadership drives change. Thus, as testimony to the power of a label, Thompson (1999, p. 112) notes the significance of leadership in the US school reform movement. The newly formed NPBEA, for example, gave deliberate priority to the notion of 'educational leadership', rather than 'educational administration'. The rationale for this choice was to 'differentiate from old stereotypes' and to be 'an accurate descriptor of the role actually required of school leaders today'. Leadership was seen as the core responsibility of principals and superintendents. 'A concept that had fallen on hard times among academics because no overarching theory proved adequate, leadership was becoming ever more critical to the success of individual school.' Hence, the NPBEA actively advocated the teaching and practice of core skills, attributes and processes of effective leadership, rather than general leadership theory.

But this kind of appropriation of leadership does not go without saying. Before they are leaders, principals are appointed as managerial job-holders. As was pointed out in the Introduction, management is logically prior to leadership because it is a legally prior relationship. That is, principals act as the agents of their employers (i.e., departments, ministries or school districts) and operate within an authority relationship with teachers. The details of that relationship are usually spelt out in an employment contract. Thus, like all managers, within the framework of such an employment contract, a principal 'is authorized to get work done through employed subordinates for whose work [she or] he is held accountable' (Jaques, 1970, p. 133). Employment contracts, however, generally do not specify the means of authorisation for securing the accountable ends. Leadership, along with persuasion, force, power, dominance, influence, etc., may indeed be one of those means, but it need not be. Organisational leadership is generally held by commentators to be a form of work-related influence, but rarely is influence the sole preserve of those who exercise the managerial prerogative. Principals and other school administrators may be leaders, therefore, but they are not automatically so by virtue of being administrators and managers, for the status of leader is ascribed by others on the basis of an individual's perceived attributes and performance (Gronn, 1999b, pp. 1–20).

Hero Paradigm

The idea of the hero paradigm is part of the continuing search for leader effectiveness. The hero paradigm derives from the assumption that effective performance by individuals, groups and organisations depends on 'leadership by an individual with the skills to find the right path and motivate others to take it' (Yukl, 1999, p. 292). The corollary of this assumption is that influence tends to be thought of as uni-directional from leader to followers, with the result that 'there is little interest in describing reciprocal influence processes or shared leadership'. One of English's (2000, p. 162, original emphasis) criticisms of the ISLLC standards is that they legitimate a conception of leader-followership in which a leader 'does to them and for them, but never *with them* as co-equals', a claim denied by the chair of the ISLLC (Murphy, 2000, pp. 413–14).

Heroic individualism goes to the heart of what it means to be a transformational leader. In the new world order of the restructured, learner-centred, self-managing school the official assumption is that principals will be transformational leaders, because transformation is the extent of the change and level of engagement demanded by school systems and principals' employing authorities. A corollary of transformation in the field of leadership, is the notion that a hero figure will 'turn around' a poorly performing or underperforming organisation. This popular shorthand rhetoric attests to the presumed potency of individually focused, transformational-style leadership. An example is the UK government's Fresh Start scheme for failing schools. Experience with the programme, however, suggests that transformational heroism may well have outreached its capacity to deliver on the officially sanctioned expectations. Following an inspection by the Office for Standards in Education (OFSTED), a school deemed to be failing in the competitive national league tables (due to low student performance attainment) earns itself a fresh start. This amended status includes the acquisition of a new name, teachers, resources and a new headteacher. New heads have been dubbed 'superheads' by the British media. During 2000, amidst a blaze of media publicity, a succession of high-profile superheads resigned (*Guardian*, 15–16 March). The job appears to have been too much and the expectations too high for just one individual.

Practice of Leadership

The third point of significance regarding the language of standards is that the hero paradigm embraced by standardisers is increasingly at odds with changing work practices in the very contexts to which the standards are to apply. That is, as will be shown in more detail in the next chapter, there is a new division of labour emerging in the management and leadership of self-managing schools. This hiatus between reality and design, however, tends to be papered over. Thus, while acknowledging changed workplace circumstances, with their reference to 'heterarchical school organizations', Murphy, Yff and Shipman (2000, p. 22) attempt to reconcile these with diverse notions of servant, architect, moral educator and transformer in their leadership design, a good illustration, perhaps, of Anderson's (2001, p. 209) point that standards attempt to 'cover all bases'.

There are two senses in which the officially endorsed individual hero paradigm is out of touch with reality. The first is theoretical. The significance attached to knowledge management and learning by design theorists of organisations has led them to reconceptualise work environments as communities of practice, in which allowance is made for multiple forms of leaders and leadership (e.g., Wenger, 2000, p. 231). This changed emphasis accords with the earlier recognition by March (1984, p. 29) and Sergiovanni (1984, pp. 13–14) of the importance of the overall density or spread of an organisation's leadership capability, rather than its concentration in one or a few hands. The second sense is practical: heroic leadership does not resonate well with the phenomenon of work intensification in self-managing schools (Grace, 1995). Work intensification is indicative of a rapid escalation in the breadth, scope and complexity of the responsibilities exercised by school managers, the speed and constancy with which they must be attended to, and qualitative changes in the overall rhythm and flow of the task environment. These new patterns are a direct outcome of changed policy accountability requirements and systemic control through micromanagement. They give rise to new workplace leadership, such as leadership teams, and a range of alternative distributed leadership synergies (Yukl, 1999, pp. 292–3; Gronn, 2000; Spillane, Halverson and Diamond, 2000a) – developments which (despite its endorsement of focused individual leadership) are readily acknowledged by the leading US standardiser, the CCSSO (Council of Chief State School Officers, 2000, p. 5). Even though this hiatus between standards-based expectations of leadership and the realities of school practice is not problematic for reformers, it is likely to generate unanticipated consequences for principal succession (see below).

Playing the Standards Game

Despite the fact that 'the daily activities of a manager are rather distant from grand conceptions of organizational leadership' (March, 1984, p. 22), standards are policy levers for engineering desired changes in principals' performance. In the words of a Hong Kong discussion paper on the training of school heads: 'the end vision is to achieve a paradigm shift and transform the principal from a hierarchical manager to a visionary leader, with the ultimate aim of improving student learning' (Task Group on Training and Development of School Heads, 1999, s. 2.5). Yet whatever the avowed intention of standards, one effect of their adoption will surely be to alter the existing pattern of career incentives, rewards and mobility for school administrators. The exact rules of the new career game are still to emerge. But if the following observation by March (1984, pp. 27–8) is a reliable guide, then aspiring and incumbent principals can be expected to do whatever it takes to secure their initial and ongoing accreditation in conformity with standards, although they may not necessarily alter their behaviour in other ways:

> Long before reaching the top, an intelligent manager learns that some of the more effective ways of improving measured performance have little to do with improving product, service or technology. A system of rewards linked to precise measures is not an incentive to perform well; it is an incentive to obtain a good score.

In light of this possibility, then, what guarantee is there, from the standardisers' point of view, that standards will secure their preferred ends? At least four problems can be foreseen. Three relate to some unintended consequences of implementation. These are dealt with first. The fourth is of major significance, and is considered in more detail because it concerns the entire conceptual basis and methodological derivation of standards.

Career Demography

A key concern for policy-makers and researchers will be the longitudinal effects of standards-based preparation regimes on the demographic composition of the profession of school administration. There are two points of significance here. The first is the elitist nature of the current profile, while the second concerns a possible misalignment between the profile of the candidate pool and the profile of the communities to be served by that pool.

On the first point, both the earlier ascriptive and meritocratic formation systems were attacked vehemently for creating demographically homogenised occupational profiles. Ascriptive arrangements resulted in leader cohorts dominated overwhelmingly by high-status, privileged white males, and the merit-based systems which succeeded them have also been attacked for disadvantaging both women and ethnic minorities (Blount, 1998; Bredeson, 1996, pp. 271–2; Tyack and Hanson, 1982). A key question for research and policy will be whether the new arrangements are seen to be compounding or alleviating this discrimination. Such perceptions strike at the heart of the credibility and legitimacy of customised designer-leadership. On the second point, Bredeson (1996, p. 258) notes the traditionally homogenous nature of US school administration candidate pools and claims that in the mid-1990s this 'demographic mismatch between school administrators and students in public schools is even greater'. This disjuncture between the orientation and social composition of the membership of a professional elite, and the mass public it serves may prejudice the legitimacy of the former. Another critical question for research, therefore, will be the extent to which standards-based leadership preparation will deliver school administrator occupational profiles that reflect the demographic composition of societies. Both of these points hinge partly on the judgments of those who will select the candidates.

Selecting School Leaders

March (1984, p. 27) observes that, because they tend to reward similar attributes, organisational promotion systems filter out variation amongst managers. One result of this homogenisation is that 'it is difficult to know unambiguously that a particular manager makes a difference'. For this reason, policies which mandate adherence to tightly defined standards framework models of leadership, as a condition of principal promotion – and which, ironically, single out key individuals intended to make a difference – are likely to narrow the range of variation even further. Thus, in regard to selection by school governors in the UK – where the previous tradition of diverse and plural forms of voluntarist professional preparation has been eroded, and legitimate practice is now standardised – Gunter (1999, p. 257) queries whether an effect of standards will be a reduced range of differences amongst potential appointees to diverse school communities. In light of the previous point, a key issue, therefore, will be whether community expectations of social heterogeneity can be reconciled with the likelihood of homogenised attributes and skills amongst the recruits of standards-based preparation.

   This issue is likely to bite, so to speak, in the selection of aspiring principals and other school leaders. There are two main implications of homogeneity: one for site- or district-based selection panels and another for policy-makers. First, the world views and values which inform the personnel decisions of site-based selection panels, in Gouldnerian terms, are as likely to be local as cosmopolitan. Selection panels tend to be composed of elected representatives of school community interests and are convened on an ad hoc basis to fill occasional vacancies. The members usually lack consistent experience in making selection judgements. In these circumstances, selectors' assumptions about candidate 'fit' can be expected to accord priority to the needs of local communities (Gronn, 1986). As a corollary, the second implication is that the intrusion of localism presents a potential problem for policy-makers. This is the possibility of slippage, in that criteria other than those which are standards related might drive decision-making. This kind of outcome may be less of a problem in circumstances in which policy guidelines require selection panels to shortlist only those candidates satisfactorily assessed and accredited as having met national standards. In the absence of such a requirement, however, and in the absence of any additional requirement designed to ensure that selection criteria should reflect the content and stipulations embodied in sets of standards, actual selection preferences may well be only loosely aligned with the preferred outcomes of standards-based training and development policies.

Recruiting School Leaders

Another potential for policy misalignment – the third unintended consequence of the adoption of standards – is that standards may compound, rather than alleviate, the difficulties being experienced around the world in recruiting school administrators, especially principals. In the UK, for example, both Brundrett (2001, p. 238) and Bush (1999, p. 246) have suggested that a daunting standards-driven headship training regime may have a negative impact on headship recruitment.

There are two components to current recruitment difficulties. As will be shown in Chapter 3, not only is there a dearth in the numbers of prospective principals applying for vacancies, but the quality of the applicants has also declined. At the time of writing, the extent of the empirical evidence regarding shortages of prospective recruits to the principalship is sparse (although see Cooley and Shen, 2000; Pounder and Merrill, 2001). On the other hand, the problem has been given wide coverage in publications such as *Education Week*, in the USA, and *The Times* and *Guardian* in the UK. A number of factors have contributed to these shortages, including: an ageing teaching service, incentives to exit the service created by pension and superannuation scheme entitlements, concerns about the incommensurability of levels of remuneration and the responsibilities exercised by principals, and, particularly, the exhaustive personal demands created by work intensification. The significance of this latter factor is highlighted in the author's research in Victoria,[3] and increased work intensity is frequently cited in newspaper editorials and reports on the recruitment crisis. In this climate, a key question is: to what extent will the adoption of standards for principals exacerbate these difficulties of recruitment? That is, will a possible unintended effect of standards be to compound the effects of work demands and pressures, by making the role *even less* attractive and appealing as a career option? Even though there has been no systematic research into the implementation of the ISLLC standards, Murphy, Yff and Shipman (2000, p. 30) report a survey in which 'some states' registered these very concerns about the negative impact of standards on administrator recruitment. In the USA, there are nearly 200 knowledge, disposition and performance indicators in the ISLLC *Standards*, while in Victoria there are more than 50 behavioural descriptors expected of government school leaders (Hay Group, 2000) and in the UK there are approximately 90 dot point requirements listed in the *National Standards for Headteachers* to be met by principals. Given their perceptions of an already beleaguered and overworked principalship, what will be effect of such elaborately detailed statements of expectations of the principal's role on experienced teachers' own career ambitions?

Normative or Evidence-based Standards?

In the early-1970s, Mintzberg (1973, p. 3) queried the absence of a substantive knowledge base of day-to-day managerial practice. Nearly three decades later in educational administration, this same sought-after knowledge base is still missing. Apart from a brief flowering of research modelled on Mintzberg's structured observation during the 1980s, there is a dearth of naturalistic studies of day-to-day administration, and of the structuring, flow and pace of the work (see Chapter 4). Of even more concern is the absence of a naturalistically-grounded knowledge base as the empirical foundation for some standards and capability statements.

Standards authorities rely on data produced by researchers and some members of the profession, but also, increasingly, by international management consultancy firms. The preferred means of data collection have been survey instruments, informant interviews and focus groups. An important question is whether these sources yield accurate information on workplace practice. Argyris and Schon (1978), for example, showed how reliance solely on informants' self-reports of their behaviour yields imagined or preferred accounts, in the form of espoused theories, rather than theories-in-use derived from clinical observations. The significance of this point has been entirely lost on the Hay Group, for example, the consultants who drafted the NCSL's Capability Dictionary and Victoria's Excellence in School Leadership report. In neither instance was any observation of school leadership practice undertaken to ascertain what school personnel *actually* did (i.e., how they performed their work as part of a job analysis), as opposed to what they *said or claimed* to do. Suchman (1995, p. 43) made the pertinent observation in regard to automated work design systems (the products of business process engineering) that practitioners adapt to standards-based design criteria by devising workarounds: 'a form of on-the-job innovation that reveals the tension between the standards for a job and the realities of doing the work'. Discrepancies between standards and reality occur because designers 'tend to think organizationally rather than employing work thinking, the fund of knowledge about details of work process that are generally not incorporated into work process designs', when the real question in customising the work for practitioners is: what does it actually take to get a job done?

Apologists for standards have rejected this hiatus between normative standards and the realities of practice as a basis for criticism. Murphy and Shipman (1999, p. 217; and see Murphy, Yff and Shipman, 2000, p. 24), for example, addressed the issue in relation to the ISLLC and claimed that to have proceeded 'by mapping the existing leadership terrain' in the devising of standards for the ISLLC 'would not be wise':

> Examining current domains of responsibility and partitioning out the multi-faceted elements of the job would, we came to believe, both advantage the status quo in the profession (which we judged as an undesirable state) and push issues of learning and teaching to a distant corner of the profession (where they have lain fallow for much of the last 75 years).

Instead, leadership had to be reconstituted in line with learner-driven conceptions of schooling. Thus, the ISLLC standards development work considered what the leadership of schools 'might look like' while 'still honoring the realities of the existing workplace'. A similar tension between norms and reality was evident in the design of the SLLA assessment regime linked to the ISLLC standards. According to Tannenbaum (1999, p. 240), the SLLA is intended to be a test of beginning principals, and to the extent that licensure assessment is based on 'the current state of professional practice' as performed by a competent practitioner, there is strain between standards and assessment. The ISLLC standards enshrine statements of desired effective school leadership (i.e., what ought to be), whereas the SLLA deals with what is. To have used the standards in the initial framework of professional practice, on the other hand, 'could have set a level of expectation exceeding what is justifiable for beginning-level practitioners'.

Whether, and in what way, these kinds of tensions will be resolved is unclear. One development which may bring matters to a head is an emerging interest in evidence-informed policy and practice (EIPP). Briefly, EIPP proponents commend it as an approach to making decisions about client needs in various realms of professional practice on the basis of the most reliably tested and widely accepted evidence of 'what works'. Stimulated by the establishment of the Cochrane Collaboration – an international consortium of scholars which conducts reviews of health-care interventions – and the newly formed Campbell Collaboration in the social sciences (February 2000), debate over the desirability and feasibility of EIPP has quickened, particularly in the UK (see Davies, 1999; Pirrie, 2001). The main selling point of EIPP for UK school reformers, educationalists and politicians is its potential for generating cumulative, rather than additive, knowledge of practice. The notion of accumulated knowledge has an obvious pragmatic appeal to grant-funding agencies and regulatory authorities in schooling. On the other hand, official or quasi-official sanction of EIPP as an orthodoxy may simply come to sustain a bifurcated view of knowledge as either 'acceptable' and legitimate or as 'dangerous' and lacking in utility. Taken at face value, knowledge that is cumulative is empirically substantive, rather than normative, knowledge. In the event that EIPP takes off, standardisers will need a basis other than desirability with which to ground their requirements in line with the new empiricism.

At the time of writing, the one standards project known to the author which best addresses the problems associated with the normative–empirical hiatus highlighted in this section of the chapter is the Professional Standards for School Principals (PSSP) project at Edith Cowan University in Western Australia. The first stage of the project has been to develop a standards framework. The creation of an assessment regime forms Stage 2 of the project (Louden and Wildy, 1999a, p. 401). Unlike the two main examples discussed earlier, the PSSP framework is anchored around a series of short descriptive vignettes which were collected during consultation with hundreds of Western Australian principals. Vignettes are based on the job descriptions of principals, rather than fixed statements encapsulating idealised behaviour. They depict a range of typical incidents (e.g., 'taking a risk', 'the hangover') and provide illustrative hypothetical decision responses by principals. Samples of principals have rated these responses as low, medium or high. In this way, the PSSP framework acknowledges the reality of qualitative variations in performance. During the development phase, principals also identified a series of moral dispositions (e.g., 'courage and decisiveness') and interpersonal skills (e.g., 'listening') displayed in each of the vignettes. The significance of this recognition is that 'within a single incident principals may demonstrate a whole range of competencies which [in other standards frameworks] appear as separate items on separate lists' (Louden and Wildy, 1999b, p. 102). In these and other related ways, the PSSP project has sought to devise standards anchored in contextualised incidents, displaying varying levels of performance, and illustrating multiple leadership attributes, which have been validated through extensive consultation.

Designing the Future

In a political climate conducive to greater regulation and the decreased autonomy of the professions, standards are being used increasingly to do the work of regulating the members of key occupational groups. Standards for the preparation and development of school leaders represent the principal instrument by which public authorities are customising their needs for leadership in key sectors such as schooling. This approach to customising requirements has been characterised in this chapter as a process of designer-leadership which, when compared to two previous historical modes of leader formation, reveals a logic of tight coupling in which a machinery of preferred outcome statements drives judgements about proficiency and levels of performance. Unlike previous arrangements governed by ascriptive and achievement norms, little is left to chance in customised approaches to leader-making.

The recent period of transition to customised leadership-by-design systems has been marked by a realignment and repositioning of existing sets of interests. In many ways, the university sector has had to make the biggest adjustment of all. In both the UK and the USA, for example, universities have been the target of a barrage of criticisms concerned with school pupil performance and the alleged inadequacies of university preparation programmes (Bredeson, 1996, pp. 256–7; Murphy, 1990). So severe has been the level of disenchantment with academia that, in some instances, training and standards authorities (e.g., the TTA in the UK) have threatened to bypass the sector entirely (Brundrett, 2001, p. 237; McCarthy, 1998, p. 135). In the eyes of commentators, the new qualifications for the profession, such as HEADLAMP, NPQH and LPSH, are to be understood as simply that: as qualifications rather than as programmes, and as professional qualifications framed around competencies, rather than academic ones, as well. This characteristic presents a challenge for universities as they seek to reposition themselves in the training market (Bolam, 1997, p. 278; Brundrett, 2001, p. 238). The kinds of difficulties experienced by UK universities in making this transition have been mitigated to some extent by the willingness of the Labour government (1997–), unlike its Conservative predecessor, to articulate training provision with university courses (Bush, 1998, pp. 330–1).

Unlike the UK, at the time of writing there is little data available on the implementation of the new ISSLC standards in the USA other than a telephone survey conducted by Murphy, Yff and Shipman (2000). On the other hand, the battery of profession-generated initiatives is seen by its proponents as compelling the field to 'move toward implementing the vision for school leadership that the standards convey' (Latham and Pearlman, 1999, p. 246). Indeed, some institutions have even had their charters to prepare school administrators withdrawn and some states (e.g., Mississippi) are considered likely to tie their accreditation of leadership preparation programmes to graduate performance assessment on the SLLA (McCarthy, 1998, p. 123; Murphy and Shipman, 1999, p. 220). These developments point to the possible re-emergence of a version of the historically discredited phenomenon of 'teaching to the test'. The logic is not yet inexorable but, as providers in a highly competitive training market, the temptation for some university programmes to concentrate solely on the learning of model answers and finding ways of making students test-proficient, in order to satisfy accreditation and assessment requirements for certification and licensure, may prove difficult to resist. On this point, it is noteworthy that, as part of its contract with the ISLLC, the ETS provides candidate information bulletins outlining samples of actual assessment questions, scoring guides used to evaluate responses and sample candidate answers from field trials. While such measures are designed to 'obviate fairness concerns by providing test takers with critical, detailed information about what they need to know to perform well on the assessment' (Latham and Pearlman, 1999, p. 252), a recent analysis of the 'right' answers concludes that sample items reward managerial 'spin', rather than sensitivity to community concerns about social justice (Anderson, 2001).

The final point is that the global adoption of standards and designer-leadership is likely to reinforce existing patterns of intercultural borrowing and global knowledge diffusion. In education policy generally, and in school reform particularly, there are numerous examples of policy copying, cloning and borrowing of regulatory frameworks and processes, following site visitations, study tours, electronic networking and so on amongst national agencies and authorities. In early 2001, for example, delegations from the NCSL visited leadership centres, and consulted with employers and professional groups in eight nations (including Australia, the USA, Singapore and Hong Kong) prior to pooling evidence of good practice at a symposium in April 2001. Likewise, in the framing of its recent discussion paper on principal leadership training, a Hong Kong task force visited England, Scotland, Australia and Singapore with a view to studying training programmes before framing its recommendations (Task Group on Training and Development of School Heads, 1999). With respect to the development, adoption, implementation and monitoring of standards, it is too early to know whether these kinds of links will be conducive to a convergence of global practices or whether the ongoing search for examples of best or preferred practice will reinforce patterns of divergence, or hybridisation. These possible developments are of crucial significance for commentators and practitioners concerned with the diminution and loss of cultural distinctiveness. A closely related issue is whether, given the traditional pattern of influence of the English-speaking world in the creation and diffusion of educational administration as a field of study, the move around the globe to mandated administrator preparation programmes will further consolidate the existing western hegemony of ideas. The examples of designer-leadership discussed in this chapter suggest that, in regard to the diffusion of standards frameworks for the regulation of professional practice, at least some western nations have already begun to set the pace.

Notes

1 This chapter is a slightly amended version of Gronn (2002a).

2 This and the next two subsections draw on Gronn (2002c) and Gronn (1999b, pp. 44–64).

3 As part of the 'Readiness for Leadership' project funded by the Monash University Small Grants Scheme.

2   A Distributed View of Leadership

In education and the social sciences, the study of leadership has been dominated since its inception by the notion of focused leadership. At the core of this understanding, with which the design systems considered in the previous chapter are conceptually aligned, is a deeply entrenched commitment to a unit of analysis comprising a solo or stand-alone leader. Confirmation of this claim can be found in Rost's (1993) recent comprehensive review of the literature. Rost (1993, p. 70) noted that, despite signs of an incipient challenge to mainstream analyses of leadership at the end of the 1970s (on which see Gronn, 2002d), more than 130 books published in the next decade reinforced the conventional message that 'leadership is basically doing what the leader wants done'. In contrast with this orthodox conception, the argument of this chapter is that commentators and practitioners would be better served by an expanded understanding of leadership and a revised unit of analysis. As an alternative to focused leadership or the hero paradigm, therefore, I propose a unit of analysis which includes distributed forms of leadership.

Notwithstanding Rost's pessimism about the 1980s, the next decade saw a surge of interest in a range of distributed phenomena amongst organisational theorists and researchers. Some commentators drew attention to distributed decision-making (e.g., Committee on Human Factors, 1990) while others investigated distributed cognition (e.g., Hutchins, 1996). Still others made brief mention of shared or distributed leadership (e.g., Bryman, 1996, p. 283–4; Miller, 1998, p. 4). But apart from these scattered references, and except for Gronn (2000; 2002b) and Spillane, Halverson and Diamond (2000a; 2000b), there are few extended, analytical discussions of the concept of distributed leadership. This paucity of coverage is puzzling, for the idea of dispersed or distributed leadership is not new. Indeed, the possibility of leadership displaying a distributed pattern was first raised as far back as the 1950s by the late C.A. Gibb (1913–94), an Australian social psychologist, in his entry on leadership in first edition of the *Handbook of Social Psychology* (Gibb, 1954) and repeated subsequently in the second edition (Gibb, 1969).

In this chapter, I begin with a discussion of the idea of the division of labour. I then suggest how changes in the division of labour are creating new workplace interdependencies and how, as a consequence, these both require and facilitate the adoption of different mechanisms of co-ordination. This overall process is known as the articulation of work. Next, I indicate how in this new working environment leadership increasingly observes a distributed pattern, in either of two main forms: multiple or concertive forms of action. In the remainder of the chapter I concentrate mostly on the second of these alternatives, and I distinguish three types of concertive actions: spontaneous collaboration, intuitive working relations and institutionalised practices. Within the category of institutionalised practices, I outline the differences between the most commonly available ways of managing work, including departments, divisions, crews, committees and teams, the last two of which are accorded separate treatment in Chapters 5 and 6. Finally, I provide a taxonomy of some of the more informal and lesser known examples of concertive action, and discuss a range of the potential synergies and tensions to which these give rise.

Division of Labour

The idea of the division of labour means the totality of the work to be performed in a particular sphere of human endeavour, its arrangement into segmented and specialised tasks, along with the requisite technological capability (i.e., tools and information) to complete those tasks. A division of labour only comes into being when two or more people are required to perform the work for, as Sayles (1964, pp. 46–7) noted, 'as long as a single individual can do all the work necessary to complete some task, such as a plumber or accountant who is in business for himself, no organization is needed'. The establishment of a division of labour, however, creates the need for a system of management 'to coordinate and integrate the activities of the various people who together make up the work system'. It is these activities and the specific form of the division of labour which 'determine the job of the administrator'.

Division of Rights and the Division of Labour

It is important to distinguish the division of labour from the division of rights or authority. In reality, the two ideas interrelate in the processes of work articulation (Strauss, 1985, p. 10), although in some discussions the distinction between them tends to be elided (e.g., Hales, 1989). The division of rights is a realm of jurisdiction, and concerns the authority and accountability for the allocation of work and resources. A division of rights exists if 'the legitimate power and responsibility to make decisions are distributed unequally within the [work] group' (Newton and Levinson, 1973, p. 117). This absence of parity of rights means that 'actors can claim, impose, assume, manipulate for, argue and negotiate over various types of work and portions of arcs [of work]' (Strauss, 1985, p. 9). The division of labour, on the other hand, is concerned with the completion of tasks in respect of the overall pattern of work. The right to prescribe and allocate tasks, then, is different from the performance of them. While the division of labour may include positions named or labelled as part of a division of rights, allowance has to be made for the emergence of 'informal, implicitly defined positions'. Thus, 'it is "understood" that Member X functions as assistant to the chief, or that Member Y attends meetings but does no work' (Newton and Levinson, 1973, p. 117). Treatment of the two realms as equivalent, therefore, confuses the right to define or prescribe a division of labour with the actual conduct or operation of that division of labour. Another way of putting this is to say that 'the division of labour defines boundaries, and the division of authority locates responsibility for regulating them' (Newton and Levinson, 1973, pp. 130–1).

As people working within a division of labour solve their problems and learn from their experiences, and as particular work circumstances generate new problems, the architecture of that division of labour changes, despite the human predilection for predictability and regularity. That same division of labour will also change due to the adoption of new technologies. Taken together, these elements constitute the technical side of the division of labour. It is for these reasons of ongoing modification that the division of labour gives the appearance of being governed by an evolutionary imperative. But there is also a social component of the division of labour which provides scope for discretion in the determination of its form, so that one should be wary of too literal an interpretation of expressions such as 'the evolving division of labour'. This social component comes into play when individuals and groups, acting on the basis of their values and interests, decide to configure the work tasks in preferred ways (e.g., their scheduling, physical alignment) and to utilise particular technologies. Needless to say, these relations are an important source of social and organisational power. The division of labour also manifests a dynamic property in which the processes of fragmentation and fusion operate dialectically. As tasks begin to proliferate, for example, or are modified qualitatively or become redundant due to external factors in the task environment, the technical side of the division of labour differentiates itself with the creation of still more specialist tasks. The rate and form of task differentiation are partly determined by decisions about appropriate and desirable ways of reorganising and configuring the work, both through the integrating of tasks and the reorganisation of the required labour (Sayer and Walker, 1992, pp. 15–17). It is this inherent duality of differentiation–integration which is the source of newly emerging forms of role interdependence and co-ordination, and which determines an organisation's overall pattern of leadership. But why might the leadership generated by that imperative of differentiation–integration be expected to take a distributed form?

A Distributed Division of Labour

There are two points to note here. The first is the likelihood that leadership has always been distributed, although most commentators have simply not countenanced this prospect. After all, however else they might be thought of, the forms of concertive action to be considered shortly – i.e., departments, divisions, crews, committees and teams – are also time-honoured ways of distributing work and providing forums for numerous individuals, acting either singly or in collaboration, to display leadership. The point is that, until recently, this possibility has not been recognised for what it is. On the other hand, while the recent phase of workplace restructuring appears to have triggered a re-awakening of interest in distributed practice amongst commentators, an earlier generation of theorists was alert to the possibility that distribution may be inherent in the very nature of what it means to organise. In their study of an executive role constellation, for example, Hodgson, Levinson and Zaleznik (1965, pp. 391–2) noted how interdependence in the administration of their case study medical psychiatric hospital resulted from the assignment of employees 'to formally defined aggregates of individuals that prompt the interlocking of roles', by required contacts with workplace peers and by a tendency for employees to gravitate to compatible colleagues. And the core thesis that emerged from Sayles's (1964, p. 258) field observations of managers in a division of a large US corporation was that 'the modern manager is placed in a network of mutually dependent relationships', a form of words with a strong contemporary ring to it. On this very point of interdependence, which is to be considered in detail in a moment, Carlson (1951, p. 96) described how one of the managing directors he was observing transferred two divisional heads to another floor 'because he wanted them to work more independently', but also had two others relocated adjacent to his own office 'because he needed to be in close contact with them for his own work'. Even more poignantly, perhaps, Stewart (1988, p. 45) described how one of the companies in her sample contained 'a large division [which] was run jointly by four line managers', with the consequence that they each spent 'a lot of time in consultation'.

The significance of the interdependence highlighted by these examples, regardless of the formal demarcation and assignment of duties in individual job descriptions, is that they point to the role of informal working relations in accomplishing work tasks. The need for these relations to be factored into a revised unit of analysis is further underscored by Sayles's (1964) highlighting of managers' interrelationships (p. 28), his claim that organisational results are 'joint products' which cannot be individually disaggregated (p. 42) and by his suggestion that, 'to be of real value, most work has to be coordinated and undertaken interdependently' (p. 115). A key implication of these illustrations seems to be that, in order to get to the bottom of the division of labour, and what managers and leaders do, and how they accomplish it, researchers need to understand organisations in process terms, rather than as entities. Certainly, process and relational approaches have been acknowledged in recent reviews of leadership (e.g., Hunt and Dodge, 2001, p. 443) as the most fruitful new developments in the field. A process perspective is a reaction to what Hosking (1988, p. 150) has termed top-down, 'physicalist' views of organisations. By contrast, a processual understanding of leadership recognises that 'organisation' is as much a structural outcome of action, as a vehicle for it, and that leadership is but one of a number of structuring reactions to flows of environmental stimuli, with the priority of focus being on 'influential "acts of organizing"' which 'contribute to the structuring of interactions and relationships, activities and sentiments' (Hosking, 1988, p. 147).

Re-Articulating the Division of Labour

The most important recent change to the technical side of the division of labour in numerous workplaces, including schools, has been the introduction of networked computing. As one of the principals in Gurr's (2000, p. 72) sample remarked: 'the effect has been very profound in terms of providing us with information but also requiring us to do all the data input and it's been incredible ... and the complexity of what we're being asked to do you can't do it manually'. On the one hand, networked computing creates complex information-rich working environments which prioritise computation, scanning and search routines as firms and human service organisations reposition themselves in fast-paced, fiercely competitive markets. On the other hand, networked computing bridges traditional barriers to simultaneous collaboration (e.g., distance, different time zones, geographic separation) between isolated employees and dispersed organisational units (Committee on Human Factors, 1990, p. 5). These developments have seen the emergence of new approaches to the study of work practice, most notably computer-supported co-operative work (CSCW) studies. One important effect of information-rich and complex work environments has been to intensify the pattern of knowledge fragmentation and dispersal, to which Hayek (1945, p. 519) was one of the first commentators to draw attention, and to provide the impetus for devising alternative modes of articulating the flow of work, in particular the redefinition and reintegration of tasks.

Work Articulation

Work articulation is part of the more inclusive and generic problem of work design and has been defined by Strauss (1988, p. 164, original emphases) as 'the overall process of putting *all* the work elements together *and* keeping them together'. This process entails 'the specifics of putting together tasks, task sequences, task clusters – even aligning larger units such as lines of work and subprojects – in the service of work flow'. It is this maintenance of 'continuity of flows', according to Sayles (1964, p. 259), which is the prime objective of the manager. Typically, it is during periods of work re-articulation that new forms of interdependence and co-ordination emerge and alter the existing pattern of work flow.

Interdependence   For an individual employee or group of employees to be dependent means that they are constrained from acting autonomously. These constraints provide evidence of the interplay of the divisions of rights and labour, and they govern both the completion of tasks and the separation of roles. With respect to task execution, Thompson (1967, pp. 54–5) distinguished three common types of interdependence: pooled, sequential and reciprocal. Pooled interdependence means that in the formal allocation of the overall work the totality of individuals and units (e.g., departments and divisions) is dependent on fellow individuals and units for the organisation's performance. Thus, the underperformance of one unit may prejudice the well-being of all the others. Sequential interdependence means that, in the work flow, for C to act requires A's and B's prior actions, while with reciprocity, each unit generates work for, and receives work from, the other units. With individual role interdependence – the subject matter of this subsection – reciprocal dependence takes one of two main forms: first, two or more organisation members' responsibilities may overlap; second, their responsibilities may complement one another.

Overlapping interdependent role-related conduct has been shown to occur due to mutual needs for information and support (Stewart, 1991b, p. 128). One consequence of role overlap is redundant effort. Heller and Firestone (1995, p. 66), for example, found that leadership in eight US elementary schools was displayed by a number of people, 'sometimes in a jointly coordinated manner and sometimes with relatively little communication'. Redundancy can be a virtue, however, because it provides mutual reinforcement, so that 'the more of each [leadership function] that is done, the better, and doing one helps accomplish others' (Heller and Firestone, 1995, p. 83). A second advantage of role overlap is that it reduces the likelihood of errors in decision-making, because when two or more people's roles overlap there is a greater likelihood of them cross-checking each other's performance.

Complementary interdependent role behaviour was a strong feature of the working relations between three members of Hodgson, Levinson and Zaleznik's (1965) executive role constellation. Here, complementarity was advantageous because it enabled the interdependent executives to capitalise on the range of their individual strengths. The data from this study suggest that role complementarity operates at two levels, the material and the emotional. First, role set members rework the physical differentiation of tasks to create a pooled resource of skills and attributes. By capitalising on their particular competencies, each person performs specialised labour in a concerted approach to task accomplishment. An added advantage of specialisation within a role set is that, while the members may rely on the strengths of their peers, they are likely to enhance their lesser skills due to frequent shared talk and observation of each other in a range of venues. Second, because each person shares the effects of the unit's successful and unsuccessful collaborative efforts, the role set members also experience common emotions. Such negotiated working relationships cement the trust which is conducive to a non-threatening climate of emotional support amongst peers (see Chapter 7).

The significance of both forms of role interdependence is twofold. First, the more comprehensive the breadth of the interdependence amongst the agents, the greater the difficulty, as Simon (1991, p. 33) noted, of measuring 'their separate contributions to the achievement of organizational goals'. Second, the greater the extent of organisation-wide interdependence, the greater the density of the reserves of overall leadership capability. And density, as March (1984, p. 29) suggested, is what 'makes an organization function well'.

Co-ordination   Co-ordination means 'managing dependencies between activities' (Malone and Crowston, 1994, p. 90), and encompasses the design, elaboration, allocation, oversight and monitoring of the performance of an organisation's technical core. It is significant because the overall pattern of co-ordination and the effectiveness with which work is performed are 'functions of the control system utilized' (Sayles, 1964, p. 235).

In a particular work context, the co-ordination mechanisms utilised, singly or in combination, will vary according to the interdependencies experienced, the activities to be managed and the extent of their routinisation. The elements to be co-ordinated include the personnel, resources, raw materials, trajectories, tasks and output required to complete activities. The range of co-ordination mechanisms includes scheduling (e.g., synchronising of practices), sequencing (e.g., task alignment), planning, bidding (e.g., by internal cost centres), standardising (e.g., units of resource, quality control), information management, and consultation and communication. There are appropriate modes of co-ordination for particular forms of task interdependence (Thompson, 1967, p. 64), such as pooled inter-dependence co-ordinated by means of standardisation and sequential by means of planning. Co-ordination patterns in diverse communities of practice, however, change from time to time. At Alinsu, a medical insurance firm, for example, co-ordination of the interdependent work of claims technicians and claims processors drifted in search of a requisite mode of engagement. Initially, techni-cians working with processors were thought to prejudice consistency of technical advice, but their subsequent segregation isolated technicians and resulted in work overload (due to indiscriminate advice referrals). Eventually, the co-location of both groups in a common work area resulted in the balancing of consultation with uniform information provision (Wenger, 1999, pp. 116–17).

Work co-ordination may be either explicit, as at Alinsu, or implicit. Explicit co-ordination mechanisms are stipulated in the duty statements based on managers' employment contracts. In reality, however, a considerable amount of work co-ordination can be implicit and informal. Thus, 'secretaries on research projects are commonly regarded as invaluable, if usually unsung, heroic coordinators' (Strauss, 1988, p. 169). Implicit co-ordination occurs because role definitions either misidentify, or fail to anticipate, the nature and scope of the exigencies of work performance. An analysis of a job's history would reveal the normalisation of implicit co-ordination as a tacit component of routine work. Such normality fuels the common impression that things get done automatically, with the irony that 'the better the work is done, the less visible it is to those who benefit from it' (Suchman, 1995, p. 58). An illustration is the example of the office secretary just given. Despite their invisibility and gendered subordination in serving the career interests of (mostly male) managers, secretaries' relations with managers illus-trate role interdependence, because in numerous instances secretaries are exten-sions of a boss's working capacity (Golding, 1986, pp. 101–2).

In the same way that the conventional discourse of office work may gloss these realities of secretarial practice, so the conventional rhetoric associated with leader-followership obscures the reality of pressures conducive to distribution. This is because the problem of co-ordination in expanding, open-ended and dis-persed information environments has changed. It can now be typified as less one of hierarchical consolidation of knowledge, than one of 'those "lower down" finding more and more ways of getting connected and interrelating the knowledge each one has' (Tsoukas, 1996, p. 22).

Division of Leadership Labour

In the kinds of circumstances and work processes just described, and consistent with the idea of an expanded unit of analysis, the status of 'leader' may continue to be ascribed to one heroic individual or it is equally likely to be attributed to an aggregate of individuals, to a small numbers of individuals acting in concert or to larger plural-member organisational groupings. In each case, the basis of the attribution is the influence ascribed by organisation members to one or the other of these focal units. The source of this attribution of legitimate influence by the attributing agents may be either direct experience, through first-hand engagement with the particular focal unit, or vicarious experience, and thus derived from the individual or unit's reputed, presumed or imagined capacity for leadership. The scope of the attributed influence encompasses the workplace-related activities defined by the employment contracts which operate in particular contexts. These activities may be confined to one of the hierarchically descending domains or levels in Hunt's (1991, pp. 25–40) multi-level leadership model (i.e., systems, organisational and direct) or they may cut across two or three domains. The individuals or multi-person units to whom influence is attributed includes, potentially, every organisation member and not just managerial role incumbents. Thus, managers may be leaders but not necessarily by virtue of being managers, for management denotes an authority, rather than an influence, relationship (Coleman, 1990, pp. 65–81). Finally, the duration of the influence attributed to one or other of these units may be of short-term or extended duration.

Distributed Leadership as Numerically Multiple Actions

If focused leadership means that only one individual is attributed with the status of leader, a numerical understanding of distributed leadership means that the aggregated leadership of an organisation is dispersed among some, many or even all of its members (Wenger, 2000, p. 231). This numerical understanding of distributed leadership does not privilege the work of particular individuals or categories of persons, nor is there a presumption about which individual's behaviour carries more weight with colleagues. Rather, the possibility that all organisation members may be leaders means, potentially, that: 'a telephone operator, a receptionist, a salesperson, and a chief executive is each from their different positions representing the system to the outside world and reflecting pictures of the outside world back into the system' (Miller, 1998, p. 4). This multiple sense of distributed leadership is the most common usage in the growing number of references to distributed leadership in the literature. Its attractiveness, as Yukl, a recent critic of the heroic leader paradigm, notes is that it 'does not require an individual who can perform all of the essential leadership functions, only a set of people who can collectively perform them' (Yukl, 1999, pp. 292–3). Thus:

> Some leadership functions (e.g., making important decisions) may be shared by several members of a group, some leadership functions may be allocated to individual members, and a particular leadership function may be performed by different people at different times. The leadership actions of any individual leader are much less important than the collective leadership provided by members of the organization. (Yukl, 1999, pp. 292–3)

These and other advantages have prompted the CCSSO, for example, in its promotion of preparation standards for school leaders, to pay lip-service at least to this multiple understanding of distributed leadership (Council of Chief State School Officers, 2000, p. 5).

Distributed Leadership as Concertive Action

Distributed leadership in its numerical sense may be seen as equivalent to the sum of its parts (i.e., the sum of the attributed influence). But distributed leadership can also be construed holistically, as conduct comprising joint or concertive action, rather than aggregated, individual acts. At least three forms of concertive action provide evidence of distributed leadership. First, there are collaborative modes of engagement which arise spontaneously in the workplace. Second, there is the intuitive understanding that develops as part of close working relations amongst colleagues. Third, there are a number of structural relations and institutionalised arrangements which constitute attempts to regularise distributed action.

Spontaneous Collaboration   Spillane, Halverson and Diamond (2000b, p. 6, original emphasis) refer to school leadership as distributed practice. This idea means that leadership is evident in the interaction of many leaders, so that 'leaders' practice is *stretched over* the social and situational contexts of the school; it is not simply a function of what a school principal, or indeed any other individual leader, knows and does'. The concertively aligned conduct which exemplifies this stretching is evident in a number of ways and in the accomplishment of numerous tasks. These may be regular and anticipated (e.g., budget meetings, staff appraisals) or unanticipated (e.g., crises, major problems), and they vary in scale, complexity and scope. One way is when sets of two or three individuals with differing skill and abilities, perhaps from across different organisational levels, pool their expertise and regularise their conduct to solve a problem, after which they may disband. These occasions provide opportunities for brief bursts of synergy which may be the extent of their engagement or they trigger ongoing collaboration. Burns (1996, p. 1) cites the example of a person who, 'because of certain motivations of her own combined with a certain self-confidence, takes the first step toward change, out of a state of equilibrium in the web [of relations]' and triggers interactions which may later crystallise into a routine.

Intuitive Working Relations   In the second instance, intuitive understandings are known to emerge over time when two or more organisation members rely on each other and develop a close working relationship. In this instance, leadership is manifest in the shared role space encompassed by their partnership. It is the working partnership of the focal unit which is attributed with leadership by colleagues, and the partners are aware of themselves as co-leaders. Fondas and Stewart's (1994) notion of a role set, which encompasses the dynamic interplay of the role perceptions and expectations of set members is helpful here. Shared roles emerge when set members capitalise on their opportunities for reliance on others (e.g., by balancing each other's skill gaps) or because they are constrained to do so (e.g., due to aforementioned overlapping role responsibilities). Intuitive working relations are analogous to intimate interpersonal relations (e.g., marriages and friendships) where two or more members act as a joint working unit within an implicit framework of understanding. In such relationships, Gabarro (1978 p. 294) found that the influence of one person on another was 'very much dependent on how much that person was trusted by the other'.

Institutionalised Practices   The third concertive form of distributed leadership is evident in the range of collaborative practices utilised within organisations. Some of these are formalised while others operate on an ad hoc basis, although it is often difficult to draw a hard and fast line between the two. Informal arrangements may exist side by side with formal decision-making machinery, as in the case of temporary task forces, or at some point in time these may be regularised and incorporated into an organisation's framework of governance. Regardless of how and why such practices are institutionalised, concertively acting units, both formal and informal, may be the focus of organisation members' attributions of leadership.

Concertive Action by Formal Units

These units are known as joint or multi-member work units. Their distributed work is executed in one of two main ways: by co-performance or collective performance. Co-performance means that bodily co-present unit members co-ordinate their actions in shared time, place and space. These circumstances are conducive to synchronised and simultaneous task-related actions. Collective performance, on the other hand, entails jointly co-ordinated action in work contexts in which the unit members need not be co-present nor simultaneously in attendance. Instead, they may be geographically dispersed and possibly separated across time and cultural zones. An example may be a multi-campus school or university. In order to guarantee synchronicity in these circumstances, work is co-ordinated by a mix of delegation of authority, personal visits and site inspections and, increasingly, computer-networked communications systems (Allcorn, 1997). This latter category includes video-conferencing and electronic group mailing. As yet, however, the full implications of the new group sizes and boundaries, and patterns of influence and identity norms facilitated by synchronous and asynchronous electronic systems are unclear (although see Finholt and Sproull, 1990). On the other hand, the new electronic protocols open up a range of new task possibilities. For corporate managers, for example, 'meeting through a video screen can demonstrably lead to lower costs and higher productivity' (Van Vree, 1999, p. 201). Nonetheless, because of physical dispersal and indirect supervision and control, a significant proportion of joint work is still likely to be performed independently, sequentially or in parallel time by members.

Defining Joint Work Units   There are two main criteria for distinguishing joint work units: the tasks they perform and the membership composition that performs them. For individuals, unit membership facilitates both participation and identity formation in a community of practice (Wenger, 1999). In their work, the members of units are conscious of their 'groupness', and that they are part of something which is more than a mere plurality or multiple of themselves

(Sandelands and St Clair, 1993). Two important attributes of membership which influence the strength of members' participation in, and the extent of their identification with, a work unit are the circumstances of a unit's formation and the basis of its membership recruitment. With regard to the latter, the legitimacy of a unit for its members will be influenced in part by whether the unit has arisen out of circumstances of design or adaptation. In the first of these possibilities, the membership tends to be prescribed, compulsory, mandated and authorised prospectively. The second case covers post-hoc, retrospective authorisation of informally emergent groupings. In respect of recruitment, the basis of unit membership is significant for each member's commitment and generally takes one of three forms: self-selection, election and appointment or nomination.

With respect to tasks, the two critical features of work units are the tools or instruments which facilitate the completion of tasks and the extent or duration of the task to be performed. There are two main types of tools: standardised or discretionary. This distinction refers to the degree to which a task can be reduced to standard operating procedures or automated routines, on the one hand, which may be uniform across work contexts, or the degree to which a task is open-ended, variable and provides latitude for judgement. These attributes of tools provide an indication of the extent of the dispensability or redundancy of organisation members in the performance of a task. The duration property of a task is a measure of its rarity and is concerned with the extent to which a particular task is a one-off or unique phenomenon requiring special or temporary measures, or whether it is an item demanding ongoing arrangements. Duration, therefore, indicates the degree to which a task has been institutionalised.

Five Joint Work Units

The combination of these different sets of attributes and the two principal modes of accomplishing joint work, co-performance and collective performance, generates a matrix of criteria for distinguishing the five work units referred to earlier (see Figure 2.1).

Departments   Of these five formations, departments and divisions can be dealt with quickly. These are the largest units in numerical membership. Traditionally, both departments and divisions have either co-performed or, when the membership has been dispersed geographically (e.g., across divisions of a firm), collectively performed their joint work. As is suggested in Figure 2.2, departmental tasks are usually discretionary and permanent (although they may include some temporary work), and the membership is usually mandated and appointed (cells 2, 3, 4, 5 and 9 but also 11, 12, 13, 14 and 18 if membership is dispersed). In schools and universities, for example, departments constitute cohesive knowledge communities sub-divided into intellectually demarcated domains that bound and structure networks of relationships and conversations (Siskin, 1994).

Divisions   Divisions are normally numerically larger than departments and their membership, at least in firms, is constituted on specialist functional lines (e.g.,

			Multi-member joint work units	
			Co-performing	Collectively performing
TASK	Tools	Standardised	1	10
		Discretionary	2	11
	Duration	Temporary	3	12
		Permanent	4	13
MEMBERSHIP	Origin	Mandated	5	14
		Emergent	6	15
	Recruitment	Self-selected	7	16
		Elected	8	17
		Appointed	9	18

FIGURE 2.1   Criteria for distinguishing formal joint work units

			Co-performing	Collectively performing
TASK	Tools	Standardised	1	10
		Discretionary	2	11
	Duration	Temporary	3	12
		Permanent	4	13
MEMBERSHIP	Origin	Mandated	5	14
		Emergent	6	15
	Recruitment	Self-selected	7	16
		Elected	8	17
		Appointed	9	18

FIGURE 2.2   Departments

production, marketing, sales etc.). As is shown in Figure 2.3, divisions comprise a mix of standardised and discretionary, but mostly permanent, tasks and a mandated and usually permanent membership (cells 1, 2, 4, 5 and 9 but also 10, 11, 13, 14 and 18 if membership is dispersed). Divisional structures often prove to be dysfunctional for multi-divisional organisations, especially when their members privilege their own particular area of expertise ahead of parallel specialisms, which may even be treated as rival priority areas in the contest for resources. In many instances these have been precisely the kinds of circumstances that have prompted the establishment of cross-functional teams in order to better co-ordinate production and to improve overall performance levels (Donnellon, 1996, pp. 51–7). In corporate contexts, however, long-standing divisional loyal-ties seem to have thwarted such cross-functional team initiatives (Donnellon, 1996, pp. 83–122), although Kruse and Louis (1997, p. 271) found that in education

			Co-performing	Collectively performing
TASK	Tools	Standardised	1	10
		Discretionary	2	11
	Duration	Temporary	3	12
		Permanent	4	13
MEMBERSHIP	Origin	Mandated	5	14
		Emergent	6	15
	Recruitment	Self-selected	7	16
		Elected	8	17
		Appointed	9	18

FIGURE 2.3 Divisions

successful teacher teaming shifted the primary loyalty of teachers to the new interdisciplinary team and away from traditional subunits and the larger school community.

Crews Crews co-perform joint work which is standardised and permanent, and work which is anticipated, to the extent that it is computed and represented in procedural manual form. As Figure 2.4 indicates, crew membership is usually mandated and appointed (cells 1, 4, 5 and 9). Crews operate typically in circumstances in which the work to be performed is arranged in rostered shifts. The division of labour in crewing can be so finely grained and reduced to simple, replicable Taylorite-type operations that, to all intents and purposes, the members of one shift will perform the learned tasks and routines in exactly the same way as another. Thus, 'the demands of Saturday night may dictate a staff of 4 wait personnel, 3 cooks and 2 dishwashers—but not any *particular* cooks or dishwashers' (Arrow and McGrath, 1995, p. 388, original emphasis). This standardisation, of course, is the essence of the fast-food industry and, perhaps, is best exemplified by McDonald's. But crews do not only operate in well-defined, as opposed to ill-defined or complex, problem domains. All other factors being equal (especially training and preparation), interchangeability of shift membership tends not to reduce the capacity of crews to manage sophisticated organisational systems – e.g., amphibious helicopter transports (Hutchins, 1996) and aircraft carriers (Weick and Roberts, 1995), systems which require heedful, as opposed to robot-like, crew member relationships.

Committees Like crews, committees co-perform joint work, except that committee work is discretionary. This discretionary labour is usually bounded by a formally or conventionally defined remit or brief. Committees are not free-standing but are invariably appendages to a hierarchical line role or superior governing body, under the aegis of which they exercise delegated authority. Unlike crews, committees execute delegated tasks in scheduled meeting formats rather than in scheduled or

			Co-performing	Collectively performing
TASK	Tools	Standardised	1	10
		Discretionary	2	11
	Duration	Temporary	3	12
		Permanent	4	13
MEMBERSHIP	Origin	Mandated	5	14
		Emergent	6	15
	Recruitment	Self-selected	7	16
		Elected	8	17
		Appointed	9	18

FIGURE 2.4   Crews

			Co-performing	Collectively performing
TASK	Tools	Standardised	1	10
		Discretionary	2	11
	Duration	Temporary	3	12
		Permanent	4	13
MEMBERSHIP	Origin	Mandated	5	14
		Emergent	6	15
	Recruitment	Self-selected	7	16
		Elected	8	17
		Appointed	9	18

FIGURE 2.5   Committees

rostered shifts. The work of committees is organised either on a permanent basis, as in the instance of the standing committee, or on a temporary basis, as with advisory or sub-committees. Committee membership is usually mandated, and provision is made for either election or appointment, or a combination of both, depending on the priority attached to principles of interest representation in various contexts. Unlike crews, in which particular personnel are more dispensable due the standardised nature of the tasks performed, importance is attached to the retention of the collective memory of discretionary task performance in committees by procedures for regularising membership turnover and replacement. Committees, therefore, combine the attributes of cells 2, 3, 4, 5, 8 or 9 (see Figure 2.5)

Teams   Teams, to begin with, are like committees in that they are principally co-performing work units. Increasingly, however, due to electronic and computerised network technologies, team and committee members are able to transcend

			Co-performing	Collectively performing
TASK	Tools	Standardised	1	10
		Discretionary	2	11
	Duration	Temporary	3	12
		Permanent	4	13
MEMBERSHIP	Origins	Mandated	5	14
		Emergent	6	15
	Recruitment	Self-selected	7	16
		Elected	8	17
		Appointed	9	18

FIGURE 2.6   Teams

the barriers of time, space, culture and place to perform their joint work collectively (Townsend, DeMarie and Hendrickson, 1998). Team tasks, like those of committees, are discretionary and – despite the preference for labelling top or executive level advisory bodies as 'teams' – the lifespan of teams tends to be temporary rather than permanent. In this respect a team resembles a task force or a working party whose membership is assembled on the basis of its collective expertise for the life of a project or working brief. The flexibility of teams as work units stems from their membership attributes. These features, however, constitute both a strength and a weakness. Teams whose membership basis is emergent and the membership self-selected, as in the case of one highly successful public sector work team (Gronn, 1998), are more likely to achieve the kinds of interactional synergy desired by many team proponents. Such teams, however, prove highly vulnerable to membership changes, with the same kind of effect that prompts sporting coaches to bemoan the loss of particular members through injury or suspension as upsetting the desired team balance. Teams may also be mandated rather than emerge informally and spontaneously, and their memberships are appointed. For all of the above reasons, teams embody the properties represented in cells 2, 3, 5 or 6, 7 or 9 (see Figure 2.6).

Concertive Action by Informal Units

In addition to these formal structures, some equally important informal, quasi-institutionalised working arrangements are also expressions of distributed leadership. In all forms of concertive action, formal and informal, the unit members endeavour to act conjointly, but conjoint action is much easier to sustain in small-sized work groups. While the exact numerical threshold in face to face groupings at which the intensity of the interpersonal emotions and norms changes its character is unclear, additions and subtractions to the membership affect the interplay of small numbers significantly. Moreover, size increases also create a greater likelihood of schism and the pursuit of factional interests. And while the aggregated

Concertive action	Mode of conjoint agency: co-performance			
	2-member form	3-member form	4-member form	5>-member form
Intuitive working relations	Chitayat (1985) George and George (1964) Powell (1997) Stewart (1991a; and 1991b) Heenan and Bennis (1999)	Hodgson, Levinson and Zaleznik (1965)		
Institutional- ised practices	Doyle and Myers (1999) Zainu'ddin (1981)		Murnighan and Conlon (1991) Newton and Levinson (1973)	Shapin (1989) Vanderslice (1988)

	Mode of conjoint agency: collective performance			
	2-member form	3-member form	4-member form	5>-member form
Intuitive working relations	Gronn (1999a)			
Institutional- ised practices			Birnbaum (1992) Denis, Langley and Cazale (1996) Denis, Lamothe and Langley (2001)	Brown (1989) Brown and Hosking (1986)

FIGURE 2.7   A taxonomy of informal joint work units

skills and values-base is enlarged and diversified, increased membership size ensures that more energy is likely to be expended on the maintenance of a sense of collective definition. Conjoint agency means that the members synchronise their actions by having regard to their own plans, those of their peers and by reference to their awareness of themselves as a working unit. The Committee on Human Factors (1990, pp. 38–47) distinguished between two-member and multi-member distributed work systems. In Figure 2.7, this distinction has been modi-fied to allow for three-, four- and five-or-more-member units.

Figure 2.7 synthesises some examples of informal joint work units from edu-cation and other spheres of work. There are four points to note. First, spontaneous collaboration has been excluded due to a paucity of documented cases. Second, the examples are intended to be illustrative, rather than exhaustive, of aspects of the actual negotiated division of leadership labour between agents. Third, in respect of organisational levels, the examples are skewed (unintentionally) towards upper echelon, formal leader-manager incumbencies. Fourth, while the evidence in the publications from which the examples are taken suggests that it was the holistic units of analysis (i.e., sets of concertively acting agents) which were ascribed with leadership, and not just individuals, evidence of internal and external reciprocal influence is unevenly reported across the case studies.

The division of leadership labour between individuals and sets of agents summarised in Figure 2.7 is as follows.

Co-performance–intuitive working relations:

- Part-time board chairs and full-time chief executive officers (CEOs): Israeli companies (Chitayat, 1985), and UK district health authorities (Stewart, 1991a; 1991 b).
- Heads of state and informal advisers: US President Woodrow Wilson and Colonel Edward Mandell House (George and George, 1964).
- Heads of government and deputies: former Australian Prime Minister, Gough Whitlam, and Deputy Prime Minister, Lance Barnard (Powell, 1997).
- Full-time CEOs and chief operating officers (COOs), and sports coaches and deputies: US corporations and sports teams (Heenan and Bennis, 1999).
- Medical administrators: a US psychiatric teaching hospital (Hodgson, Levinson and Zaleznik, 1965).

Co-performance–institutionalised practices:

- Co-principals: an Australian Catholic secondary school (Doyle and Myers, 1999).
- Dual control clergyman presidents and headmasters: colonial Australian Methodist schools (Zainu'ddin, 1981).
- Musicians: UK string quartets (Murnighan and Conlon, 1991).
- Health professionals: relations between a management group and clinical research teams in a US psychiatric hospital ward (Newton and Levinson, 1973).
- Scientists and technicians: research laboratory of seventeenth-century English chemist, Robert Boyle (Shapin, 1989).
- Worker co-operative members: a US restaurant collective (Vanderslice, 1988).

Collective performance–intuitive working relations:

- School heads and heads of campus: an Australian multi-campus boys' boarding school (Gronn, 1999a).
- University governors, presidents, managers and faculty: US universities and colleges (Birnbaum, 1992).
- Boards, CEOs, medical councils and health care professionals: Canadian provincial hospitals (Denis, Langley and Cazale, 1996; Denis, Lamothe and Langley, 2001).

Collective performance–institutionalised practices:

- Members of social movement organisations: UK women's centres (Brown, 1989; Brown and Hosking, 1986).

Distributed Leadership Synergies

Two important features of the conjoint agency manifested in these different patterns of informal working relations are interpersonal reciprocal influence and synergy. Reciprocal influence means the influence of two or more individuals on one another and it occurs in a manner akin to a virtuous cycle or zigzagging spiral. Thus, A influences B and C, and is influenced in turn by them (i.e., A < > B, A < > C and also B < > C) with each person subsequently bearing the accumulated effects of successive phases of influence when they begin influencing one another once again. Unfortunately, little can be said about reciprocal influence from the studies listed in Figure 2.7 because in most cases this was not the main focus of the authors. In regard to synergy, on the other hand, an elusive although much sought-after phenomenon amongst commentators, a few suggestions can be made. According to Follett (1973, p. 162), synergy is manifest when each unit member 'calls out something from the other, releases something, frees something, opens the way for the expression of latent capacities and possibilities'. As an illustration, a first-time leading teacher informant in the Monash Readiness for Leadership research project described how she and a more experienced female colleague had shared the role of junior level co-ordinator in a primary school:

> It worked really well. We were very compatible personalities. I think that was a, that was why it worked so well. And she was a very understanding lady and a great mentor and a fantastic person to learn from. So it was a really good opportunity for me and I think that's what gave me the experience to be able to get the level 2 position when I applied for it here later in the year (LT#7).

The two women had divided up the responsibilities between them and 'tried to match, sort of, some of the duties so we weren't overlapping': 'there were a lot of things we did together and there was lots of things that I sought her advice on. And [it] also worked the other way round, that she asked me about things' (LT#7). Both teachers 'had similar values and that was perhaps a big part of it' and they both had 'a common interest in putting kids first' (LT#7).

The studies in Figure 2.7 suggest that there are two main types of distributed leadership synergies which are worthy of comment: synergies based on role incumbency and synergies anchored in personal relations (see Figure 2.8).

Cross-hierarchy

Cross-hierarchical synergies entail the negotiation of role boundaries. The unit members negotiate their role boundaries either by blurring or expanding them.

Role blurring   Role blurring occurred in the constellation formed by three senior hospital psychiatrists depicted by Hodgson, Levinson and Zaleznik (1965, p. xii). This executive triumvirate operated as 'a relatively integrated whole' and displayed role-task specialisation, differentiation and complementarity. Complementary specialisation allowed each man to act as he preferred and as he was best equipped, within a jointly agreed-upon framework of activities in pursuit of the interests of the hospital. Extensive role blurring meant that 'each member of the system could, in part, impose his own personality on the system', but there was 'a limit to the extent of any one individual's control' of that system (Hodgson, Levinson and Zaleznik, 1965, p. 287). As is suggested by this example, the case of leading teacher #7, and as was evident in the 'odd couple' relationship between J.R. Darling (headmaster) and E.H. Montgomery (master in charge) during the

Synergies	
Role-related	Personally-related
Cross-hierarchy Trusteeship Parity of relations Separation of powers	Friendship

FIGURE 2.8   Distributed leadership synergies

foundation of the Timbertop campus of the Geelong Grammar School in Australia in the early 1950s, the factors which account for the depth of trust in role constellations and couples include shared values, complementary temperaments, requisite psychological space and previous experience of collaboration (Gronn, 1999a, pp. 54–7). Despite the fact that Darling and Montgomery were separated by 200 miles, had no telephone connection (at least initially) and relied mostly on the postal service for their communications, the two men evolved a close working relationship in which Montgomery made on-site decisions within a broad framework reflecting his chief's wishes. From other examples of couples, it appears that when one or more of these four factors are absent, the members fail to develop a requisite level of trust and merely 'bring out the worst in each other' (Krantz, 1989, p. 164).

Boundary expansion   Boundary expansion, by contrast, requires the preparedness of organisational superiors to include junior colleagues within the locus of their authority. A good example (to be considered in Chapter 7) is senior management teams (SMTs) in UK secondary schools. The impulse for the heads' establishment of teams is that while heads exercise sole authority for overall school operations, and responsibility for student learning and the work of teachers, within a policy framework of local school management, they depend on other senior staff to accomplish their numerous accountabilities (Wallace and Hall, 1994).

Friendship

Friendship is the only example of a personally related synergy documented in the studies in Figure 2.7. Other possible instances might include those derived from familial relations, such as the intuitive understanding that often exists between siblings and twins. Depending on the degree of calculation they display, most friendships seek to capitalise on the advantages of mutual attraction and compatible personal attributes.

Career- and work-based friendships are common. They cut across or are absorbed into organisation members' role relations. A classic example of a friendship which became the basis for professional working relations was Woodrow Wilson's attachment to Colonel House. House, an inveterate schemer, political kingmaker and playmaker, hit it off with Wilson at their first meeting in late 1911. Interestingly, throughout their friendship, House studiously avoided

Wilson's offers of formal positions preferring instead, as he noted in his diary, to remain 'free to advise the President about matters in general'. The need to shun official positions was essential, House once confided, 'if he wanted to retain his personal influence over Wilson' (George and George, 1964, p. 110). His goal was to be part of his president's 'personal sphere of power' yet, even though he studied Wilson's character closely, he once said that he 'could never really understand him' (George and George, 1964, p. 124). As well as mutually shared affection, the two men's friendship was fuelled by self-interest and ambition on both sides. In more general terms, however, the grounding of friendships in at least some of the factors associated with trust in couples and constellations would appear to be necessary, particularly if work-related friendship synergies are to be immune to such calculus.

Trusteeship

Trusteeship encompasses the working relations between CEOs or their equivalents and the chairs of the governing bodies who appoint them, and to which they are accountable.

Greenleaf (1977, p. 103) sees the essence of trusteeship as oversight of executive power and as necessary to check the 'corrupting influence' of power on executives and to prevent harm to 'those affected by its use'. With that end in mind, the ideal synergy would be one in which trustees, and in particular their board chairs, were proactive, rather than reactive, in their stewardship of organisations. Despite the 'legal fiction' that boards are the agents of stockholders, the reality is that they are 'most often the creatures of top management' (Coleman, 1990, p. 563). This assessment was confirmed in Chitayat's (1985, p. 69) study of working relations between CEOs and chairs. Relations in the public sector, however, may approach more closely Greenleaf's ideal. In public health in the UK, the most common pattern of relations between board chairs and district general managers (DGMs) was found to be 'mutual dependence', and analogous to a kind of marriage (Stewart, 1991a, p. 518). The creative tension in their partnerships stemmed from the chairs' need for information, and the DGMs' reliance on their chairs for the conduct of the health authorities and the interpretation of the chair's role. Both individuals shared the leadership of public health in their districts. As with the negotiated division of labour – both psychological and task related – in Hodgson, Levinson and Zaleznik's (1965) constellation and Gronn's (1999a) couple, the strength of the DGM–chair synergy was anchored in the interplay of perceptions and expectations within the role set. In particular, in DGM–chair partnerships the success of working relations depended on whether one of the two conceived of the relationship 'in that way' and 'which of them should undertake certain kinds of work' (Stewart, 1991a, p. 525).

Parity of Relations

Two alternatives to role sharing by crossing hierarchical boundaries are to dispense with hierarchies and create a situation of parity of relations, or to establish multiple parallel institutional structures, analogous to a constitutional arrangement founded on a separation of powers doctrine. Each possibility generates its own unique synergies.

Three studies in the taxonomy provide some indication of the different dimensions of, and tensions inherent in, the distributed leadership of different sized membership groups which operate in conformity with parity of relations principles. Coleman (1990) notes that as the membership size of groups increases, group incentive structures depend on greater amounts of zeal to enforce norms designed to guarantee action in concert. Starting at the lower end of group size, a musical string quartet operates as a self-governing interdependent work group whose work 'is done only as a unit' in which members use 'each other's outputs as their own inputs' (Murnighan and Conlon, 1991, p. 165). Here, the incentive to work as a unit stems from the members' shared interest in excellence and fidelity to a composition while striving for a distinctive interpretation of a musical score. Performance tensions emerge because quartets have to cope with two paradoxes. The first is the first violinist's duality of role as a musician who provides a lead, as the publicly acknowledged ensemble leader, but who, likewise, is just one-fourth of a quartet's membership. The second paradox concerns the second fiddle, who may be as equally proficient as the first violinist, but who is subordinate in status and also only one-fourth of the membership. Next on the scale of ascending membership size is Vanderslice's (1988) Moosewood collective. Here, 18 members of a restaurant co-operative tried to sever the link between leadership and leaders, by establishing a turn-taking system of leadership, and by rotating all tasks and responsibilities. In order to abolish followership and to be 'leaderful', thereby institutionalising leadership without bosses, policy and operational decisions at Moosewood were made consensually (Vanderslice, 1988, p. 685). When the membership numbers get really big, however, as in social movements, the durability of collective self-management is genuinely put to the test. Such movements strive to achieve 'enough order, but not too much' (Brown and Hosking, 1986, p. 73), and seek to avoid the twin evils of elitism and structurelessness. Nonetheless, when trying to walk this fine line, their rejection of fixed roles, adoption of minimal structures, encouragement of the participation of all, resort to rotating meeting chairs and achievement of solidarity through networking still requires skilled performers. Sometimes a sufficiency of these emerges, but on other occasions it does not. The vitality and longevity of such social movements depends on a successful combination of spontaneous collaboration and the numerical version of distributed leadership distinguished at the outset of this chapter.

Separation of Powers

With the exception of friendship, the synergies considered so far have been the products of either vertical or horizontal systems of authority. A different kind of synergy is in evidence, however, when authority is segmented, as in a separation of powers arrangement.

The segmentation, rather than the concentration, of authority creates a 'pluralistic domain' (Denis, Lamothe and Langley, 2001, p. 809) of multiple agents pursuing different objectives in fluid relationships. This situation generates qualitatively different kinds of tensions. These are evident in boundary disputes between separate authorities over jurisdictional ambiguities and in the alliances pursued by different sets of agents. An example of the former is the conflict concerned with the competing priorities of research and care which arose between a psychiatric ward management group and three clinical teams in a hospital ward, and the question of whether the ideologies of research and care were even compatible (Newton and Levinson, 1973). An instance of the latter tension is found in the numerous sources of leadership in universities, and in the power balances that emerge periodically between different constituencies within an at times unwieldy university structure (e.g., departments, faculties, colleges, professorial boards, senates, councils and offices of presidents). One result of this pattern of dispersed authority, Birnbaum's (1992, p. 124) research found, was that 'institutions could improve even when their presidents were not considered particularly effective'. An important long-term consequence of a separation of power arrangement is that strategic change becomes 'sporadic and unpredictable', as Denis, Lamothe and Langley (2001, p. 810) discovered in their investigation of Canadian health-care. With provincial authority for overall health-care delivery shared between CEOs, hospital boards, physician-elected medical councils and a range of other clinical health professionals, significant change depended on 'a tightly knit leadership group that can act in concert' (Denis, Lamothe and Langley, 2001, p. 817). A decade's research, however, revealed shifting institution-based patterns of collective leadership of varying strength by different combinations of actors which resulted in only sporadic achievement of change.

Divisions of Distributed Labour

The aim of this Chapter has been to consider a range of forms of distributed practice which might be encompassed within an expanded unit of analysis in leadership. In doing so, the discussion has concentrated on the language of leadership, rather than followership. The purpose was to avoid reliance on an orthodox discourse which, a priori, asserts or presumes the existence of a binary division of leadership labour. This purpose was informed by the belief that conventional dualisms such as 'leader–followers' and 'leadership–followership' no longer meaningfully reflect the emerging realities of the workplace. How, for example, is the notion of a leader and followers, or even leaders and followers, to be reconciled with this characterization, by a first-time campus principal from the Readiness project, of the relationship between the campuses of a multi-campus secondary college of nearly 3000 students? 'We're a little bit like Australia (laughs). We're a bit like the states and the federation that meet with the Commonwealth. The Commonwealth and state government really' (NEWPRIN-#10). In this particular college, in addition to the college principal, there were a number of other campus principals, and college and campus assistant principals. Collectively, they have wrestled with issues of college-wide corporate identity:

[Recently] we've been looking a lot more at, at 'How do we become a college'? So, part of our responsibility, things that we do, is that we meet once a week. All the campus principals and [the principal] we meet every Monday morning for a talkfest. And we spend the whole morning every week going through all the issues that, that are college issues that we need to work together on. We have one charter[1] for the college and we, what we do with that is we have improvement focuses. And then from those focuses we have each developed a campus action plan, so what's important for our campus in this area. (NEWPRIN#10)

This group of school administrators has also striven to find a workable balance between overall college control and site-based autonomy:

We, we're trying to develop a way that we take some college responsibility as well as campus responsibility. So, for example, one of the new campus principals who'll take over next year is very good in IT [information technology] so she'll look after the IT side of things and guide the rest of us along. Another one is very good and has a lot of experience with integration [of students with special needs] so she will probably run the college integration program as one of her responsibilities. And I'll probably assist [the college principal] with staffing or finance or something like that. So we're looking at doing that. (NEWPRIN#10)

These excerpts provide a glimpse of a number of aspects of the changes in the division of labour outlined in detail in this chapter. Here, first, is an apparatus which exists for most of the school's working week as a collectively perform-ing work unit, except that on this weekly occasion it assembles as a co-performing grouping. Second, the comments reveal evidence of a number aspects of collective and co-performance, such as interdependent relations between individual role incumbents and between organisational units, differentiation of specialist roles between individuals working in complementary ways in an effort to capitalise on aggregated strengths, synergistic partnerships between individuals with particular expertise, and discursive co-ordination of the activi-ties of the structural parts and wholes through scheduled forums and inter-connected plans. Third, as a role set, the school personnel are shown to be negotiating and ordering their shared role space. Finally, and perhaps most importantly, the example reinforces the significance of two points noted earlier: Simon's (1991) comment on the difficulty of disaggregating individual contri-butions to complex collaborative endeavour and March's (1984) observation about the need for an organisation-wide density of leadership capability. In short, what is depicted here is a set of lateral co-ordination relationships in which, potentially, everyone in attendance may exercise leadership, singly or in combination. In this set of working relations, the familiar mental territory and terminology associated with rank and hierarchy, such as 'superior' and 'subordinate', as Kanter (1989, p. 85) suggested, 'hardly seem accurate'. Moreover, in this context, the on-the-ground credibility of the recently endorsed heroic leadership by design prototypes discussed in the previous Chapter begins to look suspect.

3   The Disengagement of Leaders[1]

Coincidental with the high hopes invested in design specification systems for educational leaders discussed in Chapter 1 and in the face of the distributed realities of work practice just outlined, is the increasing incidence of what commentators refer to as employee abstention and withdrawal. In respect of school leadership succession and development, this phenomenon expresses itself as disengagement from leadership or the growing reluctance of teachers to consider as career possibilities senior level institutional roles which carry with them expectations of leadership. In practical terms, disengagement is manifest in the inability of education systems to recruit sufficient prospective principals and superintendents. Young and McLeod (2001, p. 462) have provided what is perhaps the most forthright assertion to date of the seriousness of leadership disengagement. They claim that in the USA, for example, 'across the nation, state legislators and administrator organizations have determined that a leadership crisis exists in educational administration'. And in the UK, Jones (1999, p. 488) has referred to school heads' perceptions that their deputies are 'shunning headship'.

Certainly, something appears to be happening in the school sectors of a number of countries, for this terminology is unprecedented and, as the evidence to be considered shortly indicates, these examples can be multiplied. On the other hand, it is not precisely clear what that something is, nor why it is occurring. One explanation may simply be that the 'vision thing', as the former US President George Bush once called it, has ceased to capture people's imagination. This possibility is implicit in the title of a recent chapter by the veteran Tavistock Institute theorist and commentator, Eric Miller, 'The leader with the vision: Is time running out?', in which he detects a collapse in employees' commitment to their places of employment. Thus, in organisations which once conferred meaning and were important sources of individual and collective identity, employees have become 'untamed' and top management 'the objects of rage', contempt or disregard (Miller, 1998, p. 12). These sentiments are also echoed in the title of a recent chapter by Dunford (1999, p. 73), who quotes a disgruntled corporate manager voicing his feelings of dispensability: 'If you want loyalty, get a dog!'. The vehemence of this remark indicates the depth of the sense of betrayal experienced. But if so, why might this be?

In order to answer this question and to begin to understand the reasons for these sentiments, I commence this chapter with a discussion of the concept of disengagement. Here I draw on findings from research in progress on leadership readiness. Next, I provide some indication of the extent of the quantitative and qualitative dimensions of the phenomenon of disengagement evident in supply and demand data from a sample of school systems in Australia, the UK and North

America. Finally, I consider a range of possible explanations for disengagement, in particular the relationship between two phenomena: the erosion of traditional workplace career identities and the intensification of leadership work.

Eschewing Leadership

As part of the Monash Readiness for Leadership project, an investigation was undertaken in Victorian government schools into the factors which impeded or facilitated the accession of school personnel to senior level administrative roles. Interviews were conducted with a sample of 36 regional officials, experienced principals (> 5 years in role), newly appointed first-time principals and newly appointed first-time leading teachers[2] in an urban region of the Victorian Department of Education, Employment and Training (DEET). The region (referred to here as 'METRO') is an administrative area comprising nearly 250 schools, including more than 40 secondary colleges, about 180 primary schools and a number of specialist schools catering for the needs of children with a variety of disabilities. METRO contains just over 110,000 students or about 20 per cent of the overall student population of Victoria, around one-third of whom come from language backgrounds other than English. There are some 10,000 DEET employees in METRO, of whom about 8,000 are teachers. METRO is a region in which, in the words of one official, 'we basically would be seeing a 15% turnover of our principal class people each term [in a four-term school year]' due to factors such as resignations, retirements and employment leave. This person continued: 'we have been tracking this now for two years and it has been reasonably constant'. For 2001, when the research took place, METRO officials had set themselves three strategic priority activities, the third of which was 'Support for leadership development and succession planning'. This priority encompassed a number of professional development (PD) programmes for leading teachers and principals, some of which were offered in formal partnership with a major tertiary provider.

In order to pinpoint the kinds of subjective or personal factors involved when teachers decide to pursue, or to abstain from pursuing, senior-level career positions in schools, the aim was to establish how samples of newly appointed, first-time principals and leading teachers self-assessed their leadership attributes and capacities. A related aim was to ascertain whether (and if so how) experienced principals identified leadership attributes and capacities amongst their colleagues. This section of the chapter draws on the principals' data. Eleven experienced principals (seven males, four secondary and three primary, and four females, two secondary and two primary) expressed interest in the project and each person was interviewed for about an hour. The principals provided a demographic profile of their schools and were then asked a series of questions which I had already grouped into three main areas: perceptions regarding teachers whose aspirations were career bound, teachers who were believed to be place bound and principals' strategies for spotting potential talent amongst junior staff. The career-bound–place-bound distinction is used in the research literature to differentiate sources of career satisfaction: mobility between career roles on the one hand, and place holding or the maintenance and extension of existing roles, on the other. The distinction was not intended to convey evaluative judgements about different approaches to career management. A semi-structured interview approach was used. This was designed to be broadly consistent for each informant in respect of question order and wording, but also sufficiently flexible to seek other information if the principals deviated or strayed from the anticipated line of inquiry. There were five main sources of information for the experienced principals' perceptions. These were: their experiences in their own schools; recent experiences in their previous schools; attendance at METRO principal briefings; their membership of principal selection panels in other schools; their principals' association and informal professional networks.

In respect of leadership in schools, experienced principals perceive two broad and dissonant orientations amongst their staff: a culture of disengagement and a culture of aspiration. Each orientation and its subthemes are summarised in turn. Disengagement refers to teachers who prefer to 'keep their heads down' by continuing to perform their current roles, and who are perceived as unwilling, for a variety of reasons, to take on new, different or higher-level responsibilities.

Disengagement

Disengagement is not unlike Sennett's (2002) notion of institutional resignation, a recent product of flat (i.e., delayered) and short (i.e., short-term time frame) organisations and systems of organisations: 'Flat and short have a paradoxical effect: they energise people at the top, and depress people lower down.' The strands that comprise a culture of institutional disengagement range from the benign to the antagonistic. At the benign end of the spectrum, some teachers, as working professionals, are seen as deriving an understandable sense of classroom fulfilment from their work, in which satisfaction is its own reward, as one principal observed (EXPPRIN#8): 'The thing they get the primary good feelings from is really managing their class very effectively and then having a productive year in that regard. That's where the most satisfaction comes I think.' A related strand here is a feeling of personal comfort. The reason teachers do not put up their hands, so to speak, to take on additional responsibilities outside of their classrooms is because they are basically reconciled to what they are doing, as this principal reported (EXPPRIN#2): 'For a lot of them they're, they're earning enough to be comfortable and they don't see a need to do anything other than that.' Sometimes this kind of comfort was seen to derive from the longevity of an appointment in a school (EXPPRIN#8): 'You can have, particularly in a school with very stable staff, you can get people locked into positions for too long a period.' From an institutional perspective, then, this evidence of 'self-regard' represents an expression of Galbraith's (1992, p. 17) notion of contentment.

But as this last principal's observation also suggests, a closely related explanation for not wanting to move outside of one's comfort zone is the experience of being part of a stable staffing structure. On the other hand, that feeling of stability may well mask a sense of insecurity (EXPPRIN#4):

The people who were [teachers in the previous career levels] 1–12³ have been where they are, and will be where they are, for quite some time. I think that now they have been where they are for such a period of time the thought of going somewhere and having to learn about the structures of a new school, and the operation of a new school, and knowledge of a new school is a daunting prospect. They're in a sense afraid. People are afraid of that move: you know where the whiteboard markers are and the disks are kept, and you know the kids in the school, and it's very comfortable to do that.

This same principal drew my attention to the ageing statistical profile of the teaching force in METRO (EXPPRIN#4):

Now, I, I think what's happening with these people is that they're making a quality decision themselves. They're saying: 'I mightn't get as much money but I have control of what I am doing. I'm comfortable in what I am doing. I don't see that taking the next step is going to, at the end of the day, advantage me in a way that's worth taking me outside my comfort zone'.

This principal continued (EXPPRIN#4):

And I've perhaps got three reasons for saying that. They haven't sought to go outside their comfort zone in the time that they have been teaching. There've been all sorts of opportunities through advertisement of positions in other schools and generally they haven't tried to do that. When there were leading teacher positions advertised in this school there was just, there were only two people who applied for them who were internal people to the school. And thirdly, I think they look at the workload of principal class people and the range of responsibilities of principal class people, and whilst they might not like all of the things that have to be done in a classroom that go with being predominantly a classroom teacher, they don't see that it is worth taking the next step.

On the other hand, the explanation for contentment may be as simple, as another experienced principal put it, as the classroom experience consuming all of the teachers' time and energy (EXPPRIN#5):

They have grown up in a culture where they can go into that classroom and close the door. Teaching's a very demanding, challenging, wearing down process, and they've been ground down to the bloody, absolute base level and they are just in survival mode. Even though they could go in and manage a classroom without difficulty. I mean we've people here who can go in, they can manage a classroom without any difficulties, but they use all sorts of excuses why they shouldn't go on [to other roles].

When trying to account for the unwillingness of their staff to put themselves forward for leadership roles, the experienced principals pointed to a number of disincentives. These included family circumstances – such as mid-career teachers having to care for elderly, or even dying, parents or young teenagers – and quality of life concerns. It should be remembered that the experienced principals were themselves prone to the effects of contentment, especially if their appointment had been in one school for a long time. I spoke to a couple of people who had been principals of the one school for nearly two decades. One said to me (EXPPRIN#8):

So once again if you're comfortable and you are getting good vibes from where you are, and all of those things, you naturally, you tend to stay. But I sort of counteract that a bit by continually trying to change things. Well I have to, you know what I mean? Because you've got to, to progress you have to change.

And in another instance, a very experienced principal confessed, in effect, to fostering a culture of contentment amongst his staff (EXPPRIN#9):

My whole emphasis, and this is where you come to an experienced principal, is telling them that their main role is teaching. And I want them to be as good as they can be as classroom teachers, and I would worry about, and I have worried over, because I've been around a long time, for teachers who are devoting too much time to things that are taking them away from their classroom duties. I feel, I believe strongly that they are teachers first, and that teaching is extremely challenging, and if they do that part of their career's work well the rest of it, as far as promotion and moving through, will fall into place for them.

In the UK, following the implementation of the National Curriculum, Jeffrey and Woods (1996) documented teachers' experiences of de-professionalisation undergone during an OFSTED inspection. One experienced Victorian principal detected a similar sense of de-professionalisation amongst staff. Towards the polarity of antagonism, then, were staff who lamented their lack of worth (EXP-PRIN#3): 'The teachers feel that their professional judgment's not valued, not acknowledged and not valued, and I think the principal class feels exactly the same.' Closely associated with lament was an attitude of abstention, or a calculated refusal on the part of teachers to countenance senior level responsibilities. Sometimes, as in this next example, the explanation for this response was that teachers did not like what they saw (EXPPRIN#1):

Now I have, of the leading teachers I do have [four substantive and three on higher duties], I know because I have spoken to them all, none of them at this stage are interested in pursuing principal class positions, which is a bit, disappointing is not quite the right word, but a bit of a shame because three of them particularly I think would make, at least initially, very good assistant principals and probably as they developed very good principals. And when I've asked them why they're not interested they just look at you and laugh and they go, you know: 'We see what you guys put up with, we know what you get paid, and it's not worth it.' And that's a fairly common response. I think they look at the hours, the responsibilities, the complexities of working with staff, parents and the Department of Education as well as students. They've got lots of interest groups or the client groups, or whatever you want to call them around the place, and I think they look at that and look at what they're doing and think 'I'd much rather be here and be more sane'.

Such teachers were turned off by the thought of administration (EXPPRIN#3):

A lot of teachers think that you only get leadership roles if you are good at admin, and teachers don't value admin activity. They don't, they don't see that all the work they do can come undone if it's not well planned for. A lot of people don't want any more work. Teachers are absoluteľy exhausted.

In some cases, abstention stemmed from strong negative feelings (EXPPRIN-#10): 'I've got a significant number of people on subdivision 12 or there-abouts who've been around for a long time. And it doesn't matter what events I structure they are cynical.' Occasionally, this kind of cynicism hardened into a more calculated 'them and us' mindset, as is evident in this comment (EXPPRIN#2):

> I think it's a combination of things. But I think there's, there's a resistance to the struc-ture or structures that we have had over recent years, probably over the last eight or nine years I suppose, in what sort of career paths are offered. And for a lot of them they see the extra responsibility or the extra work that's involved in picking up a higher level position as not matched fairly by the salary levels. So they tend to say: 'Well we'll just stay where we are because we know what we're doing. We might be able to pick up a bit of extra money by doing something else and that's as far as we want to go.'

This sense of them-and-us was sometimes fuelled by an industrial agenda (EXPPRIN#2):

> It's a very strong union school … and leading teachers are often seen by many staff members as being not real staff members because they are leading teachers. So you have got a lot of people who say: 'If I applied for that position I'd be put in that camp and I don't want that.' Okay, so it's safer to stay here, because they tend to be not accepted as well as they should be.

While these extracts may provide few indications of the incidence of disengage-ment, they do communicate a vivid sense of what principals see themselves as having to deal with. In particular, the notion of disengagement takes us right to the heart of what it means to be a good organisational citizen, a current hot topic amongst organisation theorists and institutional economists. Organ (1990, p. 46) has defined organisational citizenship behaviour (OCB) as 'organizationally beneficial behaviors and gestures that can neither be enforced on the basis of for-mal role obligations nor elicited by contractual guarantee of recompense'. From the perspective of utility maximisation theorists the above OCB data might be dismissed as evidence of the problem of 'suboptimal employee effort' (Tomer, 1998, p. 827) – a problem, because from this standpoint an uncommitted employee is typically viewed negatively as a potential free-rider. But an alter-native to this atomised perspective on reality is a view of social capital anchored in relations of trust. Trust in one's employer, for example, may be eroded by per-ceptions of unfair treatment, in which case 'where managers feel that the implicit [career] contract has been breached, they might feel betrayed and reject overtures for commitment' (Dunford, 1999, p. 73). On this line of reasoning (to be devel-oped further shortly), where professional occupational groups (such as teachers) have been stigmatised by governments of a New Right persuasion as publicly subsidised monopolies engaged in provider capture, as they were in the UK and

Victoria during the 1980s and 1990s, disengagement represents an understandable response to unfair treatment, particularly amongst an older, twilight-of-career generation of teachers. On the other hand, disengagement appears to have been less evident amongst a younger, less aggrieved generation of career mobile teachers.

Aspiration

Increasingly, principals find themselves managing a cultural dichotomy: disengagement juxtaposed to a nascent culture of individual aspiration. In schools with smaller staff numbers these differences are evident but spotty. In schools where the numbers of staff approach a critical mass of leading teachers and experienced teachers with responsibility (ETWRs),[4] on the other hand, particularly in the larger secondary colleges, the attitudinal fault lines have solidified. As with the disengagement of the older guard, the aspirational outlook of the younger Turks has a range of elements to it. And underlying all of these, for those teachers striving for something beyond and different from their current roles, a process of personal professional identity construction is occurring. Traditionally, however, the collegialism of teaching has meant that, from early in their careers, teachers have constructed their professional identities in highly robust school-based, union-based and subject association-based peer cultures. Such collegiality often serves to position the individual as an extension of a peer or reference group, a connection which may thwart or impede young teachers' personal career ideals (EXPPRIN#3):

> Often people underestimate their own capacity, because they are very social and they're team players. Some people, and I think that that's a disadvantage of the notion of teamwork, I don't think teamwork is the sole way to go about things. But teachers often can't do a thing unless it's as part of a team. For instance, there were half a dozen of them here. Now I left at 8 o'clock last Thursday night, they were still here, and I think they were generating, you know, the same response to the [ETWR] criteria. They can't do it alone, and the reason they can't do it alone is not that they can't do it alone but they have been told for so long to work in teams: 'How do you co-operate with teams? What's your contribution to teams? Do team planning. Make sure that you're doing the same as the other teacher in our year level or the parents will come and say "Why is this class doing something and not the other?"' But teachers are social. They will knock tall poppies. They will shore up and nurture. I don't mind them shoring up and nurturing people who are struggling, but to shore up and nurture and cover for the lazy ones is very annoying, but they'll do that because that's their prime value. They're committed to team collegiality.

In these socialisation circumstances, it has been the exception for youthful entrants to bring well-formed identities to teaching, although that trend may be changing (EXPPRIN#3):

> The Level 1 person who is in that category just sees that she is very capable. And she is very capable. She's absolutely right, she's a risk taker, she's able to tackle a range of things, she's been in and out of DEET employment [and] in private industry. She is

Level 1 only because she has done those things. She is 35, so if she'd stayed in teaching from the age of 18 she would have been at the top of the tree now, so she's disadvantaged as a result of her own skills. And, she sees herself as having those capacities.

As has been suggested, one major contrast between disengagement and aspiration is that these orientations appear to be generation related. The significance of that contrast is less the differences in age, however, than the fact that these polarities express the distinct training and induction experiences of separate, time-bound career cohorts (EXPPRIN#8):

One of the advantages I think, with some of the new graduates we are getting as against perhaps people who have been at Level 12 for a long time, is they might be more open-minded as they come out [from their university preparation programmes]. And I think they see the career path as not necessarily stopping within the classroom.

These differences were also seen as reflecting the particular labour market relations which obtain when teacher education graduates enter the profession (EXPPRIN#10):

Most of them have probably had that wider life experience. A number of, of them have travelled. And I think, no I think they just, they've done, they've taken a while to get the career they want, they've maybe had to fill in with other sorts of jobs, and they're keen to make an impression I think. I think they are hungry for the work more so than what, in my day it wasn't what you, it wasn't whether you could get a job it was what you were going to do. There were so many jobs available. And we, we, we grew up in the era when every-one owed us a living, and they don't have that attitude. They also don't feel aggrieved at the thought of being on a short-term contract. They don't walk into the classroom with an immediate chip on their shoulders because no one has offered them ongoing employment for the rest of their lives. They know that they've got to, they'll have, got to cobble together their career and it, and a lot of it's up to them. And that's one sort of good thing that has come out of the insecurity in employment in a way. I think that they, they do it because they like teaching and because they know that the job is there to be done.

This experienced principal continued (EXPPRIN#10):

The difference between these, these people really and the ones who were first year out in my day is, a lot of these people couldn't get jobs in their very first couple of years so they've done things, they've travelled, and they've had a bit of life experience, which makes them interesting and it also makes them understand, appreciate teaching as a career. The challenges of it, that it's not just about money, because some of them have done other things which may have brought them more money.

Unlike the older teachers, some of whom were reluctant to apply for the new ETWR positions, principals reported that their younger charges were far less diffident about seeking new challenges (EXPPRIN#5):

[Young teachers] are still working on issues to do with the classroom. But why I say that about them is because they are prepared to take on additional responsibilities all the time.

They're prepared to take on responsibilities leading other groups of teachers, they're prepared to expand their points of view about a whole range of issues to do with the, the much broader context of where secondary education has sort of got itself placed. That would indicate to me that they're, they're developing that whole sort of concept of the broader issues of education in, in, in the socio-economic context which it, in the political context in which it finds itself. They certainly have the skills too, they certainly even now demonstrate the skills to me to be able to manage all the sorts of issues that they would face when they got into a more senior position as an assistant principal or principal or whatever.

Two other examples of youthful vigour, in a primary and secondary school respectively, were (EXPPRIN#11):

She came into the school at the beginning of last year. And, a fairly young teacher but with a very mature outlook, very calm disposition. Probably a higher degree of academic and professional orientation than I'd seen in a number of beginning teachers, and all teachers for that matter, for some time. I actually was not on the selection panel for her, it was another group of staff, and probably the assistant principal who led that, that selection panel, so I really didn't know much about her other than what I had been informed about her along the process. So the assessment that I have made since has basically been my own, but she certainly has led up, led up to the expectations of what that selection group or panel had, and delivered it since. So she, because of her interpersonal skills, her intelligence, and her experience in her, a short period of her career that she had had in other educational settings, I think has stood her in very good stead to take opportunities to not only demonstrate leadership potential but to be a leader. I think she's got a long way to go. And the reason I say that, she, she's able to influence. She, within a very short space of time, because of her interpersonal skills and her maturity and her communication skills, and the experience she's had in other education settings, she was able to influence a group of teachers around her fairly significantly in a fairly short space of time. Teachers that in my assessment probably needed to be a bit more professional in their approach, a bit more communicative, a bit more of a team and so forth. And she was able to influence those factors quite significantly within a couple of terms, as well as attend very successfully to the major teaching and learning tasks in that particular classroom last year, which was extremely challenging. So she had the ability with her peers, and she was also able to demonstrate very good organisational skills and teaching and learning in her own classroom.

And (EXPPRIN#10):

Almost all of [the new young teachers] have taken on something. One is in his second year. He came from [interstate] and he is actually a [football] umpire. Very enthusiastic guy. So I was able to create an ongoing position because I'd hate to lose him, he is the Year 8 co-ordinator, he is looking after 130 students, he is doing a great job. He has, I don't know why but he's prepared to make a career in the state secondary education. He loves it here. He has been offered jobs in private schools, they've tried to poach him, because he is high profile, he's, he's, he umpires the second league down ... So pretty high profile, he likes, he sees himself as having a career here.

In broad terms, then, these experienced principals were working with two groups of colleagues whose attitudes reflected the different generational circumstances of their professional induction. On the one hand, there was an older group of baby-boomers, the survivors of protracted industrial campaigns for professional recognition in the 1970s and 1980s, many of them embittered at the erosion of their hard-won conditions, due to massive personnel downsizing, contracting out of educational services and diminution of resources by the recently (1999) defeated New Right-style state government. This disillusioned group was disengaging itself by jogging – i.e., moving forward, but at a time and pace of its own choosing rather than by going flat out (EXPPRIN#4):

> And, and the kids who are in schools at the moment, I think some of them are being dealt a disservice by the joggers because they are saying: 'Well, three years, four years, I'll take some long service leave that I've got accumulated, I've been teaching what I have been teaching so I know what that's all about, just let me go and let me do it.' And I don't necessarily know that they are firing up in the way that they should be. And that's quite a challenge for principal class people in schools.

This kind of coasting along amounted to time-serving (EXPPRIN#5):

> Then there is another group of people who are sitting on, say, [Level] 2–6, and these are the people who have been teaching for quite a period time, who just want to continue teaching. And they're are probably your most difficult ones to, in actual fact, move to change. They would rather see the world sort of just wash past them as a general sort of statement.

On the other hand, there were the youthful enthusiasts, the more 'Me, Inc.' inclined group, whose apparent capacity to take things in their stride, was consistent with the previous government's aspirations for enterprise culture schooling. Every now and then, the two attitudes collided, with abrasive results (EXPPRIN#3):

> And the one person at, the Level 1 teacher here who does identify where she's at, and she's doing other things and great things, she stood up and took a PD session towards the end of last year. And I can't remember the context but it was appropriate for her to say, she said: 'Actually I don't care what you all think. I don't, it just doesn't bother me. In fact I'm not interested in going out for dinner at night. I'd rather be at home working on my Excel spreadsheet.' And they all laughed and booed her and she's not unsociable. But she had a confidence to say: 'I'm not constricted by the need to be a part of the team.'

For experienced principals, then, these micro-level excerpts represent perceptions of an emerging set of imperatives at the pointy end of self-managed or site-managed schooling. But what happens when we invert the line of vision? How does disengagement appear when viewed from the perspective of the wider educational landscape?

Who wants to be a Leader?

In the opening lines of Roger McGough's poem, *The Leader*, the urge to be accorded leader status is captured in the kind of primitive, insistent whining normally associated with demanding children:

I wanna be a leader
I wanna be a leader
Can I be the leader?
Can I?

This fairy-tale wish is granted in the poem and the ecstasy of the questioner knows no bounds ('Yippee, I'm, the leader'), except that there is just one snag: McGough ends his poem with the new-found leader feeling at a loss and asking 'OK what shall we do?' In the case of teachers, fewer and fewer of them are voicing the kind of desire verbalised by McGough's imaginary child. Moreover, unlike in the poem, teachers are very much aware of what leaders have to do, for they know there is a lot that the new design standards expect them to do (see Chapter 1), and that, as I hope to show, is a large part of the problem.

The effect of the actual and potential disengagement of teachers from leadership roles is to reduce the supply of suitable candidates for role vacancies. Currently, the demand for replacements appears to be outstripping supply and there is an excess of vacancies over appointable candidates. Public awareness of this looming shortage of school leaders began to emerge in education systems in the English-speaking world in the late-1990s. What started as a trickle of concern has now become a steady stream, although not yet a flood. Typical of journalists' reports appearing in *Education Week*, the US digest of educational events, have been such headlines as 'Principals' shoes are hard to fill, study finds' (18 March 1998) and 'Demand for principals growing, but candidates aren't applying' (3 March 1999). Similar gloomy headlines have appeared consistently in the *Times Education Supplement* over the last three years or so, such as 'Shortage of heads worsens' (11 September 1998) and 'Headship beggars can't be choosers' (11 February 2000). In these reports, a range of quantitative and qualitative difficulties associated with the demand for principals, deputy principals and superintendents have been cited. While the incidence and severity of the difficulties experienced with leadership supply differ for primary and secondary schools, the quantitative factors reported include:

- reduced numbers of applications for advertised principal vacancies in a growing percentage of schools
- a consequent diminution of the numbers of candidates worthy of short listing
- an increasing percentage of schools failing to appoint after their first advertisement for vacancies, and
- growing numbers of temporary principal and deputy or vice principal approvals.

The following qualitative factors have been cited:

- a diminution of the numbers of quality applicants
- an inability to recruit minority candidates.

In some instances, the combined effects of these trends have been exacerbated by two additional factors: first, pension scheme provisions; second, the changing

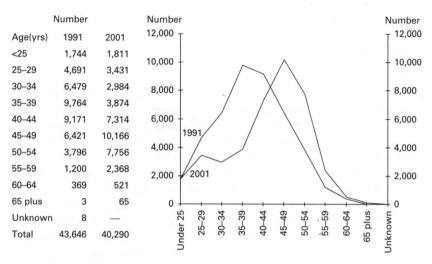

Age(yrs)	Number 1991	Number 2001
<25	1,744	1,811
25–29	4,691	3,431
30–34	6,479	2,984
35–39	9,764	3,874
40–44	9,171	7,314
45–49	6,421	10,166
50–54	3,796	7,756
55–59	1,200	2,368
60–64	369	521
65 plus	3	65
Unknown	8	—
Total	43,646	40,290

FIGURE 3.1   *Number of teaching service staff (including principal class) receiving pay by five-year age groups as at June 1991 and 2001*

TABLE 3.1   *Number of teaching staff (including principal class) receiving pay by age group as at June 1991, 1996 and 2001*

	1991	1996	2001
Under 25	1,744	916	1,811
25–29	4,691	2,548	3,431
30–34	6,479	3,557	2,984
35–39	9,764	6,426	3,874
40–44	9,171	9,705	7,314
45–49	6,421	8,093	10,166
50–54	3,796	4,944	7,756
55–59	1,200	1,220	2,368
60–64	369	236	521
65 plus	3	12	65
Unknown	8	—	—
Total	43,646	37,657	40,290
Mean age	39.7	42.2	43.5

demographics of the teaching service. The impact of pension and superannuation entitlements on existing and prospective numbers of principals in Victoria, for example, is evident in the following data.[5] In respect of pension entitlements, the columns for 1991 and 2001 in Figure 3.1 indicate the extent of the attrition of teaching service members between the age bands 50–54 and 55–59. In 1991, for example, there were 6,421 teachers aged 45–49. A decade later, when that 45–49 cohort had aged to become the 55–59 age band, there were just 2,368 teachers. This difference represented a loss of 63 per cent. The main cause of this dramatic loss of personnel is the incentive to exit at or before age 54.11 created by the provisions of the state superannuation scheme. As regards the demographic profile

TABLE 3.2   *Number of principal class members receiving pay by age group as at June 1991, 1996 and 2001*

Age (years)	1991	1996	2001
25–29		6	5
30–34	6	32	22
35–39	87	159	85
40–44	355	636	393
45–49	639	920	962
50–54	589	905	1,052
55–59	122	142	271
60–64	22	16	37
65 plus	—	—	3
Total	1820	2,816	2,830
Mean age	48.5	47.8	49.5

of teaching, Figure 3.1 shows the 'greying' of the Victorian service. In 1991, more than half of the total teaching service was employed in the 35–39, 40–44 and 45–49 age bands (i.e., 58 per cent or 25,356). By 2001, the bulge created by these bands had aged, so that more than half the total service (reduced by more than 3,000 during the decade) was located in the 40–44, 45–49 and 50–54 age bands (i.e., 63 per cent or 25,236).

Further confirmation of greying can be seen in Table 3.1. First, the mean age of teachers increased by nearly four years over the decade 1991–2001. Second, by 1996 the total number of teachers had fallen by about 14 per cent (or 6,000) compared with 1991, with the losses in that five-year period absorbed by the younger to mid-career age bands: i.e., < 25 (42 per cent or 742), 25–29 (45 per cent or 2,143), 30–34 (45 per cent or 2,922) and 35–39 (34 per cent or 3,338). While the 2001 column indicates that the < 25 and 25–29 cohorts have recovered significantly since 1996, the proportion of teachers under age 40 (i.e., bands < 25 to 35–39) was considerably less in 2001 compared with a decade earlier. In 1991, 51 per cent of teachers (or 22, 678) were aged less than 40 and 36 per cent (or 13,447) in 1996. In 2001, however, the corresponding figure was only 30 per cent (or 12,100). It would appear, therefore, that the young aspiring generation of teachers on whom the experienced principals interviewed earlier were pinning their faith as future leaders represents a diminishing proportion of the service.

Not only is the Victorian teaching service greying but, as the data in Table 3.2 indicate, the principal class is becoming even greyer. There are a number of features to note. First, the average age of principal class members increased during the decade to nearly 50. Second, for each of the three five-year periods, two-thirds or more of the principal class were aged between 45 and 54, with the percentage increasing in 2001: i.e., 67 per cent (or 1228) in 1991, 65 per cent (or 1825) in 1996 and 71 per cent (or 2014) in 2001. Third, while the percentage of principals aged 45 and over had risen by 2001, there was a corresponding decrease of younger principals in the 40–44 age band. Thus, in 1991 20 per cent of principals were aged 40–44 and this proportion increased to 23 per cent in 1996, but by 2001 it had fallen back sharply to only 14 per cent. The increase of

3 per cent in this age band between 1991 and 1996 probably reflected an infusion of 'new blood' into the service to fill the vacancies created by the numerous principals taking up the voluntary departure packages offered by the previous government from 1993. This youthful trend, however, did not persist through to 2001. Fourth, the very low numbers of principals in the age bands between 25 and 39 suggest that most principals take up their appointments when they are about 40 years old. Given the pattern of superannuation-induced attrition at 54.11, therefore, first-time appointees can generally anticipate principalships lasting for a maximum of about 15 years or an average of two to three appointments at most. But with the demographic bulging occurring at ages 45–49 and 50–54, with the average age of principals now 50 and a significant increase in retirements expected by 2006, the career profile of the principalship is likely to change dramatically. Now that 30 per cent of the current teaching service is aged under 40, for example, as is suggested in Table 3.1, a sizeable cohort of relatively junior and inexperienced teachers may have to fast-track themselves, or will have to be fast-tracked by DEET, through to the principal class.

Formal recognition by employer authorities and professional associations of the existence, nature and extent of the supply problems typified by these data has been patchy and uneven. One of the most comprehensive responses has been a Canadian report commissioned by the Ontario Principals' Council (Williams, 2001), with its title, *Unrecognized Exodus, Unaccepted Accountability*, reflecting, respectively, the related themes of delayed official acknowledgement of shortages and the disengagement or opting out addressed in this chapter. The statistical picture in Ontario is consistent with that in Victoria. Data on the provincial pool of principal certificate holders suggest that the mean age of certificate holders is 51, an estimated 49 per cent of them (about 8,000 persons) are expected to retire from the pool by 2005 and that the average annual rate of new certificate completions is just over 700. In short, 'the number of replacement qualified persons over the five year period [to 2005] is only 44 per cent of those projected to retire' (Williams, 2001, p. 6). Confirmation for this pattern was obtained in a survey of approximately 950 practising primary and secondary principals and deputy principals, the results of which led Williams (2001, pp. 9–10) to conclude that 'there will be a serious looming problem in filling key leadership positions for the province's public school boards'. Not only that, but the possible replacements, as in Victoria, are likely to be 'very inexperienced', thereby creating 'an ongoing, massive professional development challenge' (Williams, 2001, p. 25).

Intensification of Work

This evidence from Victoria and Ontario points to an emerging crisis for school leadership. The question of why that crisis exists and why it has emerged so quickly, let alone what can be done about it, is less clear. Williams asked 92 teacher respondents identified by Ontario principals and vice-principals as qualified for the principalship and vice-principalship, but who decided not to pursue these career options, to list the deterrents and disincentives that had caused them to abstain. Their suggestions complemented the explanations provided by the Victorian principals for teachers' disengagement. Together, these point towards the increasing intensification of professional work.

The second part of this book will expound on and illustrate some key features of the dynamics of work intensification. In the remainder of this chapter my purpose is to explain what this phenomenon signifies and why I think it is the key to understanding leadership disengagement. Intensification means that work becomes harder and harder to perform. The paradox of intensification, however, is that at the same time as the experience of working becomes ever more personally taxing, like moths attracted to a flame, people tend to become, and are willing to become, consumed by it. Unless one is predisposed to opt out or withdraw, then intensification beckons like a siren call. A good example of what I mean was provided by one of the new principals interviewed for the Readiness project. It was a Friday morning when I spoke to her. Early on, after telling me she had already worked four 12-hour days that week, as well as spending all of the previous Sunday at the school, at the very end of the interview, NEWPRIN#4 rattled off a summary of all the things she had had to do so far that year (it was late May, barely four months into the school year). This included having to read and respond to hundreds of DEET e-mail messages, which she proudly showed me, all neatly sorted and filed in their plastic colour-coded ring binders. She then concluded her shopping list of deeds by exclaiming how 'it just goes on and on', after which, to my surprise, she remarked, 'But I love it'.

Significance of Intensification

Intensification now goes with the territory of what it means to be a leader and a manager. It is partly about task overload, not just in the sense of occasionally having more things to do than there are hours in the day to do them, but also the experience of a never-ending treadmill effect, in which the awareness of overloading is constant, sustained and compounded by numerous deadlines with incredibly short lead times. In these circumstances, Clarke and Newman (1997, p. 74) note, the management of one's emotions becomes vital – hence the recent rash of popular books on the theme of emotional intelligence:

> To compete in the managerial career stakes now means demonstrating commitment through long (often excessive) hours of work and being able to cope with high stress. Staying on to be present at the crucial meeting to deal with the latest crisis has to take precedence over familial, relationship or community commitments. Whether the meeting is effective or not is sometimes less significant than being seen to have the commitment to be there. Such intensification, linked to career uncertainty and occupational fragility, has a profound effect on both men and women, with implications for their children, partners and parents as well as their own quality of life.

But not only is this new work regime of lived intensity physically and emotionally draining for individuals, it is also highly cognitively demanding. 'The team form of work', according to Donnellon (1996, p. 221), as opposed to the 'functional work' of tightly defined individual job descriptions, for example, intensifies the workplace in two main ways. First, it increases the 'salience of the task demands', or people's sense of the significance of the consequences of what they are doing. This awareness occurs because team members acquire 'a broader perspective on their own work' and come to see it as 'more meaningful than was previously the case'. While this kind of engagement can be experienced as both mentally challenging and exhilarating, it can also be potentially intimidating and draining, because so much energy is invested and yet a decision may go wrong. Second, the team provides its members with the security of cohort membership for taking collective action. Such safety in numbers may even 'challenge managerial perspectives and/or commands that would have a negative impact on the team's performance of its task', thereby providing a secure cover for risk-taking but, as we will see in Chapter 6, it also subjects each individual to the discipline of team norms and, in some work contexts, to heightened and sophisticated regimes of managerial surveillance.

Explaining Intensification

Intensification is partly the result of participative work practices in which organisations, in effect, renegotiate the work contract by doing away with much direct line supervision in return for which their workers are invited 'to give more of themselves to their work: to give more time, to give more energy, to identify strongly with the goals and needs of their organization, and to learn how to collaborate effectively with coworkers' (Barker, 1999, p. 11). And there's the rub, identify: for the point about intensification is that it changes what it means to be a professional, with that change being experienced as a loss, rather than a gain, in discretionary autonomy and the assumption of what many commentators regard as a de-professionalised or proletarianised status. In this new implicit contractual arrangement, a clutch of top-level managers provides the overall steering capacity, while everyone else does the rowing beneath a set of norm-governed strategic and visionary rubrics. Transposed across an entire school system of self-managing units, principals might be able to provide some limited organisational steering as part of this new deal but, in reality, they find themselves reduced to head rowers. To go with the momentum of the work flow resulting from intensification in these circumstances, therefore, requires each of the individual rowers to reconstruct their professional identities and career trajectories.

Coping with Intensification

As yet, there are no fully articulated typologies of how school leaders and potential school leaders are coping with intensified work. Clearly, at one end of the spectrum would be the kind of aging teacher flight response witnessed by the experienced principals reported earlier on. At the other end would be the kind of super-leadership displayed by NEWPRIN#4 (and legitimised, as we saw, by the rising bar of the new design specifications). After her 'But I love it' utterance, the remainder of the interview went like this:

GRONN: It's obvious that you do!
NEWPRIN#4:   I really love my job but I get frustrated ... I cope quite well but then
               I don't have other demands in my life.
GRONN: If you get ill?
NEWPRIN#4:   If I get ill well nothing, nothing will get done. It will all be piled up.
               Because I've got an AP [assistant principal], but she teaches, she
               takes phys ed [physical education] and supports my grade 5 and 6.

The words 'It will all be piled up' here should not be taken as implying the complete dependence of her staff on NEWPRIN#4's focused leadership, nor as a lack of distributed leadership for, as she had explained to me earlier in the interview, she and her AP tried to tag-team their relationship as much as possible. Rather, the words signal the absence of the requisite resources if all of the responsibilities demanded of a small, self-managing primary school are to be properly fulfilled. After all, if intensification is the result of the lean side of 'lean and mean' under steering and rowing, then having less resources stands for the mean side. Hence the feelings of frustration ('but I get frustrated') that are the flipside of the coin of intensification. The other point to note in her remarks is the vulnerability of an intensified work order. Should a CEO or, as in this case, its school principal equivalent, fall ill, or if domestic concerns intrude – which they did not in this case ('I don't have other demands in my life'), but as they did in numerous instances in Hochschild's (1997) time bind study at Amerco – then the organisational edifice is exposed as potentially brittle.

Boyle and Woods (1996) provide another example of a super-leader, Chris, an English lower primary school principal with a self-chosen 0.5 teaching load and who was the absolute acme of 'omni-awareness', with 'first-hand insight into all aspects of school life, a physical presence in all areas, and experience of other roles within the institution as well' (Boyle and Woods, 1996, p. 553). At one point Chris confessed to (bragged about?) working an 80-hour week. Personally imposed effort norms like this one suggest that, if they are not prepared to exercise the flight option, then at least to some extent, intensification requires such people to connive in their own enslavement to their work. Accountability under steering and rowing works less by direct control but by placing the onus squarely on the individual who self-manages to shape up. But manoeuvrability and the freedom to negotiate space on one's own terms are hard for an intensified self to find. It took Chris nearly four years to retranslate her sense of persecutory guilt, the sense that 'the system's gotcha!' or was peering over her shoulder, into feelings of depressive guilt – guilt resulting from an awareness that there were sometimes other important priorities apart from jumping when she thought the powers that be were wanting her to. Somewhere further back along the spectrum of responses to work intensification there are to be found those rare birds such as Riseborough's (1993) Stan D. Fast, a colourful example of an English principal who succeeded in immunising his school from the blandishments of the policy steerers. Or, there might even be occasional instances of principals collaborating on behalf of their schools in an effort to subvert official policies (Wallace, 1998). But these recalcitrant cases appear to be the exceptions.

The New Work Order

The experience of NEWPRIN#4 is emblematic, then, of the new work of educational leaders: long hours, endless demands, punishing pace and continual frustration. Most of the new and experienced principals whom I interviewed worked exceeding long hours. They arrive at school very early in the morning, they often leave after dark and they work most weekends. From a leadership development and succession point of view in schools, the experienced principals were worried about the consequences of their onerous work routines. Consumed by tasks and demands, they felt that they were not always displaying sound leadership practice. In this respect, as this next reflection from EXPPRIN#11 makes clear, they are voicing a sense of Boyle and Woods's (1996) depressive guilt (the sense that 'I'm letting my colleagues down by not attending to their needs') and persecutory guilt (the sense that 'It's my responsibility to help mould the next generation of school leaders'):

> My concern is that you are modelling the wrong things. You are not modelling what I would say would be … often enough I suppose … effective good leadership. Because you are so tied up with administration and the frustrations of administration workload rather than having the ability to model leadership. You do it every day, but to be good leaders you need to be freed up to be much better leaders in our system. And I have a major concern about that, where I am really concerned that I am perhaps putting potential leaders in the school off. They don't want the workload. They don't want the conflict. They don't want that much challenge.

This sense of *mea culpa* is understandable but, as Williams (2001, p. 20) notes, potential candidates 'clearly are picking up negative sentiments and comments from their own principals and vice principals during moments of frustration'.

The effect of work intensification, then, is to expand the role space of the individual job-holder, as Stewart (1991a) calls it, but without increasing the number of occupants to fill the inflated space. Distributed leadership, as we have seen, is in part a response to this expansion of space and proliferation of tasks. The five highest ranked of 22 dissatisfiers cited by Williams's (2001, p. 11) Ontario principals and vice-principals are instructive in this regard. These (with the percentage of the sample dissatisfied in brackets) were: 'Adequacy of time to plan for provincially mandated changes' (92 per cent), 'Number of curriculum changes mandated by the province' (86 per cent), 'Adequacy of time to work with students' (83 per cent), 'Amount of in-school staff support for the principals given workload requirements' (79 per cent) and 'Amount of time the job requires' (78 per cent). Ostensibly, the critical resource cited here is time, rather than space, but one reason for the scarcity of time is that respondents claim there is simply too much to do in the time available. That is, each individual's role space is overflowing with task demands. The deterrents cited by the sample of abstainers were not inconsistent with these five nominations. These include concern at the number of provincial government reforms, the unreasonable pace of reform and shortcomings in the mode of implementation (Williams, 2001, p. 21).

The New Work Order and Careers

Research into the links between professional identity formation, perceptions of intensified work and the decision to seek or abstain from career roles entailing leadership is still in its infancy. The concepts of career boundarylessness and do-it-yourself careers increasingly preoccupy career theorists. Recent research into corporate sector career patterns, however, suggests that while some younger managers are more predisposed to the ideas of mobile employability and marketable career portfolios, pronouncements of the redundancy of traditional bureaucrati-cally structured careers may be premature (Wajcman and Martin, 2001). In light of these developments, the conventional wisdom that teachers will inevitably apply for career promotions may be questionable, as Draper and McMichael's (2000) research has acknowledged. Noteworthy in this respect were the responses of two first-time leading teachers interviewed for the Readiness project to questions about their future career intentions. LT#3, for example, was a young man in his early-thirties who had been teaching for over 10 years and who had recently been appointed head of a subject department in a secondary school, following a three-year stint teaching in an overseas school. Did he aspire to becoming a member of the principal class? Not really. After working for a while as a leading teacher, he thought it highly likely that he would leave education altogether and commence a small business. Likewise with LT#7, who was quoted in Chapter 2. Did being a leading teacher represent the summit of her ambitions? No. As a young teacher, also in her early thirties, she had already worked in a number of different educa-tion systems and in a variety of schools. Seeking an assistant principal role was a future career possibility, but she was equally likely to depart education and try her hand at other work.

In summary, the intensification of school leaders' engagement with their work has recently been acknowledged by practitioners and researchers. Its personal significance for individual leaders and its wider institutional and systemic signifi-cance in loosening teachers' professional OCB commitment to the pursuit of pos-sible future leader roles is being recognised by educational employers, albeit belatedly. As yet, however, there have been few detailed analyses of the dynamics of intensification in school leadership practice and how these factors play them-selves out. My intention in the remainder of this book is to rectify that lacuna. Accordingly, in the following chapters I synthesise a body of research with a view to better illuminating the dynamics of leadership practice. In contrast with the architectural framework outlined to this point in the discussion, I have grouped this material around the theme of 'the ecology of leadership'. Without seeking to overdraw the analogy with organisms and their environments in the natural world, the notion of ecology is intended to convey a naturalistic approach to understanding some dimensions of school leaders' work. That is, the discus-sion tends to privilege action-oriented, on-the-hoof, *in situ* accounts of leaders as they go about their work: in essence, lead*ing* rather than leader*ship*. Inevitably, but unavoidably, even within a focus on practice, not every aspect can be con-sidered, and so the discussion is necessarily selective. Mindful of the kinds of grandiose assumptions that form part of the new normative design specifications dealt with in Chapter 1, I have chosen to discuss what researchers have shown leaders to *actually* do, as opposed to what they *should* do (Chapter 4). Equally mindful of importance of distribution, I dwell on what the research community has to say about committee and team work (Chapters 5 and 6). Finally, given the recent interest in the emotional costs of workplace restructuring and reform, I say something about the feelings of leaders (Chapter 7). In this quest for economy of discussion space, one of the obvious gaps is any separate treatment of the ethical and valuational aspects of work intensification. Rather than ignore these features altogether, the most workable compromise in the space available was to draw on the growing body of conceptual and policy critique in the domain of school leadership, and interweave it, where appropriate, into the body of the discussion.

Notes

1 An earlier version of this chapter was presented as a seminar paper to the annual meeting of the National Educational Leadership Development Network, Melbourne, 21 June 2000.

2 Leading teachers are generally the most experienced and senior teachers in primary and secondary schools. Appointments to leading teacher vacancies are made by a school-based selection panel. Leading teachers exercise responsibilities for a significant level or area of school operations, such as subject or programme co-ordination, pastoral care, student welfare or headship of a subject department. Leading teachers comprise the pool of potential recruits to advertised principal and deputy principal vacancies.

3 As part of a new industrial agreement, a revised career structure for teachers came into force in Victoria from January 2001, with the previous 12-step incremental scale for teachers classified as Level 1 now divided into Beginning Teacher (1-1-1-6) and Experienced Teacher (2-1-2-6) categories.

4 Inserted between the Leading Teacher and Experienced Teacher categories in the new career structure was the new Experienced Teacher With Responsibility classification, known as ETWR.

5 Kindly provided by the Workforce Development Branch of DEET and cited with permission.

PART 2

THE ECOLOGY OF LEADERSHIP

---

4   What do Leaders do?

A focus on leading invites a consideration of process. The most appropriate way to further an understanding of process is to address the question: what do leaders do? This chapter synthesises a body of research by commentators who have posed this, or a very similarly worded, question such as what do managers do? and some ancillary questions, e.g., how do leaders go about or accomplish this doing? and why do leaders do what they do? These kinds of questions necessitate an analysis of action. And action, which incorporates the agency of social actors, as was suggested in Chapter 2, also entails an appreciation of context. Immediately, however, we confront two dilemmas, each forming part of a current battle for the control, reconstruction and engineering of professional practice. The first concerns, what is for many reformers, the invalidity of existing practice. The dilemma arises here because the kind of logic that informs the normative standards rubrics described in Chapter 1, under which I have suggested school leaders will be required increasingly to operate, denies the relevance or significance of context. Indeed, standards are vehicles for reconstituting and delegitimating contextualised practice in order to 'reshape the conception of educational leadership for schools throughout the nation' (Murphy, Yff and Shipman, 2000, p. 25). On the other hand, rather than being subjected to control by norms, the second dilemma for the study of practice is a counter-trend to mandate practitioner control by research-based evidence. As Levačić and Glatter (2001, p. 13) have noted, these two broad strategies for control are at odds with each other for, 'despite the wealth of research into headteachers over the past 20 years … there is no evidence that it had any influence on the construction of standards'.

At the time of writing, the movement for EIPP in education, and in school leadership, is in its infancy.[1] As with standards, debate over the meaning, desirability and feasibility of an evidence-informed approach to practice is gathering momentum. Interest in EIPP in school leadership is likely to be driven in large measure by models of practice and their (direct and indirect) impact, if any, on indicators of aspects of school effectiveness. Leaving aside contentious issues concerned with the causal relation between action and outcomes, in particular unintended consequences, and what counts as evidence of effectiveness, the actions of school leaders are inextricably bound up with, and in large measure determined by, educational values and policy ends. To what extent, in these circumstances, then, will valid research and evidence exclude work informed by alternative values and ideologies, including those which are critical of government policy (see Wallace, 2001a)? From either of these perspectives, norms or evidence, research into processes in natural settings becomes highly relevant. With the former recent policy initiative in mind, for example, an understanding of workplace realities may reveal the extent to which standards-derived expectations of leadership are reasonable, given the demands on school leaders as they endeavour to cope with intensified work. These features of leadership practice may also call into question the validity and utility of standards as levers for institutional change. With the emerging interest in EIPP in mind, on the other hand, naturalistic research will be helpful in indicating which contextual factors act as barriers or bridges to the uptake of evidence-informed propositional knowledge. Of even greater significance, however, is the possibility that the findings of context-oriented research may question the feasibility of school-level actors making evidence-informed decisions, particularly within the circumscribed limits on action created by the constraints of national and systemic policies (Levačić and Glatter, 2001, p. 10).

With these considerations in mind, in the next two sections I undertake a critical review of research into the work of leaders and managers in non-educational and educational settings. Here, the emphasis is on what this material reveals about the division of leadership labour and the dynamics of leaders' work. As mentioned in the Introduction, discussions of leadership usually also invite consideration of management, and vice versa. The research reviewed is no exception. In much of it the main focus is on the role of managers, but in numerous instances there is an expectation (and evidence) that a significant component of what managers do is to lead. Both non-educational and educational areas of activity are considered in this review, because research in the former domain has provided the stimulus for many investigations in the latter. In this appraisal I touch on both substantive and methodological issues, and gaps in accumulating knowledge. Further, I link the discussion to the earlier architectural themes. In the third section, I address the unresolved issues raised by research into managers' work, especially those which concern the agency of leaders and managers, and the range of factors which both constrain and enable leaders' autonomy and discretion. The overall object of this research synthesis is to assess the adequacy of the current knowledge base as a possible departure point for evidence-informed judgements about practice. In the final section, as a means of redirecting future research into managers' and leaders' work, there is a brief outline of an alternative framework for understanding leadership practice which draws on recent discussions of activity theory. Here I argue that the focus of analysis should be activity systems, rather than the work patterns of individuals considered as isolated actors.

The Realities of Leading and Managing

Leading and managing have always been experienced as intensely demanding forms of work. The biographies and autobiographical recollections of practitioners substantiate this claim. A long legacy of research into managerial practice also reveals evidence of intensification. In these senses, then, work intensification is not news. But a close inspection of this latter body of material reveals both continuities and discontinuities. The phenomenon of work intensification shares much in common with previous analyses of practice while also displaying features that deviate markedly.[2]

Researching Work Practices

The evidential base on which to substantiate claims of continuity extends as far back as Carlson's (1951) pioneering study of nine Swedish managing directors. The reasons given for this enduring interest in managerial work practices since that time have varied. Stewart (1988, p. 113), for example, has suggested that 'knowing what managing is really like' would stimulate self-improvement on the part of practitioners and would help them to diagnose inefficient performance. For Stewart, as well as for Sayles (1964, p. 205), management afforded considerable scope for agency. For this reason, practitioners were mistaken in believing that (Stewart, 1988, p. 119): 'everything they do is a demand, that is work they must do. They fail to recognise that much of what they do reflects their own personal interests and experience. It is in reality a choice that might not be exercised by someone else in the job'. Time was an important unit of measure in Carlson's work and in subsequent studies, and so this potential for inefficiency to which Stewart (1988, pp. 120–35) drew attention provided the stimulus for the strong interest in developmental and consultative programmes in time management in the 1980s.

Another attraction in studying work practice has been that it represents a reaction to the prescriptive nature of much early management theory and the search for normative principles of management. This characteristic accounts in part for the enthusiastic reception accorded Mintzberg's (1973), *The Nature of Managerial Work*. In what now reads as a scarcely credible assertion, in his review of Mintzberg's book Weick (1974, p. 111) claimed that 'nowhere in the literature do we have any useful empirical statements of just what managers do. And it is this void that Mintzberg set out to fill'. Here, Weick had overlooked not only Carlson (1951) but also the earlier edition of Stewart's (1988) *Managers and their Jobs*, along with the two important pioneering studies by Sayles (1964) and Hodgson, Levinson and Zaleznik (1965). Sayles (1964, p. 241), whose book *Managerial Behavior*, Mintzberg (1973, p. 218) considered 'stands apart from all the others', provided the most succinct justification for the study of managerial work practices, when he wrote that 'abstract job descriptions and departmental "charters" do not determine who does what as much as do evolving patterns of work relationships'.

Origins of Work Practice Research

Interest in the work practices of managers had quickened towards the end of the Second World War and, in Carlson's (1951, pp. 13–17) case, his research was driven by the need for adequate preparation and education of private sector executives, and with the aim of improving their training and selection. Precise knowledge of 'how executive work is carried out' (Carlson, 1951, p. 16) would alone satisfy this purpose, but that knowledge had to be procured without influencing or interfering with the executives' normal working behaviour. This was easier said than done and it caused Carlson to wrestle with a number of problems that have continued to plague researchers. He decided to observe the managing directors for four weeks in their work locales, along with the persons with whom they interacted, their modes of communication, the subject matter of these communications and action taken in relation to that subject matter. But observation was by no means straightforward. His major difficulties arose out of knowing what to count as 'work'. First, what about when an executive spent time alone? 'We shall never find out either what the managing director does when he [*sic*] works by himself', said Carlson (1951, p. 36) 'or which problems he specially wants to talk to other people about.' For this reason, 'continuous interviews' were used to supplement observations. Second, it was virtually impossible to log every telephone call or contact, particularly when the executives were on inspection tours or engaged off site. In these instances, what was a managing director to request his secretary to record for him on the researchers' contact record when he returned the following morning (Carlson, 1951, pp. 41–2)?

> Was reading of memoranda and trade journals work only when it was done in his office or without disturbance at his home in the evenings, or was it also when he did it in the train going to and from his office? Was it work when he discussed the firm's affairs with a colleague or a subordinate during a Sunday walk?

Third, there were problems in defining contacts. What was the duration of a contact, for example, when an executive met several people simultaneously or when another person met him while he was engaged with someone else?

Carlson's use of 'observation' was misleading, for it did not mean literally being watched by a third party; instead, he relied on the executives to complete self-report questionnaires (in the form of single-card summaries) on which they were to record details of matters handled and actions taken. Analysis of these revealed that, on average, a normal day at the office was just under 10 hours (excluding weekend work at home), with about one-third of the time spent working outside the firm (Carlson, 1951, pp. 63–4). The executives spent varying intervals of time alone in their offices, during which they 'scarcely had time to start on a new task or to sit down and light a cigarette before they were interrupted by a visitor or a telephone call'. The net effect of their 'excessive working load' was that, over the long term, all but one managing director believed they 'could not continue with their present amount of work' (Carlson, 1951, pp. 73–4, 75). Carlson confessed quite candidly to the weaknesses of his study, one of which was that he ignored the social system operating in each firm and had considered the point of view of only one actor, so that when an executive sought information, such procurement might be regarded by a subordinate as 'decision taking' or 'receiving orders'. This possibility prompted him to conclude that a full understanding of executive actions necessitated observation of them 'in relation to the simultaneous actions of other people in the organisation' (Carlson, 1951, p. 118).

Three years later, Burns (1954) did just that in a British engineering factory. By slightly modifying Carlson's approach, he studied the social system of a senior executive group comprising a manager and three immediate subordinates at the head of a 128-person strong department. Again, the executives self-recorded their interactions, this time for five weeks, thereby generating (as in Carlson's case) statements of opinions about their behaviour, as opposed to statements of behaviour. Burns found exactly as Carlson had predicted, so that when the record forms for the executives' exchanges were cross-referenced they revealed discrepant interpretations of the same events. In a reversal of Carlson's order of reporting, perhaps in keeping with wider cultural differences in status maintenance in their respective countries, Burns (1954, p. 95) noted that 'half the time, what the manager thought he was giving as instructions or decisions was being treated as information or advice'. Interestingly, he believed his data undermined the significance of vertical, dyadic authority relations between superiors and subordinates and instead highlighted 'a complementary lateral system rendered necessary by problems and difficulties internal to the group' (Burns, 1954, p. 97).

Extended Field Studies

Sayles (1964) built on this early work and provided what is still, arguably, the best theoretically informed first-hand account of management practice. He augmented Carlson's quest for accurately grounded training programmes by asserting the need for a firm basis for personnel evaluation as his warrant for asking: 'What, then, is the manager's job; what is the nature of administration?' (Sayles, 1964, p. 14). Sayles gave as an additional justification the percipient observation that changes in the division of labour were likely to be accelerated by the foreshadowed automation of aspects of managerial work. He rejected the popular myth of organisations and managers as discretely boxed entities. When modern decisions are 'the product of actions through time on the part of many people' (Sayles, 1964, p. 27), just as Follett (1973, pp. 120–1) had claimed they were some four decades before, and problem-solving was 'a matter of flows, and processes', it made precious little sense to think of managers as performing static, well-bounded and readily defined jobs. Rather, they found themselves immersed in numerous relationships built on an expanding rate of specialisation which necessitated a greater degree of synchronisation and co-ordination of effort. The paradox of management, then, was that a developing division of labour generated simultaneous and contradictory pressures: the need for increased managerial discretion at the same time as it required overall conformity and co-ordinated effort (Sayles, 1964, p. 33). From Sayles's point of view, then, a manager was less the hierarchically defined occupant of a role who designed and initiated ordered sets of relations in accordance with the fine-grained legalisms of employment contracts, than someone who was a creature of changes in the division of labour.

Sayles conducted a more conventional anthropological study, spending several years with about 75 mainly middle managers in one division of a large US equipment manufacturer, where he 'tracked and watched' many of them for weeks at a time (Sayles, 1964, p. ix). Later, while lauding those like Sayles 'who propose to *observe* leadership behavior as their methodology for study to gain knowledge', Dubin (1979, p. 226, original emphasis) cautioned that leadership in organisations was rare and that tracking managers would probably reveal scant evidence of it: 'If one records everything observable, one will be overwhelmed by data ... The first cut at such data mass will consist of sorting it into two piles: the small stack of leadership acts, and the very large pile of acts of managing and supervising.' This balance is not an unreasonable summary of what Sayles found, although he refused to be overwhelmed for by it, unlike Carlson, Burns and others, he thought it 'not sufficient for us to know the gross quantitative dimensions of a given managerial position' (Sayles, 1964, p. 48). His managers performed three main roles. First, they participated in numerous laterally paired relationships, as Burns had discovered. As one reflected on the extent of his network dependence (Sayles, 1964, p. 43):

> Actually, I only have eighteen people directly reporting to me. These are the only ones I can give orders to. But I have to rely directly on the services of seventy-five or eighty other people in this company, if my project is going to get done. They are in turn affected by perhaps several hundred others, and I must see some of them, too, when my work is being held up.

Second, managers were leaders and, third, they were also activity and work process monitors. In the web of relations that comprised management, there were three aspects to managers' leadership, with only the first entailing direction-setting for subordinates, while the remaining two demanded responsiveness to subordinates' initiatives and representation on their behalf elsewhere in the organisation (Sayles, 1964, pp. 51–3).

The year following the publication of Sayles's book saw the appearance of a study based on a similar model of prolonged observational immersion, Hodgson, Levinson and Zaleznik's (1965) *The Executive Role Constellation*. In some ways, this book is at odds with the work of the researchers under review, none of which is referred to by the three co-authors. On the other hand, there are clear points of connection. Like Sayles, Hodgson, Levinson and Zaleznik (1965, p. 19) eschewed a 'systematic who-to-who frequency count' of executive level behaviour and focused on the character of managerial relationships and, like Burns, they concentrated in detail on the interactions between a small number of executives working cheek by jowl, in which the division of labour figures prominently in their analysis. And, once more, as with Sayles's informants, written formulations of the executive triad's role descriptions and duties 'did not enter into any of their talking or behaving' (Hodgson, Levinson and Zaleznik, 1965, p. 230). The three authors' major departure from previous work, as should be clear already from Chapter 2, was the significance they attached to the fit between personal and work-related factors in management, through the idea of role-task work, and the way in which the blending of personal and organisational needs helped cement a constellation of patterned and distributed role relations.

Research from the Late-1960s

By the late 1960s, the study of what managers do had established its own research genealogy. To this point, the subjects investigated were overwhelmingly men who managed or led mostly at executive and mid organisational levels. With the important exceptions of Sayles's emphasis on management and leadership as responses to workflows, and Hodgson, Levinson and Zaleznik's analysis of role differentiation, specialisation and complementarity, however, the division of labour had mostly not figured prominently in accounts of practice. Rather, the principal emphasis had been on documenting time usage, patterns of contacts, and the tasks and activities engaging managers. Estimates of level and scope of work intensity were variable, with intensity mostly undertheorised. Horne and Lupton (1965, p. 31), for example, in a diary study of 66 UK middle managers in industry, claimed that 'in terms of duration of work activities, managers are not overworked', whereas 'in intensity of activity they may well be overworked'. Their diary data, however, precluded full understanding of 'the degree of tension, conflict and technical difficulty in the work activities described'.

Intense managerial work patterns began to take shape in Stewart's (1988) *Managers and their Jobs* (originally published in 1967). Stewart (1988, p. 4) confined herself to the previous focus on time, for she maintained that time study 'was simpler, both conceptually and methodologically, than a study of what managers do', but she significantly widened commentators' awareness of the impact of time on overall work patterns. She began by investigating similarities and differences in the time spent on activities by, and the frequency of the activities of, 160 middle and senior managers, mainly in sales and production, in varying sized UK manufacturing firms. For four weeks, managers completed diaries and record forms. On average, they worked about 42 hours per week (Stewart, 1988, p. 15), a figure comparing favourably with Horne and Lupton's (1965, p. 30) mean of 44 hours during their single research week. She then highlighted two new phenomena. The first was job fragmentation, or the ways in which interruptions and repeated changes of subject focus, due to fleeting contacts, 'can give an exhausting sensation of o.d.t.a.a.', or 'one damn thing after another' (Stewart, 1988, p. 52). The second was the extent of the variety of work experienced due to differing job content, people, places and cyclic work patterns. The overall variations in time expenditure were sufficiently large to prompt Stewart to devise a series of typical role profiles, in the interests of appropriate preparation and training, instead of stereotypical summaries of 'the' or 'the average' manager.

Work Activity and Beyond

Intensity was given a particularly sharp focus by Mintzberg's (1973, p. 51) *The Nature of Managerial Work*, where he pithily characterised managerial activities as comprising 'brevity, variety and fragmentation'. Moreover, managers were believed to prefer this pattern of fractured, superficial, interrupted live action to the boredom of routine. Mintzberg's conclusions were drawn from his observations of five US CEOs over one continuous working week in each case: the chairman of a consultancy firm, the president of a research and development firm, the head of a hospital, the president of a consumer goods firm and a school superintendent. A closely related aphorism at about this time, which also slipped into popular discourse, was Weick's (1982, p. 235) description of management as 'fighting fires', in which a manager's actions were 'primarily oral, face-to-face, symbolic, presumptive, brief, spontaneous and blunt'.

Mintzbergian Research

Mintzberg typified the growing body of research into the manager's job as the work activity school. This school, he asserted, was characterised by inductive and systematic analysis. He devised a 'structured observation' method which was to become the hallmark of work-activity studies and gave his own research wide appeal. Mintzberg (1973, p. 227) dismissed the prolonged field immersion required by the open-ended observation of the likes of Sayles and Hodgson, Levinson and Zaleznik because 'too much is asked of the researcher'. He also discredited diaries for their supposed unreliability when they were completed at the discretion of informants, and because their design and layout, he believed, presumed the features of the work they were meant to ascertain. Structured observation, by contrast, worked as follows (Mintzberg, 1973, pp. 231–2, original emphasis):

> The researcher observes the manager as he [*sic*] performs his work. Each observed event (a verbal contact or a piece of incoming or outgoing mail) is categorized by the researcher in a number of ways (for example, duration, participants, purpose) as in the diary method, but with one important difference. *The categories are developed during the observation and after it takes place.* In effect, the researcher is influenced in his coding process, not by the standing literature or his own prior experience, but by the single event taking place before him. In addition to categorizing events, the researcher is able to record detailed information on important incidents and to collect anecdotal materials.

This kind of approach represented a compromise between the pay-off of prolonged first-hand engagement with research subjects and the alleged vagaries of diaries. Moreover, confining observation to short intensive bursts had the added advantage of enabling researchers to increase their sample size.

For each datum of evidence (managers' contacts, mail, media of communication, frequency and duration of activities), Mintzberg (1973, p. 55) asked one question: 'why did the manager do this?' The answers, when grouped 'logically', then 'emerged' as a set of 10 roles. It was the requirements of these roles which were the source of common managerial work characteristics. The 10 roles formed a gestalt, or integrated whole (Mintzberg, 1973, p. 58): 'In essence, the manager is an input-output system in which authority and status give rise to interpersonal relationships that lead to inputs (information), and these in turn lead to outputs (information and decisions). One cannot arbitrarily remove one role and expect the rest to remain intact.' Interpersonal roles included 'figurehead', 'leader' and 'liaison'; informational roles included 'monitor', 'disseminator' and 'spokesman' (*sic*); and decisional roles were 'entrepreneur', 'disturbance handler', 'resource allocator' and 'negotiator'. Leadership infused all of a manager's activities. Even though managers performed these roles intuitively, Mintzberg's hope (1973, p. 135) was that the work of senior managers might be programmed (with leadership programmes likely to be 'the most difficult to understand'). In this sense, as Willmott (1984, p. 357) observed, Mintzberg's real aim was to introduce rationality to managerial work, through the systematic redesign of the individual manager's role.

Problems with Mintzbergian Research

To graduate student researchers, for whom time was precious, the logistics of Mintzberg's structured observation were to prove more attractive than prolonged participant observation, as noted by Kotter (1982, pp. 150–1). In the late 1970s and early 1980s, a clutch of them in Australia and North America published Mintzbergian-style findings on school principals' and superintendents' work. With some variations, these confirmed his picture of frenetic intensity, however they also disclosed a number of problems with work-activity research (Gronn, 1982; 1984b; 1987). First, Mintzberg's notion of an 'event' or 'activity' was contestable. When, for example, did a verbal contact begin and end? In one case (Sproull, 1981, p. 116), an event was taken to mean a continuous focus for one minute or longer on a medium and subject content, with an activity being the sum of these events. This view lent itself to the assumption that events occurred sequentially, yet Duignan (1980, p. 20) provided an alternate image of simultaneity when he quoted a school superintendent reflecting on his 'mental juggling operation' in keeping 'the multiple strands related to various issues separate and distinct'. This example, which resonates more with Sayles's image of the manager located amidst flows of work and workplace relations, perhaps explains why Carroll and Gillen (1987, p. 43) thought managerial work was 'really mental work' and that activity measurement, narrowly conceived was 'not going to present a full picture' of it. Similarly, when confronted by simultaneous occurrences in the principal's work as difficult to disentangle as 'interruptions of interruptions', Acker (1990, p. 250) saw little point in striving for numerical precision.

A second major difficulty concerned the purpose of an activity. Who was to attribute purposes and which ones? To rely on the behavioural evidence before their eyes, as Mintzberg had enjoined researchers to do, meant, for example, that coding the purposes of principals' work activities would be 'the most exacting and most subjective stage of post-categorisation' (Willis, 1980, p. 35). In this regard, both Burns and Carlson had already shown how the attribution of seemingly innocuous labels like 'reporting' and 'informing' to interaction segments was a recipe for disputed interpretations. A third difficulty lay with the comparative quantification and measurement of managers' deeds. One consequence of this concentration on numbers was to marginalise qualitative analysis.

Discrimination between trivial and significant events in structured observation studies, for example, was rare. Some scholars were alert to this omission. Like Dubin, Martin and Willower (1981, p. 87) warned about the spectre of the researcher adrift in 'a sea of numerical appraisal' or, as Barber (1974, p. 452) was to observe so colourfully from the sphere of US president-watching: observing a president should not result in an obsession with 'how many times he brushes his teeth'. Further, there were remarkably few attempts to account for observed behavioural differences in managers' work patterns. Comparing the work of Korean and US school principals, for example, Chung and Miskel (1989, p. 57) confirmed Mintzberg's picture of variety, brevity and fragmentation, but then, rather than providing their own explanation, they appealed for additional studies to 'identify the reasons for these similarities or differences in principals' managerial behaviour'.

The most significant difficulty with structured observation research, however, stemmed from the assumption that, in the study of managerial work, the appropriate unit of analysis was the individual manager. One of the consequences of this preference for methodological individualism (which I consider in more detail shortly) was that it generated contradictory images and metaphors of managerial agency. How much freedom, for example, did managers have to structure their own preferred patterns of work, or were they relatively powerless to do so in the face of conflicting pressures, and floods of demands and requests from other people? Unlike Sayles (1964, p. 162), who likened managers to orchestra conductors, Carlson (1951, p. 52), who also began with this metaphor, rejected it in favour of CEOs as akin to puppets 'with hundreds of people pulling the strings'. Later commentators conveyed images of active managers (e.g., Martin and Willower, 1981, p. 82), while others equivocated between active and reactive (e.g., Larson et al., 1986) – including Mintzberg (1973, p. 51), for whom managers could be puppets as well as string-pullers – and a number of others showed a high proportion of principals' contacts initiated *for*, rather than *by*, them. Still others (e.g., Stewart, 1988, pp. 120–35) maintained that the destiny of managers was in their own hands and urged them to make better use of their time.

Post-Mintzbergian Research

A more proactive image of managerial work was presented in Kotter's (1982) book *The General Managers*, a study of 15 (male) US business executives in nine corporations of varying size and located mainly in the service sector. Like Sayles before him, but unlike Mintzberg, Kotter (1982, p. 153) also affirmed that 'real progress' in understanding the work of managers came from extended field study. In his case, this had entailed two years' part-time research or about 500 hours of observations of, and interviews with, general managers (GMs), and interviews with their subordinates. The work of GMs was intellectually and interpersonally demanding, and only three of the 15 CEOs worked < 55 hours per week (Kotter, 1982, p. 81). All of them were found to approach their jobs 'in roughly the same way' (Kotter, 1982, p. 60), with the two distinguishing characteristics of their roles being the development of corporate agendas (of goals, plans, projects, etc.)

and – shades of Sayles once more – the building of networks of cooperative relationships amongst various stakeholders and key interest groups. The members of networks were those people on whom the GMs 'felt dependent because of their jobs' (Kotter, 1982, p. 67). With this emphasis on interpersonal relationships, Kotter had provided 'a needed corrective' to previous work which had mostly 'abstracted [the analysis of work] from the political organization and control of the labour process' (Willmott, 1984, p. 359).

This last comment by Wilmott signalled a qualitative shift amongst commentators towards new theoretically informed understandings, as opposed to straightforward empirical descriptions, of managerial work. Developments in the 1980s and 1990s went in a number of simultaneous directions. First, the early burst of enthusiastic replication of the work activity school petered out (Kurke and Aldrich, 1983) and the approach underwent modification in research in the general management area (Martinko and Gardner, 1985) and in schooling (Hultman, 2001; Martinko and Gardner, 1990). Second, the focus of research into managers' work shifted to an evaluative concern with the work of successful or effective managers (Hales, 1986; Luthans, Rosenkrantz and Hennessey, 1985). Third, work activity study began to diversify to include such varied examples as senior civil servants (Sinclair, Baird and Alford, 1993), hospitality and hotel managers (Dann, 1991; Hales, 1987) and managers in non-western cultural settings (Boisot and Liang, 1992; Luthans, Welsh and Rosenkrantz, 1993; Shenkar et al., 1998). Finally, the work of managers was theorised in directions consistent with the thrust of Willmott's (1984, p. 357) criticism that Mintzberg had abstracted the doing of management from any explanation of its hows and whys, and that he had construed it as 'peculiarly mechanical and unconditioned by historical and contextual circumstances'. In the school sector, a residual concern with Mintzbergian work activity persisted in the 1990s in the UK (e.g., Blease and Lever, 1992; Jones, 1999; Jones and Connolly, 2001; Laws and Dennison, 1990) which, following the implementation of the Education Reform Act, 1988 and subsequent related legislation, became overlaid by broad critiques (mainly by policy sociologists) of the entire thrust of government school reform policy. It was these comments which indicated how stringent accountability requirements, as part of NPM, as the movement for the reform of public sector management became known, were exacerbating the already intensified work regimes of school leaders.

A Knowledge Base for Informed Practice?

The thrust of the above survey provides an indication of the kind of knowledge base which might be assembled with a view to facilitating evidence-informed practice. While few of the researchers within the managerial work tradition were motivated by the kinds of justifications now being offered for EIPP, a number of them did seek to derive practice-based knowledge for the improvement of training and preparation programmes (Laws and Dennison, 1990). How useful then, might the above material be for an evidence-informed approach to the improvement of management and leadership practice in education?

Characterising the Research

Clearly, the overall research picture is extremely variegated. First, there are conflicting images of managers and leaders. There exists a considerable amount of detail which is illustrative of the rhythm, flow, routine and pacing of managers' work, but there is no agreed-upon terminology amongst commentators with which to describe the experiences of leader-managers and the properties of management. And while some researchers, such as Mintzberg, have provided a standardised picture of the work of leader-managers others, such as Stewart, have emphasised the overall diversity of responsibilities and role demands. For Stewart, management as an occupational category is so varied, due to level, function and sphere of operation, as to defy meaningful generalisations. Second, there is considerable disagreement over the merits of various research methods, used either singly or in combination, let alone over the most appropriate means with which to frame investigations. Undoubtedly, these differences are the source of the conflicting findings and imagery associated with the work of leader-managers. Third, there is little agreement over the linkages between levels of analysis and whether, for example, the integrity of research is jeopardised by confining an investigation to the micro-level of practice, or whether micro- and macro-level understandings need to inform each other. Indeed, theorising on this issue was virtually non-existent until the appearance of Stewart's (1982) model of role performance as the outcome of a manager's capacity to negotiate the role demands and constraints imposed on, and opportunities available to, her or him in particular contexts. By demands, Stewart meant the job requirements and procedures, and expectations which role set members had of incumbents (Fondas and Stewart, 1994; Hales, 1987). Constraints encompassed a variety of resources and their availability, politico-legal and industrial frameworks, technology, etc., and choices entailed how and what work was done, including the discretion to emphasise certain aspects of the job and to ignore others.

Micro- and Macro-Levels of Analysis

Stewart's model was an acknowledgement that micro-level factors alone were insufficient to explain the work of managers for, as social actors, managers are constructed and positioned by macro-level factors not of their own making and largely beyond their control. Theorising on levels subsequent to the publication of Stewart's model took two broad directions. First, some commentators, arguing from the perspective of labour process theory (e.g., Whitley, 1989; Willmott, 1987), maintained that managerial actions were particularly constrained by managers' structural locations and functional roles in a capitalist economy. In the case of corporation management, managers were inextricably part of the social relations of market production. In the case of public sector agency managers, they were subject to bureaucratic legal-rational rules. These different arrangements each positioned managers as the bearers and representatives of key interests, social classes and status groups. A second line of criticism concerned deficiencies in the conceptual underpinnings of the accumulating body of field study evidence. Hales (1986, p. 105), for example, argued that researchers had failed to properly distinguish between managerial behaviour (i.e., what managers could be shown to do) and managerial jobs (i.e., managers' responsibilities and what they were expected to achieve). This discrepancy between performance and expectations provided one possible basis for appraising managers' effectiveness, and the extent to which performance was instrumental in accomplishing role expectations. Hales's (1986, p. 109) second point was that the activities which managers had been described as being constantly engaged in (e.g., desk work, tours, telephoning, corridor conversations, meetings) were hardly unique to them, so that the 'work' depicted was by no means distinctly managerial. In more recent attempts by Stewart and Hales to synthesise this research, these arguments have been broadened to encompass a range of additional factors which, to varying degrees, position managers and shape what they do. These include hierarchical level, sectoral embeddedness, functional realm, national cultural embeddedness and organisational context (Noordegraaf and Stewart, 2000), and organisational form, ownership and governance, organisational structure, and divisions of labour within management (Hales, 1989; Hales and Tamangani, 1996).

Leader-Managers' Agency

As foreshadowed earlier, the most significant issue arising from the body of research reviewed, which has been made even more contentious by recently documented experiences of work intensification, that makes life so qualitatively different and difficult for those who are now expected to provide leadership in schools, concerns the amount of and scope for the expression of leaders' self-determined, institutional level agency. In the UK, Hall and Southworth (1997, p. 151) have summarised the post-1988 situation confronting school principals (or heads), for example, as: 'the extent to which headteachers must choose to be or not to be entrepreneurs; and the extent to which a positive choice inevitably compromises their identity and activity as leading professionals, as well as to be critical of the system of which they are part'. That is, if the redesign of leadership and the reconstitution of professional identities as part of government-driven school reform are so complete and pervasive as to restrict the freedom of school personnel to deviate from official prescriptions, then the agency of the actors is significantly diminished. But what is agency, and what factors might serve to broaden or narrow the degrees of freedom for its self-determined expression?

Emirbayer and Mische (1998, p. 970, original italicised) have defined agency as a mode of 'temporally constructed engagement by actors of different structural environments' which, by means of such human faculties as habit, imagination and judgement, 'both reproduces and transforms those structures in interactive response to the problems posed by changing historical situations'. This definition means that the actions of school leaders may be instrumental in altering those wider factors which frame their work (e.g., mitigating the effects of particular policies, diversifying patterns of resource dependence, rectifying persistently declining enrolments) or they may make little or no difference, thereby reinforcing their current structural positions. As suggested, up until the early-1980s, work activity researchers basically conveyed contradictory pictures of agency, with most writers providing an underdetermined view of managers as agents. That is, managers were attributed with structural transformative, rather than reproductive, capacities. With intensification under NPM, however, school leaders' role demands have become numerically large and exceedingly complex, and the constraints they face extensive and imposing, with the result that in many instances the opportunities for widespread influence and transformative agency (as enshrined in standards statements) have been minimised (although see Barker, 2001 for a dissenting view).

Further Intensified Management

This qualitative shift is evident in the contrasting features of pre-reform era intensity, as documented by the work activity paradigm, and examples of intensified work under NPM.

Work Activity Intensity   The following examples of time demands and busyness (Laws and Dennison, 1990, p. 276) were replicated in numerous studies:

- principals' high individual weekly workloads: up to 60 hours (Willis, 1980, p. 33)
- school board CEOs' protracted (scheduled and unscheduled) meetings, frenzied activities, frequent switches of attention, torrid work tempos (McLeod, 1984, p. 175)
- principals' high volume of tasks: about 13 per hour (Peterson, 1978, p. 2)
- principals' numerous tasks of short duration: over 80 per cent lasting between one and four minutes (Martin and Willower, 1981, p. 79).

NPM Intensity   Although the picture under NPM is complex and variable in different, local quasi-marketised contexts, a handful of recent illustrations of activities which consume UK heads' and colleagues' time in a highly competitive schooling environment include:

- devising highly calculated information management and disclosure tactics in relation to school improvement profiles against benchmarked performance targets (Cullingford and Swift, 2001, pp. 281–2)
- adopting segmented, differentiated and targeted internal and external marketing strategies to retain and expand enrolment student cohorts (Maguire, Ball and Macrae, 2001)
- extensive collaborative documenting of numerous policies to ensure that schools 'meet the overwhelming demands of government directives' (Webb and Vulliamy, 1996, p. 447)
- whole school documentary preparation and collective emotional rehearsal in anticipation of OFSTED inspections (Jeffrey and Woods, 1996).

In the face of what surely appeared to be 'grasshopper-style' work patterns (i.e., successive knee-jerk responses to a procession of demands), would it not have been possible for pre-reform era principals to have delegated more of their work? As Laws and Dennison (1990, pp. 272) pointed out, such advice, even then, would have been largely gratuitous in the face of complexities and role overload, but under NPM, delegation entirely misses the point. Instead, the four dot-pointed examples highlight the need for a qualitatively different way of conceptualising leader-managers' work.

From Work Activity to Activity Systems

Rather than being construed as atomised tasks or, in traditional management discourse, as functions, a more accurate way of representing the examples of profiling, marketing, framing policies and institutional evaluation is to see them as sets of activities. As was implicit in the earlier discussion of researchers' conceptual and practical difficulties during fieldwork, a model of leader-management labour as a linear or cumulative flow of discrete, task-related individual acts provides almost 'no room and no language for representing horizontal interactions between various parallel tasks of an actor, or between different actors, or between actors and their artifacts' (Engeström, 1999, p. 64). One of the features of the work activity paradigm was that a succession of studies highlighted the very high proportion of time managers spent in meetings and conversations, so much so that 'talk as the work' (Gronn, 1983) became a hallmark of management. Curiously, however, the interactional significance of this linguistic work was lost on most researchers (see Chapter 5). Yet, conversational analysis of managers' talk indicates that management is a collectively negotiated labour process comprising sets of simultaneously occurring and interacting activities.

Activity Theory

Activity theorists such as (Engeström, 1999, p. 65) view activities as collective systems comprising three main elements: motives, actions and operations. Respectively, these terms denote the needs or purposes fulfilled by an activity, the various cognitively defined initiatives undertaken in pursuit of those purposes and the physical operations which realise the actions. Leont'ev's (1981, p. 210) much cited illustration of an activity is an animal hunt:

> When a member of a group performs his [*sic*] labour activity he also does it to satisfy one of his needs. A beater, for example, taking part in a primaeval collective hunt, was stimulated by the need for food or, perhaps, a need for clothing, which the skin of the dead animal would meet for him. At what, however, was his activity directly aimed? It may have been directed, for example, at frightening a herd of animals and sending them towards other hunters, hiding in ambush. That, properly speaking, is what should be the result of the activity of this man. And the activity of this individual member of the hunt ends with that. The rest is completed by the other members. This result, i.e. the frightening of game, etc. understandably does not in itself, and may not, lead to satisfaction of the beater's need for food, or the skin of the animal. What the processes of his activity were directed to did not, consequently, coincide with what stimulated them, i.e. did

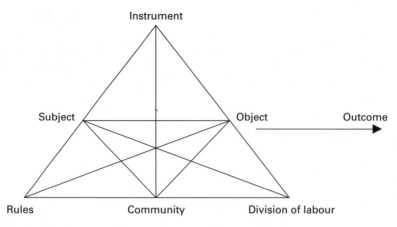

FIGURE 4.1   The mediational structure of an activity system (Engeström, 1999, p. 66)

not coincide with the motive of his activity; the two were divided from one another in this instance. Processes, the object and motive of which do not coincide with one another, we shall call 'actions'. We can say, for example, that the beater's activity is the hunt, and the frightening of game his action.

In this example, operations would include the beating of bushes and disturbing of habitat by this particular hunter, and the direct attack on and killing of the game by other hunters. While Leont'ev's description concentrates mainly on the actions of one man as a subcomponent of a larger activity system, his example highlights the centrality of the division of labour in human activity. There are two points here. First, the actions of an individual (such as a beater or shooter) only make sense from the perspective of the overall pattern or system of labour relations that comprises the activity. Thus, 'the beater's action is possible only on condition of his reflecting the link between the expected result of the action performed by him and the end result of the hunt as a whole' (Leont'ev, 1981, p. 212). Second, the labour relations between the individuals who coalesce to accomplish an activity are interdependent. Just as the actions of other hunters or shooters 'give sense to the object of the beater's action', likewise do the beater's actions 'justify and give sense to the actions of the people who ambush the game' for, 'were it not for the beaters' action, the making of an ambush would be senseless and unjustified' (Leont'ev, 1981, pp. 212–13).

An activity system model is outlined in Figure 4.1. It comprises six components. These are located at equidistant points around the perimeter of the equilateral triangle. Relations between the components are always mediated rather than direct. This mediational property means that, within a particular Community of Practice (C), the actions of individual or collective Subjects (S) in relation to their Objects (O) or pursuits are accomplished through a range of tools or Instruments (I), within a Division of labour (DofL), and are governed by tacit understandings, conventions or Rules (R). The notion of mediation is grounded in Vygotsky's

(1978, p. 30) claim that in child development 'the path from object to child and from child to object passes through another person' or, as Leont'ev (1978, p. 59) says, 'equipment mediates activity connecting man (*sic*) not only with the world of things but also with other people'.

Emergent Activity

Another aspect of the model is that it accommodates the idea of emergent activities by incorporating Vygotsky's (1978, pp. 84–91) notion of the zone of proximal development. In his discussion of the relationship between the learning and development (or maturation) of children, Vygotsky observed that all learning has a history which conditions current learning. As part of that history, the zone of proximal development is the space between two levels on a trajectory of learning: the actual (retrospective) and the potential (prospective). In the distance between the two levels lies a series of embryonic functions, with their maturation contingent upon appropriately structured learning environments. For analytical purposes, in the activity system model the zone of proximal development expresses the emergent path of potential activity development. Thus, the particular arrangements of R, C, I and DofL which obtain for actors and their objects at Time^1 (T^1) may form different configurations at T^2 and T^3 etc. If a series of activity system triangles is pictured as randomly positioned, but in a roughly ordered left–right sequence, then the zone of proximal development is the area (Engeström, 1999, p. 67): 'between actions embedded in the current activity with its historical roots and contradictions, the foreseeable activity in which the contradictions are expansively resolved, and the foreseeable activity in which the contradictions have led to contraction and destruction of opportunities'. Emergence in Leont'ev's (1978, p. 50) idea of activity is expressed in his view that an activity is both structured and dynamic. Thus, an activity has 'its own internal transitions and transformations, its own development'.

Re-Thinking Leader-Management

From the perspective of activity theory, to constitute managerial activities as units of analysis requires the decentring of individual leaders. Within a regulatory framework, such as obtains in the State of Victoria, for example, which stipulates 52 dot point accountabilities for principals, arranged in 11 sets, it is humanly impossible for just one individual to provide leadership in every instance. The preamble to the dot points admits as much: 'It is understood that all the functions will not necessarily be carried out directly by the principal'.[3] Thus, while Victorian principals are expected, as part of the 'Planning, review and accountability' set, to 'lead and manage the development of the [triennial] school charter', 'ensuring' that it meets community expectations, and to 'negotiate' its agreement and implementation with the state government,[4] it would be meaningless to conceive of them as working on a charter alone or, for that matter, that they would necessarily be directly involved in every step along the way. Charter writing, including the establishment of the required systems and processes, and the evaluation of performance and subsequent planning, represents an activity. As such it can be interpreted in activity system terms as having it own division of labour, which will afford numerous opportunities for distributed leadership (both numerical and holistic) while different individuals and groups contribute to the overall charter construction process. As Jaques (1970, p. 133) was quoted in Chapter 1 as saying, the employment contract authority of managers (and therefore principals) is 'to get work done through employed subordinates', for which they as managers are held accountable. But this requirement defines a division of rights, as opposed to a division of labour. It vests authority to oversee the totality of the work and to 'sign it off', rather than defining in minute detail how that work should be done and who should perform it.

Analysis of what leader-managers do in activity system terms, as proposed by activity theory, offers potentially greater explanatory power than the previous work activity paradigm. As has been shown, structured observation case studies generated minimalist data, and descriptions which generally yielded lists of arbitrarily defined events in which CEOs or their equivalents were observed and reported on as solo-performing actors. Research outcomes described sequentially occurring behaviours, largely devoid of contextual and stylistic factors, and mostly expunged evidence of interaction. Behaviours were classified, numerical frequencies tallied and these were then cited as evidence of, say, principals' 'instructional leadership'. An activity theory approach, by contrast, in keeping with the earlier view of distributed leadership highlights the range of jointly performing actors who contribute to various school-level outcomes. One of the aims that the work activity approach set itself was that it would document 'the important "invisibles" of principals' administrative behaviours … as they really are' (Thomas, Willis and Phillips, 1981, p. 70). But nothing better encapsulates the shortcomings of work activity than the word 'principals', for it suggests that leadership practice extends as far as just one person rather than being stretched across the organisational fabric, as Spillane and his colleagues suggested. Activity theorists are committed to a similar project of visibilising work (Engeström, 1999, pp. 68–9), only this time through the shared cognition of a number of school leaders (via their mental representations) and the diversity of the tools on which they rely, and not just with respect to the in-the-head cognition of solo actors.

In this chapter, I have shown that management and leadership have always been intensive and demanding forms of work. In many workplaces, however, including schools, contemporary practice was shown to entail qualitatively new and different dimensions of work intensification. In reviewing and critiquing a heritage of inductive field research intended to advance understanding of leader-management practice, I cast doubt on its potential to provide the basis of an accumulated evidence-informed knowledge base for management and leadership. I then proposed an alternative analytical template to facilitate a contextually grounded understanding of practice known as activity theory, which, in keeping with the spirit of distributed forms of work, I suggested was better calculated to articulate the hidden dimensions of leadership work. Having argued for a distributed unit of analysis, it remains now to consider the dynamics of the two most prominent institutionalised forms of distributed leadership, committees and teams, the first of which is the subject of the next chapter.

Notes

1 In the UK during 2001–02, the Standing Conference on Research in Educational Leadership and Management (SCRELM) has been engaged in a review of research, and mapping of the fields of educational leadership and management. The NCSL also includes a series of evidence-based discussion papers on its website.

2 The following survey is necessarily selective. For the most part, only those details which illustrate the theme of work intensity and closely related themes, in what is a vast body of research, are utilised in this chapter.

3 *Victorian Government Schools: Principal Class Handbook* (February 2001), Melbourne: DEET, p. 48.

4 Ibid., p. 49.

5   Leaders' Committees and Meetings

A meeting, remarks the writer, Malcolm Bradbury (1975), in *The History Man*, his novel about English academic life, constitutes 'an elaborate social construct'. Picture at the head of the table an ageing, slightly frazzled department chairman, Professor Marvin, 'in that curious state of suspended animation appropriate to the moment before the start of a meeting':

> Then the alarm clock of Benita Pream, the administrative assistant, pings; Professor Marvin coughs very loudly and waves his arms. He looks up and down the long table, and says: 'Can we now come to order, gentlemen?' Immediately the silence breaks; many arms go up, all around the table: there is a jabber of voices. 'May I point out, Mr Chairperson, that of the persons in this room you are addressing as "gentlemen", seven are women?' says Melissa Todoroff. 'May I suggest that the formulation "Can we come to order, persons?" or perhaps 'Can we come to order, colleagues?"' 'Doesn't the phrase itself suggest we're somehow in a state of *dis*order?' asks Roger Fundy. 'Can I ask whether under Standing Orders of Senate we are bound to terminate this meeting in three and a half hours? And, if so, whether the Chairman thinks an agenda of thirty-four items can be seriously discussed under those limitations, especially since my colleagues will presumably want to take tea?' 'On a point of information, Mr Chairman, may I point out that the tea interval is not included within the three and a half hour limitation, and also draw Dr Petworth's attention to the fact that we have concluded discussion of longer agendas in shorter times?' 'Here?' asks someone. 'May I ask if it is the wish of this meeting that we should have a window open?' The meeting has started; and it is always so. It has often been remarked by Benita Pream, who services several such departmental meetings, that those in History are distinguished by their high rate of absenteeism, those in English by the amount of wine consumed afterwards, and those in Sociology by their contentiousness. The pile drivers thump outside; the arguments within continue. The sociologists, having read Goffman, know there is a role of Chairman, and a role of Argumentative Person, and a role of Silent Person ... it is 14.20 before the meeting has decided how long it is to continue, and whether it is quorate, and if it should have the window open, and 14.30 before Professor Marvin has managed to sign the minutes of the last meeting, so that they can begin on item 1 of the agenda of this one, which concerns the appointment of external examiners for finals: 'An uncontentious example, I think,' says Professor Marvin.
>
> It is 15.05 before the uncontentious item is resolved ...

Despite the high comic farce of Bradbury's example, meetings constitute an inescapable component of what it means to lead and manage. On any working day, across the entire world, there are likely to be thousands upon thousands of different kinds of meetings occurring simultaneously in schools, universities, firms and numerous other workplaces. This need to confer is likely to be accepted with varying degrees of tolerance, bemusement and resignation: some people will no doubt welcome the opportunity to get together, and to behave in a convivial or businesslike manner, while others are likely to begrudge what they see as yet another invasion of their already tightly packed work schedules and commitments. Every one of these meetings will be conducted according to diverse sets of written and unwritten rules and conventions: these legitimations will result in encounters which are experienced as crisp and punchy in style, along with those like Bradbury's which barely even feel as though they hang together, but which must nevertheless be endured stoically. Some meetings will seem to be mercifully short and sweet, and the departing members will be keen to pat themselves on the back for their efficiency. In other cases, by contrast, people are bound to feel as though they have been short-changed by the very fact of having to be present and that, as a cultural artifact, their particular meeting has mostly limped along and ended up going nowhere. But no matter what the locale or the substantive outcomes in each instance, the vast majority of these meetings will have had at least one feature in common: their inherent fecundity, for they are more than likely to have created the need for even further meetings (Schwartzman, 1989, p. 37).

Such is the business of meetings. But why this apparent need to meet? And what is it that makes a meeting a meeting, rather than something else? Next, how is the very notion of 'meeting' accomplished? What collective cultural knowledge, for example, do those who attend meetings need to possess in order to engage in appropriate meeting behaviour? And, indeed, what counts as meeting behaviour? To some readers, these may seem like an odd set of questions to pose, for they are about the nature of the phenomenon – i.e., meetings – rather than being designed to improve the performance, or even reduce the incidence, of the phenomenon. This distinction, as Schwartzman (1989, p. 17) notes in her synthesis of meeting research, is a common one in the social sciences. It is the distinction between, on the one hand, social phenomena as resources for research and, on the other hand, as the above questions imply, the topics of research. That is, a resources view of a phenomenon means that the fact of its existence is taken for granted as largely unproblematic, whereas treating something as the object of an inquiry entails a critical analysis of both the logic of its justification and an elaboration of its core constituent elements.

This chapter is written with the latter, rather than the former, perspective in mind. In respect of meetings as social phenomena, then, for the most part the discussion eschews the kinds of understandable pragmatic priorities which leaders and managers might have in reconstituting meetings as more efficient instruments for effective decision-making and achieving their goals. The reason for this disavowal stems less from an ideological disdain for the idea of the researcher as a servant of power, with its implicit assumption that the purpose of knowledge should be to bolster the managerial prerogative, and more from the conviction that straightforward means-end rationality and instrumentalism are intellectually muddle-headed. Whole bodies of research literature reflecting a social constructionist and linguistic turn in the social sciences which appeared the 1970s and 1980s – not to mention the well-established earlier work on bounded rationality and cognitive limitations on reasoning capacity (Simon, 1976 [1945]; March and Simon, 1958) – pointed to the fact that organisational rationality is an everyday, practical working achievement (see Schwartzman, 1989, pp. 18–22). Moreover, despite the prevalent common sense and (the wishful scholarly) assumption of the existence of a causal connection between the discretionary intentions of actors, the instruments at their disposal and desired social outcomes, a considerable proportion of the actual outcomes of action (i.e., both change and a reproduced status quo) occurs for involuntary and unintended reasons.

I begin with an explanation of the ubiquitousness of meetings, I then follow with a definition of meetings, which I link with the two most frequently institutionalised meeting forums, committees and teams. Thenceforward, the discussion of meetings is confined in this chapter to committees, and to teams in Chapter 6. Next, in keeping with my earlier theme of the distributed nature of leadership, I show how committee meetings are intrinsic to the work of leaders. Following that, I synthesise the research literature on committees around the two themes of their structural and interactional properties. Finally, building on Bailey's (1965) influential and ground-breaking analysis of committees, and the operational tension between consensus and majority rule, I show how the pressures for unanimity and a collective mind need to be offset against the possibility of groupthink.

But Why Meetings?

Although the research findings of the work activity school and those who preceded them differed over aspects of leader-managers' work, they were unanimous about one thing: the high proportion of conversations and meetings during a manager's working day. Horne and Lupton (1965, p. 27), for example, found from their diary entries that 'about half the time of all our managers is spent in their own offices talking to other people or listening to them'. For this reason, they believed, rather than a quality like analytical capacity, being a middle manager called for 'the ability to shape and utilize the person-to-person channels of communication, to influence, to persuade, to facilitate' (Horne and Lupton, 1965, p. 32). Similarly, a decade earlier in the 1950s, Burns (1954, p. 78, original emphasis) had concluded in answer to the question of how his sample of four executives spent their time: '*in conversation*'. It was much the same for Stewart's (1988, p. 114) 160 managers and a similar picture was true for school administrators. In six of eight of the early structured observation studies I reviewed (Gronn, 1982), the percentage of time administrators spent talking ranged from two-thirds to three-quarters of each individual's working day. Later in-depth observational fieldwork confirmed these findings. Sayles (1964, p. 190) had observed that 'meetings drain away a great deal of time; many last as much half a day and require the attendance of a host of managerial talent' and, in his ethnography of the firm 'Playco', Morrill (1991, p. 589) noted how:

On any of their regular 10-hour work days, top managers from the same departments can be observed talking with one another in hallways, elevators, parking lots, over the phone, and in the lobbies at headquarters. Most of these conversations last less than three minutes. Colleagues who do not share the same department tend to confine their communication to frequent (three or four per week) meetings, or, in the absence of meetings, had sparse interaction.

On the basis of this evidence, I concluded (Gronn, 1982, p. 31, original emphases) that 'talk *is* the work', in that it consumes most of a manager's time and energy, that 'talk *does* the work', in that it is the main resource to get others to do things, and that 'talk *displays* the work' because it reveals evidence of administrative activity. While some of this managerial talk occurred in informal conversations, much of it took place in meetings. Nearly 40 per cent of the working time of Mintzberg's (1973, p. 39) five CEOs, for example, was consumed by scheduled or unscheduled meetings, although for Stewart's (1988, p. 28) diary sample, prearranged committee time was 'surprisingly small': only 7 per cent.

Ubiquitous Meetings

The sheer amount of time given over to meetings is one reason for examining their operation more closely yet, surprisingly, Schwartzman (1986, p. 4) claimed, 'whereas meetings appear to be everywhere, they are almost nowhere in the research literature'. Her comment is still valid in 2003. Another reason is that meetings play a vital role in the management and leadership of schools. For most of the long history of public schooling, regular teachers' meetings with administrators were rare phenomena. In fact, consultative meeting forums and advisory committees in Victorian schools really only began in the early 1970s. But for much of the last two decades or so, the most powerful collective voices in Victorian schools, particularly secondary colleges, have been the local administration committee (LAC) and the curriculum committee (CC). For part of that period LACs and CCs were mandated by the state government (Watkins, 1993, p. 137). Latterly, these bodies exist at the discretion of principals. Other components of the consultative apparatus in schools, in addition to the LAC and CC, have included local selection panels, committees to allocate higher duty responsibilities and allowances, staff meetings, sub-school meetings, and year level and subject co-ordination meetings. More recently, with government encouragement, Victorian schools have instituted leadership teams alongside, or as substitutes for, committees. These structures have multiplied the time devoted to meetings. Key questions regarding meetings, therefore, include: how do they work? What purposes do they serve? And, to what extent does meeting work count as 'real work', or is it seen as a sideshow to the main game? Do regular faculty meetings in schools, for example, as Riehl (1998, p. 122) found, provide a vehicle for institutions to rehearse and reinvent themselves, rather than accomplishing substantive work?

A third reason for understanding meeting dynamics is that school leaders and administrators often share power with committees, or have to negotiate close working relations. But shared executive authority in relation to policy and operations often invites tension, or at least creates the potential for it. In North

American school districts and in independent schools in Australia, for example, superintendents and principals and their respective governing bodies try to arrive at informal working agreements about their respective territories and professional turf. The division of labour may be as black and white as board or council responsibility for 'fabric' matters, such as finance, buildings and the maintenance of tradition, and principal responsibility for 'professional' concerns, such as curriculum, staffing, pastoral care, conduct codes and day-to-day operations, but relations between both parties are rarely ever so neatly cut and dried. Betty Archdale (1972, p. 90), retired headmistress of Abbotsleigh Girls' School, for example, recalled that: 'the number of headmasters and headmistresses who have left their schools over the past ten years owing to disagreements with their councils would, in Sydney alone, run into double figures'. By contrast, A.H. Wood, for 28 years (1939–66) the principal of Methodist Ladies' College, Melbourne, made sure he had few if any difficulties with his governing body. His school council was a large grouping which met on only one or two occasions per year. 'Real authority' lay with an eight-person executive committee, all of them men and all 'personal friends', which met once a month for an hour and a half. In the interests of efficiency when dealing with 'busy men', said Wood (1976, p. 258), 'I wrote the minutes beforehand with the anticipated decisions'.

When is a Meeting?

In Chapter 2 I distinguished five main types of joint work units: committees, teams, crews, divisions and departments. A common feature of each of these membership units, with the possible exception of crews, is that their members 'meet', mostly at set times as part of a timetabled meeting cycle, but also spontaneously. Scheduled meeting occurs in agreed time slots, is distinguished by spoken and unspoken formalities (e.g., tone and demeanour), is structured by a precirculated or tabled agenda, is transacted through rehearsed ways of speaking and is minuted or archived. By contrast, unscheduled meetings observe few or none of these conventions and leave no archival trace. Meeting constitutes the entirety of the work of committees, a significant proportion of team activity, but only a segment of the business of divisions and departments. On the other hand, teams and committees are not the only organisational formations which meet. Numerous clubs and societies, for example, including various spare time or hobby-based groups, convene regularly and adhere to meeting conventions (e.g., record-keeping, and rules concerning turn-taking and speaking rights), as do groups as diverse as shareholders, disputes resolution tribunals, workers' councils and diplomatic forums.

The Idea of 'Meeting'

As suggested by the opening excerpt from *The History Man*, 'meeting' is an occasion when varying sized aggregates of people interact or transact business. Meeting occasions have either formal or informal status, although this may be contested. There are usually recognisable beginning, ending and transition points between which people confer, but these may be the subjects of negotiation. The meeting mode of engagement, Schwartzman (1986, p. 241) notes, is normally characterised by: 'multi-party talk that is episodic in nature and participants develop or use specific conventions for regulating this talk. The meeting form frames the behavior that occurs within it as concerning the "business" of the group or organization'. Yet, despite these obvious points, meetings do not go without saying, for they are in fact learned social accomplishments. For a meeting to be a meeting, rather than another form of talk or mode of engagement, requires reflexive self-awareness on the part of those present that they are indeed constituting, sustaining and carrying off a particular social form (Cuff and Sharrock, 1985). In that sense, meetings are 'collaborative productions' (Atkinson, Cuff and Lee, 1978, p. 136). Participant reflexivity is manifest in the repertoire of readily recognisable cues for getting started such as: 'Righto', 'Er, okay' or 'Let's get under way'. This reflexivity is also apparent at another level of awareness in references to such phenomena as 'the meeting before the meeting' or 'the meeting after the meeting', where the alleged 'real' business deals are done, along with the connections between these phases, distinctions no doubt lost on any but the most experienced meeting officiandos. Meeting formats without these shared expectations, purposes and knowledge of the rules of engagement, as in one-off school reporting evenings for parents, can result in uncertainty about 'the role [participants are] expected to play and how to read the other players' (Walker, 1998, p. 176). Finally, for an organisation member to be designated as 'in a meeting' or at a 'meeting in progress', is to be in a state of temporary respite from the normal flow of events, and spatially and temporally cocooned from regular engagement. In this way, meetings structure the notion of 'unavailability' as a significant indicator of an individual's seniority and demand status.

The Historical Origins of 'Meeting'

Meeting is a product of differentiated and complex social systems. It emerges as part of the civilising process during the transition from warrior, to courtly and thence to democratic social formations, and represents the triumph of words over swords. 'Having to meet has become the fate of "civilized" people' (Van Vree, 1999, p. 197). This culture of meeting probably began to institutionalise itself earliest in the Netherlands, fuelled similar developments in France, England and Switzerland, and then blended with these to diffuse throughout northern Europe and beyond. Schwartzman's (1987, p. 272) study of a Midwest US community mental health centre showed that it was 'the meeting format that actually constituted and maintained the organization' and that most staff spent nearly half their working time in meetings, and centre management met for about 80 per cent of its time. This same image of an organisation as a hierarchical arrangement of meetings was true of an entire nation during the rise of the Dutch Republic where, following the break with Hapsburg Spain at the end of the sixteenth century, 'several thousand people from a population of about two million were obliged to meet regularly' (Van Vree, 1999, p. 190). They were members of a political network of urban administrative boards and the provincial states linked to the States-General which, in turn, were tied closely to the Dutch Reformed Church, and a network of guilds, water boards, trading companies and universities. It was from these interlocking arenas, 'built from below' (Van Vree, 1999, p. 130) and connected through multiple memberships, that the meeting rituals and practices that came to be associated with parliamentarisation (seating, chairing, speaking rights, rules of procedure, admissible conduct, etc.) emerged, were formalised in manuals of rules, and books of etiquette and manners and, in a small-scale society, spread quickly and extensively. The growth of this meeting apparatus in the transition from an agrarian to an industrial economy 'was largely unintentional and unplanned'. Interestingly, in light of my earlier analysis of the factors conducive to distributed leadership, this development occurred and was sustained due to 'the necessity to solve the complex problems of co-ordination which arose during the unprecedentedly powerful, extensive and intensive growth' (Van Vree, 1999, p. 197). As part of this emerging meeting culture, the committee became an institutionalised meeting form.

Committees

The criteria for distinguishing committees as joint work units (Chapter 2) were that they were mandated structures, whose elected or appointed memberships performed discretionary work of either a temporary or ongoing nature. Two key features of committees, including councils and boards, are their structural and interactional properties.

Structural Properties

Three attributes define a committee's zone of discretionary action and the way it will exercise its discretion. The first two derive from the order of authority within which committees are constituted. The third is determined by a committee's organisational location.

Proprietorship   The first constraint on the agency of committee members is institutional ownership: to whom or what is a committee answerable? Whenever a small decision-making structure is a creature of a larger entity, the relationship of the small to the large is one of encapsulation, rather than free-standing independence (Bailey, 1970, p. 149). An example is the school governing body or council established by statute.

The effect of proprietorship varies according to the type of committee. There are four main types: sub, standing, interest-based and ad hoc. Subcommittees or steering committees exist at the behest of a manager, agency or larger committee and usually have a limited lifespan. Their purpose is to explore, investigate, take submissions and frame recommendations for the encapsulating body. Standing committees operate with well-established terms of reference. They endure changes in membership composition. Examples include parliamentary committees which call witnesses, invite submissions, and review and audit public policy. Interest-based committees act as forums for advice, typically to government ministers or senior officials. Here, membership voice depends on the basis of membership recruitment, with independence from constituent interests ensured by invitation and appointment from above, and protection of interests safeguarded through elected representation and constituency appointed delegates. Ad hoc working groups, project management committees and task forces have brief shelf-lives and very specific remits. They are deemed to be 'far "safer" from the point of view of the administrator than is the statutory or continuing group' (Grant, 1960, p. 99) as there are less costs in rejecting their advice than in ignoring a standing committee with a firmer sense of its identity and relative independence.

Powers   The second, closely related constraint is the definition of a committee's role and, therefore, the authority with which it is vested. The key distinction here is between advisory and executive powers and duties. As regards advice, authority ends with the provision of information whereas with execution, committees are empowered to give effect to actions.

Policy committees illustrate the dilemmas associated with advice giving. The person with the power of membership appointment has a far greater chance of engineering committee consent in the formulation of policy if individuals are invited to be members, rather than interest groups being permitted to nominate their preferred representatives (Grant, 1960). On the other hand, policy consensus amongst the appointees of the interest groups to be conciliated may equally be secured because those interests attach a higher price to their participation than their voluntary abstention or political marginalisation. Withdrawal of their consent runs the risk of future non-participation and, consequently, less potential influence.

Positioning   Committees operate in qualitatively different organisational regions. These are arenas bounded 'to some degree by barriers to perception' (Goffman, 1976b, p. 109), rather than fixed physical locations. Two key regions are front- and back-stage, with 'front' denoting a public domain and 'back' signalling privileged entrée or 'behind the scenes' privacy.

These positions determine committee language patterns and behaviour. 'Up front', for example, members proclaim 'the principles by which they are 100 per cent guided', in conformity with their supporters' expectations. Front-stage behaviour is about wearing masks in order to keep up appearances. Behind closed doors, however, during detailed bargaining, where there is room for compromise, dealing and agreement, masks are dropped and concessions made with less loss of face (Bailey, 1977, p. 115). When committee members re-emerge, they contrive appearances for public consumption by denying they have backed down or given too much ground. Back-stage talk is characterised by gossip, scandal, rumour or confidences. An example is school administrators' speculation in the privacy of an office concerning the possible pregnancy of a teacher and the impact of her departure on grade allocations (Gronn, 1983, p. 7). These forms of talk highlight the problem of audience 'segregation' (Goffman, 1976b, p. 137) for leader-managers; i.e., entrusting information and regulating its distribution 'so that some arenas are public and some are private, and controlling the type of information available in each arena' (Bailey, 1977, p. 200). Should confidential information be disclosed or misused, leader-managers fall back on public excuses or justifications. These are defensive accounts for untoward actions 'in which one accepts responsibility for the act in question, but denies the pejorative quality associated with it', in the case of excuses, and 'in which one admits that the act in question is bad, wrong, or inappropriate but denies full responsibility', with justifications (Scott and Lyman, 1968, p. 47). Another tactic, to head off anticipated rather than prior difficulties, is the public disclaimer, where leaders 'display in their speech the expectation of possible responses of others to their impending conduct ... [and each] asks forbearance' (Hewitt and Stokes, 1975, p. 3).

Interactional Properties

Depending on the committee type, memberships vary in size up to a maximum of about 20–25. Size and the face-by-face spatial relations created by table seating arrangements during meetings establish a working environment in which credit and debit considerations associated with social 'face' (e.g., a member's sense of group centrality, marginality and integration) and being 'on show' shape proceedings. Within a particular organisation's framework of governance and the structural parameters just outlined, five features of committee behaviour warrant comment.

Style Depending on the members' formal or informal links with their constituencies, committees will display either an elite or arena style. Committees in elite mode, especially those with non-representative membership status, tend to adopt a closed approach. Here, members close ranks and, with only loose or informal links, if any, with external interests, devise consensus decisions by 'sense of the meeting' (Bailey, 1965, p. 1). There are difficulties with consensus, such as attitude convergence and defensiveness, as will be evident shortly from the groupthink research. Committees in arena mode, by contrast, are less secretive in their deliberations and more conscious of members' constituencies as external points of reference. In extreme cases, members may refer constantly to their interest groups for authorisation and advice, as in negotiations over school amalgamations (Gronn, 1994, pp. 72–5).

Factions In contrast with elite committee solidarity and contained disagreement within civilised meeting bounds, arena committees may splinter. In highly factionalised circumstances, such tactics as publicity seeking, information leaking and 'hanging out the dirty washing' may be used to internal advantage. On the other hand, there are pressures to soften differences in the interests of productivity. In this Victorian school council meeting, a parent (Cox) aggrieved at the practice of non-budgeted expenditure, smiled as she criticised the council president (Evans) for his support for the principal (Hughes), resulting in laughter from others (Gronn, 1984a, p. 75):

Cox:	Yes but if we've already spent [\$]3,600 and it hasn't come through yet I mean we just don't
Evans	[interrupting]: No wull
Cox:	have 750
Evans	[groping for a solution while trying to talk over others]: No wull look that's what I'm getting at we we re we review we a … we approve *some* of that money now we say make an allocation of 3 or 400 so that we can get started I mean would that enable you [Illingworth: teacher] to get started?
Illingworth:	500'd be good
Evans:	(laughs) three for five. (laughter)
Cox:	But if we haven't got 500 Jack [Evans] where's it going to come from?

Later, after the principal had interposed with 'I have a solution', Cox's reaction evoked a similar response (Gronn, 1984a, p. 76):

Cox:	I'll bet
Lewis (parent):	Tch (laughs)
Hughes:	an that is that we we simply
Cox:	(laughingly) just pay the money and shut up.

Identity   Some committees, due mainly to longevity, acquire reputation and consistency of core membership, develop a sense of collective identity (Gronn, 1985, pp. 264–5). Like the biographies of their members and organisations more generally, committees follow a life cycle or developmental career path. Bailey (1983) detected three broad stages of development. Identity maturation is evident in the extent of members' condensed and coded meeting speech. In the immature phase, members 'have difficulty communicating with one another and do little more than grunt and grimace' and convey 'large internally undiscriminated gobs of information about attitudes and feelings'. As working relations solidify during the adult phase of feelgood togetherness, committee members' messages are highly coded with 'fine discriminations'. With the onset of senility, however, members tend to turn inward, for they 'think they can read each other's mind' and see 'no point in communicating with an external world' (Bailey, 1983, p. 104).

Games   Given the strength of the human predilection for theatricality, as is attested in the opening excerpt from Malcolm Bradbury, committee meetings serve a host of unintended expressive purposes, despite their avowed instrumental justifications. Goffman (1976a, p. 508) notes that: 'often what talkers undertake to do is not to provide information to a recipient but to present dramas to an audience. Indeed, it seems that we spend most of our time not engaged in giving information but in giving shows'. One example is the devising of formalistic substitutes for action. Galbraith (1963, p. 130) described this as 'the rite of the meeting which is called not to do business but to do no business' and yet to sustain the impression of business being done. Committee meetings are also vehicles for the management and display of status, as is evident in jockeying for recognition by 'seeing who defers to whom and who gets greater rewards for like effort' (Owens and Sutton, 2001, p. 301). A good example is the battle for dominance, as evident in Hanak's (1998) study of a male Zanzibar agricultural officer's attempted usurpation of a female chair's prerogative during a village seaweed farming co-operative meeting.

Deliberations The final interactional attribute concerns the character of the conduct of committee meetings. Research attention here has necessarily been directed to features of the flow and rhythm of the multi-party talk that is peculiar to committees and meetings generally. Unlike the more generic field of conversational analysis, however, with its extensive body of ethnomethodological and socio-linguistic research findings, knowledge of the structural patterning of multi-party talk is much less fine-grained and definitive.

One feature about which there is broad agreement is the sequencing imperatives which dictate staged or phased meeting deliberations, with stages marked by various linguistic signals or cues. Stages include the pre-meeting talk of an arranging or beginning phase (particularly evident with unscheduled meetings, where agreement to meet and meeting terms have to be negotiated) during which members gather their thoughts, exchange pleasantries, clear their throats, shuffle their papers, get comfortable and come to order (Atkinson, Cuff and Lee, 1978; Cuff and Sharrock, 1985). This stage is followed by framing, at the outset of which the meeting itself and the business at hand are formally designated and legitimated. Framing also occurs throughout meeting proceedings via meta-level gambits that advise listeners 'of the general nature of the semantic information conveyed' (Keller 1981, p. 111), such as 'what I'm hearing you saying is ...' or 'am I to understand you to mean ... ?'. Next, there is an ending, or winding-down, phase for tidying up or deferring loose bits and pieces of business. This is followed, finally, by an afterwards phase over supper or drinks, or on the telephone, during which members rework the meeting and conduct 'post-mortems' (Schwartzman, 1986, p. 247). Closely connected to this intra-meeting sense of stages is the phasing or staging that is evident over the life course of a series of meetings. Rather than adhering to the popular normative presumption of an unfolding rhythm of form, norm and storm etc., Gersick's (1988) research highlighted the importance of punctuated equilibrium. Her observations of eight task force advisory committees suggested that, following an early experience of inertia, almost exactly halfway between first meetings and their official deadlines, 'in a concentrated burst of changes', groups 'dropped old patterns, reengaged with outside supervisors, adopted new perspectives on their work, and made dramatic progress' (Gersick, 1988, p. 16).

Movement between stages or phases within meetings has been shown by Bailey (1983) to depend on a range of rehearsed or non-rehearsed moves (or plays). Committee work comprises a mix of instrumental attention to tasks, and affirmative and negative feelings about those tasks. Committee deliberations zigzag between these emotions of friendliness and animosity, during which members' positioning in relation to the issues in hand is evident in the masked selves (e.g., silly, civic, tactical, moral) that they display. Verbal codes (e.g., preventative, curative and disruptive plays) signal movements into or out of the zones of rationality and emotion. The subtleties of this phased movement via code-switching depend on access to a meeting 'floor', a phenomenon defined by Edelsky (1981, p. 405, original emphasised) as 'the acknowledged what's-going-on within a psychological time/space'. Speakers' floor access rights may be contested, regulated by the meeting chair, self-selected in a speaker turn space or conferred by a preceding speaker, as in 'Well, George, that's all I have at the moment' (Francis, 1986, p. 60). Edelsky's (1981, p. 391) audiotapings of five meetings of a university standing committee disclosed two main floors: F1s, or one-speaker-at-a-time floors, and F2s, or collaborative, free-for-all floors which displayed 'much simultaneity, joint building of an answer to a question, collaboration on developing ideas ... and laughter'.

Morgenthaler's (1990) investigation of meetings of a slightly combative, activist (mixed sex) Latin American study group (LASG) and a women's study support group suggested there were also distinct gender differences in floor use. Study group women regulated meeting floors through eye contact, with speakers' and facilitators' glances signalling speaking turns and topic switches. This female-only behaviour, and women's behaviour in company with LASG males led Morgenthaler to modify Edelsky's F1s to include single-party (or sole speaker) contested exclusive F1s (as when parliamentary speaking rights pass to the next in turn) and non-exclusive F1s, with some slight variation observed in the F2s. Contrary to Morgenthaler, however, research into mixed-sex US government agency taskforce meetings revealed each sex as willing to challenge the other. Women were not verbally 'frozen out', talked more often (although for shorter times) than men, and women's preferred topics prevailed as much as men's, leading Duerst-Lahti (1990, p. 214) to conclude that women administrators had mastered co-verbal power displays and can 'play the game too'. Floors and western turn-taking make little sense in the entirely different cultural context of Australian aboriginal Pintupi meetings. Here, talk 'does not press on toward a topic, relentlessly to solve a problem', but instead is interruption-free and intended to 'sustain relations among the participants under a rubric of being related to each other' (Myers, 1986, p. 432).

Charting the universe of tactical possibilities in multi-party talk situations is currently proceeding in two main ways: forms of talk peculiar either to occupational groups, such as the professions, or to particular genres of arenas. As regards the former, two illustrations relevant to school leaders but not peculiar to the groups depicted are the meta-level conversational meeting formulations and reformulations (e.g., 'What can we agree on doing?') used by US attorneys (Bilmes, 1981, p. 270), and the clarifications ('What you are really getting at is ...') and compliments ('We do appreciate your comments') which health professionals use to blunt client criticism (Paap and Hanson, 1982). With respect to the latter, interest in the entire area of the 'the games people play' at meetings, was kick-started by the entertaining acuity of Cornford's (1973 [1908]) little treatise on academic gamesmanship, *Microcosmographia Academica*. Its 'the thin edge of the wedge', 'setting a dangerous precedent' and 'the time is not yet ripe' ploys have long been part of popular folklore. One genre of multi-party talk of particular importance for school leaders is the situated negotiation talk which occurs in arena-style committee meetings. Negotiations in industrial bargaining (as distinct from diplomacy) manifest position talk (O'Donnell, 1990, p. 224), which is co-produced (Francis, 1986, p. 62) and in which representatives of each side try to implicate the other in their side's definition of a problem. This may be resisted by problem reformulation, although sometimes the parties may be uncertain about what they want and what the other side is likely to offer (Anderson, Hughes and Sharrock, 1987, p. 155).

Summary

Like other joint work units such as divisions and departments, committees, particularly of the standing variety, play a vital role in the governance of organisations through the pooling of collective intelligence. When their remit is advice, committees mostly supplement the authority of individual leader-managers, but if their mandate is execution then they share authority. In either case, as cheek by jowl working relations and the interdependencies to which these give rise solidify through time, leader-managers and their committees are likely to be more comfortable with Bailey's (1965) sense of the meeting unanimity than the divisiveness and discomfort associated with majority rule voting. In essence, they prefer the elite, rather than the arena, mode of operation. But committees in an elite frame of mind tend to think of themselves as institutional guardians, as 'accepting responsibility for the collectivity and reaching a decision in the best interest of all' (Bailey, 1977, p. 71). This predisposition to close ranks vis-à-vis those whom they serve may be bolstered by a hostile external working environment. These kinds of pressures leave committees vulnerable to the phenomenon of groupthink.

Groupthink

'Groupthink' has a deliberately sinister Orwellian ring to it. It is concerned with the processes conducive to, and the consequences of, high degrees of attitudinal concurrence and conformity, in a range of small groups, including committees and teams. Groupthink assumes significance in meeting deliberations, for example, whenever leader-managers attach a high priority to consensual agreement and the maintenance of work unit *esprit de corps*. Because it impairs decision-making and the capacity for learning, however, groupthink is potentially bad news for committees and teams, for it 'effectively turns around some of the traditional ideas about the effectiveness of "cohesiveness" on group performance' ('t Hart, 1991, p. 256). Sure signs of groupthink are evident, according to Aldag and Fuller (1993, p. 534), when a group:

> limits its discussion to only a few alternatives. After a course of action is initially selected, members ignore new information concerning its risks and drawbacks. At the

same time, they avoid information concerning the benefits of rejected alternatives. Members make little attempt to use experts to obtain more precise information. In addition, because they are so confident that things will turn out well, group members fail to consider what may go wrong and, as such, do not develop contingency plans.

But why? What is groupthink? And how and why are joint work units susceptible to its effects?

In *Groupthink* (originally *Victims of Groupthink*), Irving Janis (1982) analysed historical and journalistic evidence of four US foreign policy debacles (abortive Bay of Pigs invasion, Korean war escalation across the 38th parallel, ill-preparedness for the Japanese attack on Pearl Harbour, and protracted engagement in, and ignominious withdrawal from, Vietnam). Later, he supplemented these events with the Watergate cover-up, and two foreign policy successes (blockade of Russian naval vessels en route to Cuba in 1962 and the Marshall aid plan for post-Second World War European recovery). With this evidence, Janis postulated the antecedents of a collective mindset he called groupthink (Janis, 1982, p. 9):

> to refer to a mode of thinking that people engage in when they are deeply involved in a cohesive ingroup, when the members' strivings for unanimity override their motivation to realistically appraise alternative courses of action ... a deterioration of mental efficiency, reality testing, and moral judgement that results from in-group pressures.

Janis (1982, p. 13, original italicised) hypothesised that 'the more amiability and esprit de corps' among policy-making in-group members, 'the greater is the danger that independent critical thinking will be replaced by groupthink', resulting 'in irrational and dehumanizing actions directed against out-groups'. To reinforce the earlier point about the effects of elitist committee pre-dispositions, 't Hart (1991, p. 264) noted that when work units 'do not have to account for their judgements and choices' then the tendency for groupthink is stronger than when such work units are required to render account.

Essentially, Janis (1982, pp. 243–5) was proposing a relationship between a series of antecedent conditions and their observable consequences. The antecedent conditions comprised three components: a cohesive group of decision-makers, structural organisational faults (e.g., group insularity, lack of impartial leadership, absence of methodical procedures) and a provocative external context (e.g., stress-inducing, low self-esteem due to previous failures, low self-efficacy). These created a predisposition towards groupthink or concurrence-seeking. Groupthink would be evident in the following eight symptoms (Janis, 1982, pp. 174–5):

1 An illusion of invulnerability, creating excessive optimism and risk-taking.
2 A belief in the group's inherent morality.
3 Collective rationalisation of information threatening to shared assumptions.
4 Stereotypical demonising of rivals or enemies as evil, weak and stupid.
5 Self-censorship of deviations from the group consensus and denial of doubts.
6 An illusion of unanimity in the absence of overt dissent.
7 Scapegoating or marginalising pressure on deviants from the group 'line'.
8 Mindguarding by members that reinforces a complacent sense of superiority.

The consequence of these antecedents would be defective decision-making, as evidenced by incomplete information search, poor risk assessment, information bias, an absence of contingency plans etc., and a low probability of successful decision outcomes.

Criticisms of Groupthink

Janis's idea has attracted a lot of attention, indeed over 700 citations alone appeared in the *Social Sciences Citation Index* for the period 1989–92 (Aldag and Fuller, 1993, p. 533). And yet, even though wide-ranging debate continues about groupthink (Street, 1997), there has been a 'relative numerical paucity of subsequent research efforts' ('t Hart, 1991, p. 259). There has been even less attention accorded it in school leadership, which is remarkable given the traditional emphasis on consultation and consensus in the professional culture of teachers. Three main lines of criticism have emerged. First, Janis has been attacked for his apparently blanket disavowal of concurrence-seeking. Langley and Pruitt (1980, p. 75), for example, claim that in group decision-making contexts some level of agreement is required for group effectiveness, in which case the real concerns about groupthink are less the fact of its existence and more to do with the timing (i.e., *when* during the decision-making chain), process (i.e., whether checks and balances have been navigated prior to agreement) and the extent of agreement. And, even were the negative consequences of concurrence-seeking to be conceded, groupthink might only be worth worrying about in cases of significant, rather than routine, decisions. In fact, according to Langley and Pruitt (1980, p. 80), Janis's groupthink diagnosis rested on only four assumptions (1, 3, 4 and 7), 'a loose bag of partially related ideas', with the precise causal contribution and relation between them unclear. This was because the four other alleged 'symptoms' (2, 5, 6 and 8) were perfectly reasonable assumptions and far from detrimental to group effectiveness. Finally, Janis had not related the incidence of groupthink to the developmental life of groups but, Langley and Pruitt hypothesised, contrary to Bailey's (1983, p. 104) view of committee senescence, groupthink was more likely to be present early in the life of a group.

The second line of criticism concerns the nature of the connection between the antecedents and the decision outcomes. Mohamed and Wiebe (1996, p. 420), for example, query whether Janis's model is a model of *process* which recounts how a phenomenon occurs, in the sense that a course of action Y depends on a set of preceding, antecedent conditions having been met. In that case, the groupthink formula, working backwards, would be 'if Y, then ABC'. If, however, there were no antecedent conditions, then there probably would not be a detrimental outcome, in which case 'if not ABC, then not Y'. This is a 'pull' model of groupthink. On the other hand, the model may be a *variance* or *causal* model, in which the forward reasoning would be 'if X, then Y', in that the outcome Y follows inexorably from the posited antecedent X. This is a *push* model. Unlike the process view, which expresses the probability of an outcome's occurrence, the causal view is deterministic. Mohamed and Wiebe incline towards the former, but they acknowledge that poor outcomes and reckless decision-making can occur despite, not just because of, groupthink and also for reasons of bad judgement, lack of information etc., so that groupthink is just one of a universe of outcome possibilities. The posited antecedents may be necessary, but not sufficient, to yield a groupthink-type outcome, therefore, and other factors may be involved (Mohamed and Wiebe, 1996, p. 424). Likewise, Neck and Moorhead (1995) suggest that groupthink occurs in some contexts when Janis's posited antecedent conditions are present, but not in others. The two critical elements and intervening factors which make the difference are the presence or absence of a closed leadership style, and adherence to methodical and structured decision-making procedures (Neck and Moorhead, 1995, p. 539). Two additional constraints on decision-makers are time and the magnitude of the decision (Neck and Moorhead, 1995, p. 545).

The third major criticism is that alternative explanations may better account for the faulty decision outcomes attributed to groupthink. Indeed, groupthink is said to provide 'a partial explanation' at best for decision debacles and cannot really explain 'why the group view coalesces around the particular policy option that it does' (Whyte, 1989, p. 51). What has to be explained is the predilection of numerically small, key advisory groups for excessively risky decisions, especially 'no win', situations. In these 'damned if you do or damned if you don't' circumstances or aversive states of affairs, the options for a group are a choice between risks and losses of varying import. In policy contexts in which the decision-makers' options begin to polarise, the pressures towards a uniformly held attitude, due to shared information and the need to maintain working relations, yield a preference for one option. With a group desiring to avoid almost certain policy failure, and loss of face and reputation, decision-makers will be inclined to take big risks, because they feel they have little or nothing to lose (Whyte, 1989, p. 48). In such polarised circumstances, therefore, the options for action boil down to either certain loss or possibly even greater loss, with the slim possibility of being able to snatch victory from the jaws of defeat if the decision-makers take a gamble. On this same point, t' Hart (1991, p. 265, original emphasis) suggested that 'it is precisely *because* the risk dimension of their actions becomes less relevant to members of decision groups caught in the groupthink syndrome, that they will not refrain from supporting alternatives that are highly risky'. For Whyte, each of the foreign policy fiascos cited by Janis are examples of loss avoidance, as much as groupthink.

Further Revisions

Other modifications to Janis's groupthink hypothesis have arisen as a result of its application to cases other than foreign policy. The most persuasive has been to account for the explosion in 1986 of the US space shuttle *Challenger*, shortly after take-off, which killed seven astronauts. Subsequently, the presidential commission of inquiry cited flawed decision-making as 'a primary contributory cause' (Moorhead, Ference and Neck, 1991, p. 540) and, as was evident from the testimonies of commission witnesses, three of Janis's antecedent conditions for groupthink were present when the decision was taken to launch the shuttle, despite technical advice to the contrary. Groupthink might also be expected to impair the effectiveness of juries, although Neck and Moorhead (1992, p. 1081) reviewed the trial of a US drug trafficker, John de Lorean, and found that 'decision-making contamination was avoided', mainly because the jurors canvassed a wide range of alternatives before arriving at a judgement and searched constantly for new information. The groupthink avoidance factor with general import that emerged was 'whether or not the group [concerned] establishes and utilizes procedures for information search and appraisal' (Neck and Moorhead, 1992, p. 1088). This second example suggests the possibility of coherence without groupthink (Bernthal and Insko, 1993) and that the challenge for group decision-making is to retain meeting coherence in order to perform effectively, but without the psychology of groupmindedness impairing members' judgements. Groups cohere emotionally and/or in respect of their tasks, and Bernthal and Insko (and see Mohamed and Wiebe, 1996, pp. 425–6) believe that Janis's model applies mainly where socio-emotional cohesion is paramount.

Consensus and Collaborative Synergies

Commentators disagree over the merits of Janis's groupthink hypothesis and continue to revise it. Aldag and Fuller (1993), for example, draw liberally on groupthink research and the literature on problem-solving, with a view to reframing the model and its components in more neutral and non-pathological language. They commend their revised version as applicable to a broad range of group problem-solving situations, with its primary purpose being descriptive rather than predictive (Aldag and Fuller, 1993, p. 546).

Difficulties

Despite the continuing refinement of groupthink, Janis's concurrence-seeking symptoms are a cause for concern wherever meetings of small group structures, such as committees, are under pressure, when solving problems, to produce 'sense of the meeting' or consensus-style outcomes. As suggested earlier, during the 1970s and 1980s, for example, consensus had strong widespread consultative and participatory appeal in many school systems. It acquired three main meanings, each giving it powerful symbolic force as a moral good. First, consensus described an outcome, an end state of numerical unanimity by an aggregate of people in accord with a policy or course of action. Second, it referred to the justification for a policy commitment, in that the policy or action was freely consented to by those in agreement. Third, consensus came to mean a process for arriving at an outcome which entailed fidelity to consultative mechanisms in which the views of all stakeholders were aired. These attributes are both a strength and a weakness of consensus. As ways of trying to find common ground between competing interests, institutionalised consensus processes may prove appealing from various industrial relations, political or other points of view, but these may not necessarily be the most effective means of utilising an organisation's collective wisdom in the interests of problem-solving, particularly if the need for concurrence becomes overriding. Consensus and concurrence-style thinking have also acquired informal currency in the assumption that workplaces are primary groups which function as surrogate families and that leader-managers should facilitate and strengthen family-like bonds amongst workers (Baum, 1991). A favourite marketing ploy of some school leaders, for example, is to cast their institution as 'the school family'.

Individualism or Groupism

Whatever its shape or form, consensus has rarely achieved universal acclaim. A vehement opponent was W.H. Whyte (1963), in his widely cited critique of the human relations movement in industry, *The Organization Man*. Whyte attacked the prominence of groups in the workplace as conducive to timid, dull and mediocre leadership and management. Group structures were an attempt to pander to employees' affiliative needs, but a by-product of their sense of belonging and togetherness was a stultifying group-mindedness. For Whyte, group dynamics was an insidious management tool for manipulating morale, motivation and loyalty. Group consensus was odious to Whyte (1963, p. 53) because:

> To concentrate on agreement is to intensify that which inhibits creativity. For any group of people to operate effectively some firm basis of agreement is necessary, and a meeting cannot be productive unless certain premises are so shared that they don't need to be discussed and the argument can be confined to areas of disagreement. But while this kind of consensus makes a group more effective in its legitimate functions, it does not make the group a creative vehicle.

Such groupism, in particular, was antithetical to individuality (Whyte, 1963, p. 59):

> Consider the abstractions that are so taken for granted as good – such as consensus, cooperation, participation, and the like. Held up as a goal without any reference to ends, they are meaningless. Why participate, for example? Like similar abstractions, participation is an empty goal unless it is gauged in relation to the job to be done. It is a means, not an end, and when treated as an end, it can become more repressive than the unadorned authoritarianism it is supposed to replace.

Likewise with consensus: the price of progress, he believed, was a 'departure from agreed-upon ways of looking at things', rather than continued agreement with them, which only served to legitimate 'the hostility to that creativity upon which we all ultimately depend' (Whyte, 1963, p. 59).

Hybrid Approaches

By the 1990s, the individualist entrepreneurial leadership for which Whyte yearned had become *de rigueur*, in both corporate and human service sector organisations, including schools. Under the impress of policies informed in part by the kinds of transformational and charismatic leadership theories enshrined in designer-leadership, consensus-style committee structures shed some of their symbolic lustre. In the search for the more flexible and informal synergistic modes of workplace collaboration considered earlier, teams began to assume prominence. Yet, despite their appeal in numerous educational settings, universities and schools, do not appear to be replacing their committees with teams, but instead, in the form of short-life working parties and advisory groups, team structures are being grafted, hybrid-like, onto existing sets of departmental and committee governance arrangements. Teams can be expected to breathe new life into consensus-style work practices because, although they differ from committees (for the reasons given in Chapter 2), they have sufficient in common with them for team meetings to be susceptible to similar kinds of psychological pressures and dynamics. For that reason, teams are also likely to have been the targets of Whyte's wrath. The purpose of the next chapter is to explore some of the distinctive features of teams and team meetings.

6   Leadership Teams

'Teams and teamwork are in', notes Cohen (1993, p. 194) and, as Barker (1999, p. 4) observes, 'the most popular planned organizing innovation is the transformation of a traditional, hierarchically based organization to a flat confederation of self-managing teams'. These observations are true of all organisational sectors, profit, not-for-profit and human service alike. Of the forms of distributed leadership considered earlier on, teams are the most prominent and popular. They represent the most recent manifestation of a heritage of collaborative modes of work practice known as autonomous or semi-autonomous work groups. The antecedents of teams go back as far as the early years of the human relations movement and socio-technical systems research on work organisation in the 1950s and 1960s. More recently, they are evident in the 'islands of autonomy' (Jenkins, 1994, p. 851) in manufacturing and production in the 1970s that included various forms of worker participation, consultation and industrial democracy.

From Chapter 2 it will be recalled that, as joint work units, teams, like committees, perform discretionary work, although they tend to have a limited lifespan and the synergies they generate are especially vulnerable to membership changes. An additional key element in their efficiency, as will be clear from the following discussion, is whether teams are mandated or imposed from above by managers, or whether the initiative for their creation comes from below. For school leaders contemplating structural changes, therefore, any simple formulaic prescription to the effect that if one changes the label then one changes the reality should be treated with caution. An existing group entity, for example, does not simply metamorphose or reconstitute itself into a team and automatically jettison all the accrued psycho-political baggage associated with its previous incarnation as, say, a staff forum or advisory committee. Thus, Hall (2001, p. 329) notes how simple solutions to management problems necessitate a 'health warning' that teamwork is 'not just about composition and games'. On the other hand, Wallace and Huckman's (1999) four UK primary heads were confident they could 'establish structures and give the group of senior managers a team label'. But as Wallace and Huckman (1999, p. 129) note, this confidence depended on their colleagues' willingness to work as a team. After considering some explanations for the recent interest in teams, the discussion appraises the justifications provided for teamwork and critically reviews a body of research into team functioning, both within and outside education. The chapter concludes with a discussion of teams as vehicles for organisational learning.

Teams Re-emerge

Workplace teams were embraced in the 1980s and 1990s for a number of reasons, most of them related to workplace restructuring and the search for flexible forms of work organisation as part of micro-economic reform. Some commentators typify this trend as the Japanisation or Scandinavianisation of work in recognition of the diffusion of clan-like and syndicate manufacturing work practices to Anglo-American economies. In the transition to a new era of post-industrialism or informationalism, a new technical mode of production is seen as the principal lever of change in the social dynamics and organisation of production relations. Castells (1996, pp. 152–60), for example, juxtaposes two ideal types or modes of production: Fordism and Toyotism (or Volvoism). The Fordist ideal of the traditional factory-based, mass-production system was distinguished by a strict hierarchical differentiation of the work of managers and employees which, crudely put, might be typified as the distinction between productivity associated with the head (intellectual labour) and the hand (manual labour). Moreover, consistent with F.W. Taylor's scientific management principle of the fragmentation of shop-floor labour into minute protocols of measurable operations, industrial employees under Fordism are said to have worked as isolated individuals at conveyor belts or assembly lines where they performed repetitious and low-level discretionary tasks demarcated by varying levels of predefined skill. The shift to Toyotism (roughly during 1970–90), however, has seen the adoption of far less rigid methods of production, flatter managerial hierarchies and a much greater reliance on employee initiatives channelled through combinations of quasi-autonomous work units. According to this line of reasoning, teams represent an explicit attempt by managers to reposition and realign workers' commitments in relation to their peers under a new enabling rhetoric and structural rubric of autonomy, participation and empowerment (Smith, 1997, pp. 323–6).

Especially important in this switch in employment paradigms, however, as pointed out in Chapter 2, has been the reconfiguration of the division of workplace labour, in particular changes in regard to the definition, and distribution and performance of tasks. Broadly, in the Fordist paradigm, the aggregate of the tasks to be performed was broken down, Taylor-like, into specific individual jobs and sets of minute operations, with the workforce matched to individual tasks and employed as job-holders. In the new emerging division of labour, however, employability and portability are substituting for employment for many, although by no means all, workers (Cappelli, 1999; Jacoby, 1999). That is, an organisation's work requirements are distributed across sets of individuals in circumstances of rapidly shifting work priorities with tasks performed jointly. This pattern usually requires the mobilisation of a requisite set of competencies for the completion of generic tasks, often of limited duration, rather than scheduled tasks to be completed in an ongoing time frame and as part of career-long individual employment contracts. An important consequence is the disruption of traditional employee ideologies of localism – in respect of definitions of time, space, place and sense of community in the workplace – during restructuring, and their allegiances and identities are reconstructed while organisation managers endeavour to respond to the direct and indirect effects of globalising imperatives (Castells, 1996, esp. pp. 240–51, 410–28, 469–78).

Sinclair (1995) has also highlighted the seductiveness of teams for leader-managers because of their promise of peak organisational performance (and see Reich, 1987, p. 83). Another source of appeal has been the idea of the employee as a 'team player' (Zaleznik, 1989, p. 268), an attractiveness stemming partly from the adoption of popular imagery of sporting team success which communicates a palpable sense of 'players being "in a groove" and almost preternaturally "in tune" with their fellow teammates' (Sandelands and St Clair, 1993, p. 436). Finally, attention parallel to operational level teams in manufacturing has been accorded the senior management team at the executive levels of organisations. The rise of the SMT is reflected in the increasing scholarly attention devoted to areas such as upper-echelon theory, elite theory and strategic leadership (see Hambrick, 1994; Pettigrew, 1992; Hambrick and Mason, 1984). Senior management teams or their equivalents are now utilised in many schools and in universities. School leadership commentators point to a variety of reasons for the introduction of SMTs. These range from 'greater managerial complexity' in school administration (Wallace and Hall, 1994, p. 183) to an explicit commitment to collaboration (Cardno, 1998, p. 47).

Justifying Teams

These wider arguments related to organisational restructuring coalesce around the argument most commonly advanced to support the introduction of teams in workplaces in either the manufacturing or service sectors, namely, that they guarantee flexibility and speedy decision-making in increasingly competitive work environments (Cohen, 1993, p. 195): 'Flexible organizations place decision-making authority in the hands of those close to sources of information and those who have the expertise to interpret and act on it. This is rarely an individual task, because changing technologies and markets have different impacts on organizational functions and disciplines.' Notice here the assertion that task performance operates collaboratively, rather than individually, and that flexibilised work environments create a new incentive and motivation structure. The claim is that joint authority to execute decisions should be sufficient to meaningfully engage employees in securing their own interests, along with those of their peers and the organisation as a whole. A virtue of the team idea, then, is that by regulating its own affairs, a team's members are empowered.

Self-management

The idea of collective empowerment grew out of claims about individual empowerment. Two of the earliest commentators to canvass the possibility of self-influencing or self-regulating behaviour on the part of individual subordinates were Manz and Sims (1980). They took as their departure point the highly influential claim about substitutes for leadership made by Kerr and Jermier (1978). Essentially, this argument was that organisational outcomes and decisions could be accounted for causally in a number of ways, only one of which might be the leadership of an individual. Manz and Sims appealed to the notion of an alleged internal locus of control – i.e., that most people for much of their working and non-working lives regulate and control their own behaviour (through self-denial, deferred gratification, etc.) and respect the rights of others – and argued in favour of ways of maximising and building on forms of employee self-control in the workplace. All kinds of benefits were likely to accrue. Thus (Manz and Sims, 1980, p. 363):

> from a cost/benefit perspective, self-management can be considered a desirable objective because it involves less expense to the organization, in terms of dollars and time, than having someone else serve as a manager. Furthermore, the employee's manager is free to address longer-term problems and issues that need attention [instead of engaging in constant direct supervision].

In practice, self-management means that 'relatively small, highly autonomous work groups that take responsibility for a product, project or service' (Salem, Lazarus and Cullen, 1992, p. 24), with the team members' relationship being one of mutual dependency. 'Employees are trained to use their skills daily to schedule, assign tasks, co-ordinate with other groups, set goals, interface with suppliers, evaluate performance, handle customers, hire new members and deal with discipline problems', with the idea being that, even though no one individual has all the skills, 'the team as a whole possesses the skills and abilities which are needed to perform any task' (Salem, Lazarus and Cullen, 1992, p. 25).

There are a number of assumptions embedded in this entire line of reasoning. The first is that employees will want, and will seek, self-control or self-management. But is something like this desired by all employees or just some? Self-management, as Barker (1999, p. 7) notes, has become necessary to secure the commitment of an increasingly educated workforce which 'does not respond well to strict forms of control'. A second assumption is that the capacity to self-manage is presumed to come naturally to employees socialised into traditional modes of organisational control. But what if self-management has to be learnt? What preconditions for learning have to be satisfied? Proponents of self-managing systems, such as Manz, Mossholder and Luthans (1987, pp. 13, 15) concede this latter possibility when they note that 'self-management is a skill that many individuals will need to develop before they can function effectively under autonomous conditions' and that the capability for self-management 'is not simply an innate quality'. A third assumption is that conditions which apply to individuals are taken to apply to collective units. That is, arguments about self-managing which were 'originally developed to explain individual differences [suddenly] migrated to a higher level of analysis' (Markham and Markham, 1995, pp. 343–4).

Self-leadership

Manz, Mossholder and Luthans (1987) developed the claimed advantages of behavioural self-regulation and self-management into an argument for self-leadership. Self-leadership was distinguished by 'the personal meaningfulness and "ownership" of the individual's governing standards' (Manz, 1986, p. 589). Whereas under self-management workers would monitor their own performance against predetermined work standards or benchmarks, as self-leaders they are able to define or determine those same standards as well as striving to attain them. Not only that, but work under self-leadership is performed because of its intrinsically appealing nature, in which case there is an inherent motivation to engage in activities that are designed to generate their own rewards – e.g., the experience of self-determination, feelings of efficacy and a sense of altruism (Manz and Sims, 1992, pp. 1128, 1131). In practice, however, attempts to secure a sense of employees' internal or personal commitment as part of avowed policies of empowerment appear to have foundered (Argyris, 1998), so that proponents would be hard put to sustain this conceptual distinction between self-management and self-leadership. Furthermore, Markham and Markham (1995, p. 346) note that 'there is very little empirical validation concerning the distinction between these two processes within organizational settings' and Dunphy and Bryant (1996, p. 693) report that they have never found any 'fully-fledged examples' of self-leading teams in their research.

Learning

Senge (1993) provided a 'wisdom of teams' justification for workplace teaming. Although empowerment was implicit in Senge's (1993, p. 234) argument, his primary concern was with collective intelligence. For Senge, team learning was one of five so-called disciplines or components of a model of the learning organisation – the others being systems thinking, a sense of personal mastery, mental modelling and shared visions. Relying on the analogue of sporting team success and jazz syncopation, of being in the groove, with unit members attuned to one another and moving together as one, the 'wisdom' of teams lay in achieving collective resonance or synergy. 'Individuals learn all the time', according to Senge (1993, p. 236) 'and yet there is no organizational learning.' Using terms such as dialogue, discussion and colleagueship to express team relationships, Senge aimed to communicate a kind of essence of creative team processes. Senge's team ideal was contrasted with the reality of defensive reasoning and routines which become deeply entrenched in many organisations, and which are the sources of rigidity, wasted effort and self-perpetuating cycles of internal politicking (here he cites liberally from the well-known work of Argyris and Schon). Senge was searching for a discourse with which to construct a model of practice built around Csikszentmihaly's (1991) idea of being in flow – a state of mind similar to the ecstasy that comes from optimal experiences.

Critiquing Teams

So much for the proponents of teams, what about the opponents? To Neumann's (1991, p. 489) deceptively simple question, 'What is it like to be on a team – and to be outside one', critics, as is shown below, have alleged that being 'on a team' is mostly oppressive for team members, at least in teams in non-educational spheres. There are few studies of being 'outside one', although teachers at Rockville County Primary School perceived the school's SMT 'almost entirely negatively' (Evans, 1998, p. 420). And mutual empowerment of those on and outside of teams, Wallace and Huckman (1999, p. 162) noted, depended on the capacity for compromise between the school-wide interests of SMTs and the sectional interests of non-SMT personnel.

Each of the following arguments reflect Bramel and Friend's (1987) thesis that the importance of particular work group formations has varied historically according to the shifting balance of the wider power and interests of management and labour. Thus, when organised labour can wring concessions from management, arguments about worker control, industrial democracy and co-determination assume prominence in management theory. At such times, commentators have advised that these mechanisms were important and that, used skilfully, managers could harness them to increase organisational productivity. But, when managerial interests have been ascendant and organised labour's demands contained, then commentators' advice to managers has switched in an effort to persuade them to ignore class solidarity and to secure workers' allegiance by more egoistic appeals to co-operate. Self-managing workplace teams illustrate this trend because of the implied personal satisfaction obtained through both individual autonomy and willing collaboration for the good of everyone. Employee team satisfaction, however, may depend in part on whether a team is mandated or emergent. A team is mandated when its composition and role is initiated and imposed on a workforce by senior management. An emergent team, by contrast, may be thought of as a 'team-that-builds-itself' (Williams, 1995) and is consolidated from an existing informal, but strongly bonded, primary group. Even though, as was pointed out in Chapter 2, the depth of members' commitment is likely to be stronger and the development of a working synergy easier in an emergent team structure, there are still few commentators who explicitly acknowledge the significance of this distinction.

Identification

Critics of self-managing teams invoke arguments concerned with identity politics. The first criticism is that, in some contexts, the self-managing team experience represents enslavement rather than empowerment. In the absence of knowledge of 'how self-managing teams construct new and functional forms of control' and 'how these forms compare with how we have conceptualized control in the past', Barker (1993, p. 414) conducted an ethnography of a small electronic component manufacturer, ISE Communications. In the late 1980s, Jack Tackett, the founder of ISE,[1] restructured his company and divided his employees into three self-managing production teams in order to implement his new vision for the future. Barker tracked and monitored this innovation over some years and found that concertive control replaced traditional hierarchical management. As we saw in Chapter 2, concertive action is jointly performed action. Concertive control at ISE meant that the laterally sanctioned authority of group consensus replaced direct supervision and, according to Barker (1993, p. 408), was experienced as 'more powerful, less apparent, and more difficult to resist than the former bureaucracy'. Over time, the three teams had reached 'a negotiated consensus on how to shape their behaviour according to a set of core values, such as the values found in the corporate vision statement'. But this consensus represented a form of collaboratively coerced compliance because, with the threat of survival hanging over the company's future, ISE employees were in no position to contest the owner's commitment to self-managing teams (Barker, 1993, p. 414). The essence of concertive control was captured in an ISE worker's description of his team's policy of low tolerance for misdemeanours (Barker, 1993, p. 408). As Ronald said: 'I don't have to sit there and look for the boss to be around; and if the boss is not around I can sit there and talk to my neighbor or do what I want. Now the whole team is around me and the whole team is observing what I am doing.' As part of concertive control, employees take the heat off their employers by punishing their recalcitrant peers. In this sense, then, 'team members had become their own masters *and* their own slaves' (Barker, 1993, p. 433, original emphasis).

Surveillance

The second criticism is that enslavement is accompanied by new and sinister forms of worker surveillance (Sewell, 1998). Identification with team core values under concertive control results in a system of generative discipline in which employees self-manage through willing compliance with team norms (Barker, 1999, p. 76): 'As the team's value consensus and particular work ethic began to penetrate and subjugate the new members' individual work ethics, this process took on a heightened intensity.' This outcome, in the face of potential job loss through failed team performance, is self-disciplined docility. In some contexts, norm-based self-discipline is complemented by a host of surveillance devices. These include: electronic monitoring of behaviour; the public use of comparative norm-based team performance data, visual displays in work station areas of quality test results which source particular errors to individual team members, coercive propagandising by ideational means to convey a sense of team duty, the use of team output target meetings to celebrate or humiliate members, and so on. The result is a chimerical regime of discipline secured by the 'gaze' of peers, as at Kay Electronics, for example, in which 'nominal autonomy and a high degree of control can co-exist' (Sewell, 1998, p. 414). At StitchCo, a UK garment manufacturer, on the other hand, where self-managing work teams were introduced as an extension of existing line control mechanisms, surveillance was less in evidence. Here, a team-based bonus scheme was introduced by management without any consultation, and self-managing teams of machinists found themselves having to pressure their colleagues to increase their output in order to maintain previous overall earnings levels. Many machinists, however, were indifferent, and even resisted these expectations (Ezzamel and Willmott, 1998, p. 385). The StitchCo case is a rare instance of successful contestation of management-imposed team self-management.

Feigned Community

A closely related criticism of workplace teams is that imposed teams, unlike the primary group team that builds itself, represent a contrived version of community. Quoting the findings of a series of ethnographies of flexibilised workplaces, Sennett (1998) deprecates such teams because, in their attempt to capitalise on adaptable work practices, they serve only to destroy long-standing and deep-seated organisational loyalties, and to corrode the character structure which for so long has formed the core of the work ethic. Sennett abhors the use of sporting team analogies by government agencies to give their blessing to team-based flexible employment in their official reports. He also cites the same kind of assembly-line pressure exerted by peers, instead of bosses cracking the whip, as does Barker, and he considers the presumed equality or parity of status between management and worker members of teams to be a fiction. Moreover, like Bramel and Friend, Sennett claims management is tolerant of teams because, from an industrial relations perspective, they are non-threatening. Thus, teams create a false sense of community as they presume a shared set of interests between employers and employees. And the irony of feigned community, when authority is diffused, is the absence of any one accountable manager, so that authority is simultaneously everywhere but nowhere (Sennett, 1998, pp. 110–17). In a strong defence of the localism which is eroded by globalising imperatives, Sennett (1998, p. 143) asserts yet another irony: 'all members of the work team are supposed to share a common motivation, and precisely that assumption weakens real communication'. Instead, 'strong bonding between people means engaging over time their differences'.

School SMTs

The experience of teams in education has been much more benign than that of industrial work teams. The volume of research findings is considerably smaller and, reflecting the recency of school teams, a literature only began accumulating from the mid-1990s. In the late-1990s, Cardno (1998, p. 53) reported a very high incidence of permanent self-styled teams in schools in New Zealand and in the UK, 'for the first time', wrote Wallace and Huckman (1996, p. 310), 'senior managers in large primary schools are embracing some notion of a team as the basis of their approach to management, in contrast to the more individualistic approaches of the past'.

As a form of shared or distributed leadership, teams tend to be viewed as a response to work intensification. Finding themselves 'ever more dependent on [their colleagues] to contribute their specialist expertise in implementing mandated reforms', UK heads, for example, have instituted SMTs (Wallace, 2001b, p. 156). Curiously, however, teams have not been part of the UK training agenda for headship. Apart from the negative instance of Rockville mentioned earlier, the documented experience of school teams has generally been benign. The most critical verdict is Wallace and Huckman's version of the de-professionalisation thesis, which is that, even where teams reflect heads' commitment to egalitarian values, they empower staff 'only in so far as [their members] work together synergistically to achieve the goals of marketisation'. In this way, teachers are manoeuvred into 'contributing voluntarily to the downfall of their collective autonomy to determine classroom practice' (Wallace and Huckman, 1999, p. 23).

Primary School SMTs

Wallace and Huckman investigated team practices in UK primary schools of 300 or more pupil enrolments via a postal survey in mid-1995 with 150 heads in south Wales and south-west England. The results revealed that SMTs had mostly been implemented since the Education Reform Act 1988, that membership varied in size from three to eight members, and that teams mainly included heads, their deputies and other senior teaching staff. Heads saw SMTs as vehicles for communication and keeping in touch with school-wide developments and, to that extent, SMTs bolstered heads' control and authority. Wallace and Huckman (1996, p. 317) distinguished five typical patterns of SMT operations spread out on a continuum with the greatest extent of head control and the least potential for staff empowerment at one end, and the reverse balance of least control and greatest potential for empowerment at the other. About 40 per cent of heads surveyed clustered around the least control/greatest potential position. Wallace and Huckman (1996, p. 321) concluded that 'while going it alone' was no longer an option for large primary school heads in the post-reform environment, 'going it in the company of a team is not a straightforward solution to the demands of managing today's schools either'. Against this big picture, Wallace and Huckman (1999) investigated the small picture in four UK primary school SMTs. Only one team, Winton, developed a strong working synergy and was located at the egalitarian end of their continuum, with Pinehill, Kingsrise and Waverley located at the hierarchical end. The Winton team emerged from a working partnership between a head and her deputy, which later expanded to a threesome with the appointment of an experienced teacher, and then became a foursome. Synergy proved possible at Winton because 'all members were given scope to give their all', but even here the proviso was that SMT members 'kept within the head's comfort zone and were willing to operate within these parameters' (Wallace and Huckman, 1999, p. 202).

Secondary School SMTs

In research into six UK secondary SMTs, Hall and Wallace (1996) conducted a field study comprising interviews with team members and observations of (nearly 50) team meetings in each school followed by longitudinal case studies in two of them, Middleton and Drake. The sample of six was nominated by two local authorities as comprising schools in which there was a strong, positive, unified commitment to teaming. As with primary SMTs, in each case the secondary teams were the creatures of school heads. Teaming was a high-risk strategy, especially for female heads. If, on the one hand, teams achieved desired levels of synergy then they bolstered heads' credibility. But if, on the other hand, they were unsuccessful then a head's credibility as a manager was strained. This latter possibility was compounded by the blurring of formal role distinctions in teams (Hall and Wallace, 1996, p. 300). Observing teams in action was thought to be a little like observing a marriage, in that 'there were high and low points and sometimes divorce hovered uncomfortably in the wings' (Hall and Wallace, 1996, p. 300). The judgement on the success or otherwise of a secondary SMT's operation rested on two criteria in the minds of members: first, the strength of individual members' contributions and second, the quality of decisions made by team members, with major decisions being taken by consensus. Overall, the six teams observed were regarded as effective by their members and, although each operated differently, teamwork proceeded smoothly. On the other hand, Hall and Wallace (1996, p. 308) observed that, as researchers, they 'went where the going was good', which raised the question of 'how is the necessary culture of teamwork to be nurtured where the going is not good?'.

Accounting for the Team Experience

What possible explanations may be advanced for the contrasting normative and empirical perspectives on teams summarised to this point?

One possibility is that different types of teams serve different purposes and that such divergent ends account for divergent perspectives. A more likely explanation is provided by Dunphy and Bryant's (1996, pp. 684–5) two criteria of level of collective skill complexity needed to perform a team task and the degree of interdependence demanded by a particular task. By interdependence they mean either the extent to which tasks can be differentiated and performed separately by individuals acting in concert or whether the individual tasks require more than one person to complete them. An example of the former would be a team of sub-school teachers collaborating to enhance the overall quality of student learning within their particular classrooms, while an example of the latter would be an emergency services team co-ordinating the rescue of a stranded yachtsman. These two criteria of complexity and interdependence are the bases of the matrix in Figure 6.1. The contrasts represented in Figure 6.1 by cells 1 (high complexity and high interdependence) and 4 (low complexity and low interdependence) capture the different experiences of service sector teams (cell 1) and manufacturing sector teams (cell 4) summarised earlier. Self-managed teaming in the circumstances depicted in cell 4 explains the vulnerability and susceptibility of team members to concertive control and surveillance pressures: i.e., persons with low-level or lower-level skills working in differentiated, same-task, work environments are arguably much more likely to feel relatively vulnerable, expendable and powerless compared with team members in cell 1-type situations.

An additional factor may be multiple membership of joint work units. In some organisations, complex task environments are conducive to the adoption of

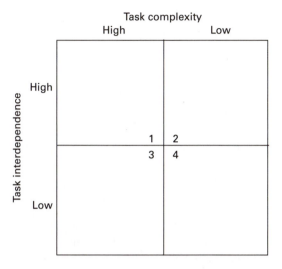

FIGURE 6.1 *Team task and skill conditions (based on Dunphy and Bryant, 1996, p. 685)*

multiple, overlapping, interdependent work units. Thus, from the point of view of the individual teacher in a moderately large school or a researcher in a university, one can be simultaneously a member of a number of distributed work units, e.g., a subject department, a course or grade level, a series of committees and a course teaching team. Such networks of cross-cutting and even countervailing allegiances tend to be less in evidence in working environments demanding lower levels of skill and task interdependence. An important effect of single or multiple unit membership is, respectively, to legitimise one or a number of reference points from which an organisation member derives a sense of employee identity. Thus, membership allegiance which is dependent on only one point of reference is likely to augment, rather than counteract, an already strong sense of personal vulnerability, particularly in a surveillance-saturated work environment. In such circumstances, individuals are more visible, there are fewer avenues of retreat from the direct or indirect supervisory 'gaze' or 'evil eye' (Hochschild, 1997, *passim*), there is less likelihood of making oneself indispensable and there are fewer opportunities to confront colleagues in diverse roles than in an environment conferring multiple memberships. In the former situation, each individual's identification eggs, so to speak, are all to be found in the one membership basket. With multiple sub-organisational memberships, by contrast, there is more possibility of an increased number and range of interdependent relationships enmeshing team members, thereby providing stronger and more diversified bases of identification.

Team Leadership

While committees are controlled by means of encapsulation and delegation, the appeal of self-managing workplace teams has been the promise of autonomy and a reduction in formal supervision. The extent of actual team autonomy, however, depends largely on the nature of team leadership and the relationship of teams to their line managers.

Teams and Managerial Authority

Self-managing teams are linked to organisational authority systems in two main ways. First, teams devise their own preferred patterns of leadership and retain a formal accountability link to an organisational manager. Second, as in the example of UK principals and their SMTs, line managers may be members (and normally formal leaders) of self-managing teams.

External links   External forms of team control vary. Team accountability, in the most liberal circumstances, may mean little more than periodic reporting to a senior manager. In this situation, when external scrutiny is low and teams self-select their members, and teams build themselves rather than being mandated, leadership is more likely to be shared or rotated, as in the health sector training team example observed by Gronn (1998). If, on the other hand, the wider organisational link entails extensive intrusion and scrutiny, then the status of 'self-management' is questionable. For this reason Dunphy and Bryant (1996, p. 688) distinguish between supervisor-centred teams and self-managed teams. Personnel external to teams usually perform such roles as coaches, facilitators or co-ordinators. In some cases the creation of these roles accompanies the introduction of teams. Thus, in a non-unionised US small parts manufacturing plant, the self-managing team co-ordinator occupied a hierarchical role 'analogous to a foreman in a more traditional plant' (Manz and Sims, 1987, p. 107). In the autonomous work groups with internally elected team leaders in this same plant, Manz and Sims (1987, pp. 113–14) observed 'a notable absence of direct commands or instructions from the co-ordinators to the team' and a form of leadership practice designed to:

> influence the team and team members to be able to do it themselves, rather than for the coordinators to exercise direct control or do it for the team. There was an abundance of deliberate and calculated efforts to foster independence rather than allow the dependence of more traditional work groups.

Here, the internal team leader co-ordinated job assignments and ensured that job materials were available. Earlier research showed external co-ordinators to be taking great pains to encourage teams to devise their own solutions to problems (Manz and Sims, 1984, pp. 416–17). On the other hand, confusion existed between co-ordinators, team members and senior managers about the co-ordination role and the fine line between 'over-direction and under-direction on the part of coordinators' (Manz and Sims, 1984, p. 420).

At ISE, by contrast, the role of external co-ordinator evolved. ISE work teams began with peer-selected co-ordinators chosen for one month to handle such information as production schedules, parts supplies and company-wide memos

(Barker, 1993, p. 421). Later, when early team talk about value consensus gave way to concertive enforcement of team work norms, co-ordinators were elected for six months. At this point (Barker, 1993, p. 426): 'The coordinator role began to take on the aura of a supervisor. People began to look to coordinators for leadership and direction.' Later still, after about four years of self-management, the co-ordinator's role was formalised into the role of facilitator. At that point, teams nominated possible facilitators who were then interviewed before selection by a committee of workers, managers and the owner, Jack Tackett. The new appointee leaders were awarded a 10 per cent per hour wage supplement and drew up duty statements for the role (Barker, 1993, p. 429). And at StitchCo, where part of the original purpose in switching to self-managing manufacturing teams had been to phase out external supervision, the supervisory role survived. Here, supervisors had to sort out internal bickering and team personality conflicts. Moreover, because team leadership was thought to be inconsistent with self-management, no team leaders had been appointed when teams were introduced. Instead, 'it was both expected and preferred that natural leaders would emerge', except that this failed to occur (Ezzamel and Willmott, 1998, p. 383). In the health-care sector, a long-standing belief amongst mental health professionals was that 'committees and other work groups are essentially incapable of productive work' and that 'the "real" work for which the group was presumably established is done outside of meetings by one or two powerful individuals' (Newton and Levinson, 1973, p. 119). Recent research (Griffiths, 1997) into the working relations between psychiatrists and two community mental health teams (comprising mainly nurses and social workers), however, suggests that such norms may be changing. Each team saw clinical psychiatric assessments as part of a team-based consultative approach to patient care. While the Team A psychiatrist refused to attend team meetings, and reinforced his authority over para-professionals in patient diagnosis, prescription and treatment, the Team B psychiatrist did attend team meetings. Team A's role was to follow up its psychiatrist's referrals. In Team B, by contrast, there was evidence of collaborative diagnosis as well as referral, and greater scope for a negotiated division of labour among team members, although this 'surface equality was undermined by strategies of subtle control' on the part of the psychiatrist (Griffiths, 1997, p. 77).

Managers as Team Leaders   Formalised authority links in which managers assume the formal role of team leader have produced different leadership tensions. As suggested earlier, the search for strategic advice in organisations has produced a combination of interconnected individual roles and conjointly performed distributed organisational work. In schools, this has meant the superimposition of 'new working practices for senior staff upon a hierarchy of formal status which is structurally reflected in salaries and conditions of service' (Wallace and Hall, 1994, p. 184).

Research evidence into SMTs conflicts and indicates a range of centripetal or centrifugal factors, both internal and external to organisations, which are conducive to team integration or fragmentation (Hambrick, 1994; 1995). Senior management teams in schools, for example, create a dilemma for heads who are responsible for overall school operations, student learning and the work of teachers by virtue of their role accountabilities. Site-based self-management, however, necessitates the establishment of SMTs to accomplish the complexities of the work. But, in making themselves dependent on their immediate subordinates, heads are vulnerable for, while 'it is up to the head to provide conditions which encourage all members to contribute fully to teamwork', 'the complementarity between individual team roles of "team leadership" and "followership" means other members must also facilitate the teamwork process'. The strength of team-work in UK schools depended on every member's capacity to cope with these dualities (Hall and Wallace, 1996, p. 304). Further, SMTs may turn out to be pseudo teams. Complementary temperaments amongst team members, time to rehearse or develop trusting working relationships, negotiated psychological space, a collective sense of humour and, especially, shared values have all been found to be conducive to successful teaming (Gronn, 1998), yet these factors can be difficult to sustain in the upper echelons of organisations. Due to their career-long socialisation into traditions of individual accountability for role perfor-mance, for example, senior managers – often very powerful and independent 'barons' within their functional fiefdoms – may resist mutual or collectivised accountability (Katzenbach, 1997, p. 86). Despite the mythology of the 'team player', there may be few incentives for top-level co-operation. On the other hand, the members of US college presidents' higher education advisory groups espoused an integrated image of themselves as 'a model of the cognitive team' embodying eight prototypical team roles: definers, analysts, interpreters, critics, synthesisers, disparity monitors, task monitors and emotional monitors. Each role contributed to overall team solidarity (Neumann, 1991, p. 487), even though college presidents were known to attach varying levels of importance to the advice emanating from such groups (Bensimon, 1991).

Team Learning

An important aspect of teaming, as highlighted earlier by the normative propo-nents of teams, is team learning. In regard to learning, commentators, on the basis of fieldwork data, have attempted to model the mechanics of team cognition. Most have utilised either Senge's (1993) five disciplines or Argyris and Schon's (1978) single-loop and double-loop learning categories (e.g., Scott, 2000) although, in an effort to provide more holistic representations of team synergy, others have developed entirely new classification schemes for learners' mental maps (e.g., Kasl, Marsick and Dechant, 1997). This trend has resulted in the inspection of team members' transcribed speech patterns and videotapes of team meetings for evidence of team learning.

A key issue for learning concerns its relationship to team leadership and, in particular, the role, if any, of team leaders in facilitating learning. Once more, commentators' views are divided, between those for whom it is vital and those (perhaps the majority) for whom leadership is of little or no consequence for learning.

Learning without Leadership

The most ambitious and extended naturalistic study of team learning has been conducted by Hutchins (1996), whose research findings, published in his much quoted book *Cognition in the Wild*, are significant for two main reasons. First, Hutchins demonstrated that cognition is a socially distributed phenomenon, rather than an attribute of individuals, in which the properties of the cognitive system required to perform a complex task lay partly outside the minds of the members of a work group. Second, he provided a detailed analysis of collaborative computational problem-solving in a very uncertain, high-risk, complex task environment in which leadership, as conventionally understood, was absent. Hutchins (1996, p. 21) labelled the co-performing work group he observed a navigation team – i.e., 'as few as one and as many as six members of the Navigation Department [comprising the navigator and seven enlisted men] working together'. According to the definitional framework outlined in Chapter 2, this grouping was in fact a crew, although a crew which exercised high order computational and problem-resolution skills, and which displayed surprisingly little of the synergy desired by the apologists for teams.

Hutchins conducted a participant observation study of ship navigation aboard the *USS Palau*. On one occasion, when entering San Diego harbour, the *Palau*'s propulsion mechanism failed. This malfunction was followed by the failure of a number of other important electrical devices, in particular an all-important direction-finding gyrocompass. This predicament meant that the bridge crew on the *Palau* had to act quickly to find alternative navigational tools in order to safely berth the 17,000-ton ship. The men from the navigation department of the *Palau* collaborated as best they could to calculate a series of lines of position so as to plot a course for the stricken vessel. As events transpired, they were so successful in doing so that eventually the *Palau* was satisfactorily brought to anchor at its intended location (Hutchins, 1996, p. 5). What emerged on the bridge of the ship, then, was an improvised division of cognitive labour – evident in the tape-recorded and transcribed dialogue between the recorder, the plotter and the helmsman – because the existing stock of computational navigation tools had failed. For Hutchins (1996, p. 349), the lesson to be derived from the incident from the point of view of organisational learning was that 'before its discovery by the system as a whole … the final configuration appears not to have been represented or understood by any of the participants'. That is, within the framework articulated earlier in this book, learning was the outcome of the co-operative cognitive endeavours and instruments of an interdependent co-performing work unit. Essentially, the incident exposed the incapacity of the conventional navigational routines – i.e., the taking of regular lines of position from compass bearings to plot a charted course – that had been regularised in naval manuals of procedure, to cope with unanticipated circumstances. Instead, a new routine evolved by virtue of the local adaptation of an existing work system to the exigencies of a crisis. The outcome of the incident was that the conditions encountered were 'quite rare' – so rare, in fact, that the solution discovered 'was not saved in the system' and not encoded as a new routine (Hutchins, 1996, p. 351).

Because they make the need for solo leadership redundant, routines are a perfect illustration of Kerr and Jermier's (1978) idea of leader substitutes in teams. Provided a task was unambiguous, routine and intrinsically satisfying, it was likely to be performed unquestioningly and with no need of a manager's leadership (Kerr and Jermier, 1978, p. 380):

> Thus, the existence of written work goals, guidelines, and ground rules (organizational formalization) and rigid rules and procedures (organizational inflexibility) may serve as substitutes for leader-provided coordination under certain conditions. Personal and group coordination modes involving the formal leader may become important only when less costly impersonal strategies are not suitable.

The eventuality allowed for by Kerr and Jermier in the last sentence of the quotation fits the example of the *Palau*. But Hutchins's (1996, p. 241) study also shows that distributed cognition is a substitute for the focused leadership of a key group member, because 'the complexity of a system may make it impossible for a single individual to integrate all the required information'. If leadership is to be an ingredient of group learning then it is much more likely to be distributed throughout an entire working group as members seek to pool their efforts to arrive at a plausible interpretation of a phenomenon which appears in the task environment (Hall, 1997, p. 329).

Learning in the Presence of Leaders

Leithwood, Steinbach and Ryan (1997) applied a framework based on Hutchins's model of adaptation to an analysis of the work of six teams in five Canadian secondary schools, in which the authors relied on interviews and a small survey rather than observations. Coded interview transcripts were used to distinguish descriptions of team performance according to evidence of their high or low potential for learning. Attempts to fit the data according to Hutchins's conception of learning, however, 'largely failed' and instead 'we found our data fitted much better a conception of team learning as "problem solving"' (Leithwood, Steinbach and Ryan, 1997, p. 311). Unlike Hutchins, these researchers attributed significant influence to a key individual in stimulating team thinking: 'the presence of at least one team member who is ready to contradict or point out the fallacies in members' thinking fosters learning'. Moreover, in contrast with the emphasis accorded superordinate positional power by Brooks (1994; and see Hall, 1997, p. 328), 'this person does not have to be the nominal leader' and may even be a neutral external facilitator (Leithwood, Steinbach and Ryan, 1997, p. 322).

Brooks (1994, p. 227) studied team learning in four case studies in a large high-technology manufacturing firm. From her observations she extrapolated two important dimensions of team learning and the production of knowledge. The first was reflective, problem-solving work undertaken during team meetings and the second was active work outside of meetings to procure and disseminate knowledge. Brooks was particularly interested in differences in the distribution of power amongst team members, and the extent to which these inhibited or enhanced members' reflections on, and actions in pursuit of, their tasks. The experience of having hierarchical superiors as co-members at team meetings stifled and intimidated some individuals from making free and open contributions. Brooks referred to this response as learning in the social or interactive domain. Power was found to be less inhibitory, however, in what she termed the technical domain, i.e., in regard to the substance of the substantive technical knowledge with which the team was dealing. In both domains 'leadership style and the power a leader could claim in relation to other team members was important on all four teams' (Brooks, 1994, p. 227).

Teams and Leadership Practice

As has been suggested, scholarly understanding of teams is recent and there is, as yet, no taxonomy for classifying the great diversity of team types. Compared with older traditions of small group and group dynamics research, for example, the overall team knowledge base is small. Indeed, the popularity of teams is 'outstripping our knowledge about them' (Ilgen et al., 1993, p. 259). In light of the current importance attached to achieving workplace synergies, the two matters currently preoccupying researchers, with significant implications for practice, are first, whether teams can avoid the perils of groupthink in work contexts depending increasingly on interdependent task performance and, second, the processes by which, as part of team building, team members come to substitute the interests of the team for their own personal interests.

Thinking and Talking like a Team

As one possible antidote to groupthink, Neck and Manz (1994) have outlined an approach that is consistent with the argument for self-leadership summarised earlier (i.e., self-direction and self-motivation to perform), known as teamthink. While groupthink may be viewed as a negative outcome of teamwork, Neck and Manz (1994, p. 935) advance teamthink as a positive outcome, in which: 'a group pattern of thinking emerges, that is more than the existence of a simple collection of individual minds'. In support of their claim, Neck and Manz highlight the importance of team members resisting distorted beliefs, engaging in positive team talk and cultivating positive team imagery in the interests of cultivating constructive appraisals of reality.

The notion of teamthink, however, is far from unproblematic. Taken at face value, it reads like a prescription for mind control with its emphasis on altering individuals' thought patterns, moments of reverie, self-talk and internal conversations, mental imagery and reflective processes. In this sense, teamthink is perfectly consistent with the self-disciplined compliance thesis advanced earlier by surveillance theorists which views managerial interests as perpetuated by team docility. The second point is that, despite the metamorphosis implied by 'emerges', in the above quotation, this word glosses the very process it purports to explain, namely, the means by which such *self*-oriented strategies translate into a state of holistic, as opposed aggregated, group-mindedness. Finally, ironically, despite their emphasis on *self*-leadership, Neck and Manz still see a vital role for 'the' team leader in engineering teamthink. Thus, a team leader should encourage the expression of diverse viewpoints, do everything to prevent members' dependence on her or him, reduce the pressure to conform and 'should not reveal his/her patterns of thought, self-dialogue, and mental imagery, early in the group's discussion to avoid creating concurrence-seeking pressure within the group' (Neck and Manz, 1994, p. 947).

Accomplishing Teamness

'Teamness', the shared awareness of membership of a concertively acting entity, is especially evident in negotiation talk. Here, typically, two parties representing opposing sets of industrial or diplomatic interests, engage in co-produced position or standpoint talk during a series of isolated and resumed meetings. Francis (1986) illustrates how team-mindedness is evident in various forms of multi-party, collegial conversational implicature. That is, using the structural property of talk known as an 'adjacency pair', as when a first pair part question such as, 'What's the time?', yields the second pair part the answer, 'Midnight', Francis shows how a sense of team identity is evident in recipients' expansion of the second pair part. That is, negotiating team members express their teamness through such verbal devices as team passes, team assists, team takeovers and team movements. In the following backstage-style extract, teamness is evident in Gambon's acceptance of a team pass (Francis, 1986, p. 64):

Meyer [union rep 1]:	These are soft chocolate, if somebody (Gambon; Well –) wants some candy.
Loring [management rep]:	No. thank you.
Gambon [union rep 2]:	Don't bribe him, Bernice.

Here, Gambon's utterance 'Don't ...' shores up the team identity of his negotiating side, through the exercise of his right to speak as a team member and protects the integrity of the team through what may be heard as an implied judgement of a colleague. In these, and a host of related ways, team members' talk shows them to be extensions of a team mind or brain.

These arguments about teamthink and implicature highlight the cognitive dimensions of teamness, but team members also align themselves emotionally with one another through identification. For Lembke and Wilson (1998, p. 929), for example, task interdependence in itself is an insufficient guarantee of teamness. Instead, team members need and want to identify with a team's collective identity and are attracted to its purpose. It is only through such identification that individuals cease to think and feel as individuals, and come to think and feel as members of a social grouping. It is that sense of identification which, in turn, becomes the source of their team productivity. Identification, therefore, means more than mere association with a collectivity, and instead entails a wholesale reworking of one's cognitive and emotional perspectives. On occasion, the depth of each team member's identification may be such as to create a 'hot group', not merely another structural entity or grouping to complement committees and teams, but more a state of contagious single-mindedness. In so-called hot groups, the source of members' identification is claimed to be 'their task', rather than one another, 'that hot groups love, along with the *process* of working on that task together' (Lipman-Blumen and Leavitt, 1999, p. 50, original emphasis). Well-bonded groups are 'hot to trot' when they labour intensely at their tasks. Moreover, because their members are 'tough-minded and realistic', both with one another and outsiders, they are 'too dynamic, too open, too full of challenge and creativity' for the unquestioning conformity of groupthink 'to solidify' (Lipman-Blumen and Leavitt, 1999, p. 43).

To end this discussion on such an up-beat, optimistic note would be to legitimate Lipman-Blumen and Leavitt's 'warm and fuzzy' view of employee bonding as the norm. But to do so would be misleading, given that there is also a well-known 'cold and prickly' side to working life. For this reason, and in order to provide a more rounded picture of leadership practice, the discussion now considers the range of emotions experienced in the workplace.

Note

1 The acronym ISE, devised by Tackett, meant 'In Search of Excellence'.

7   The Emotions of Leaders

Since the emergence of theories of management and organisations in the late nineteenth century, the existence of workplace emotions and sentiments has been acknowledged by commentators and researchers. Two sources of evidence substantiate this claim. First, for a long time, one of the earliest and most common ways of classifying the psychological dispositions of leader-managers towards their work was to see them as either task-oriented or person-oriented. That is, the priorities of leader-managers in fulfilling their accountabilities were believed to be either getting the job done or putting the interests of their employees first. Those for whom people were more important than tasks were claimed to be concerned with *how* the work was done, and therefore with the personal needs of workers and with fostering a sense of community in the workplace. Like other popular binaries, of course, this one suffered from being a false dichotomy. Some commentators were understandably reluctant to classify their research subjects in such crude black and white terms, and pointed to genuine 'fusion' types amongst leader-managers who accorded equal weight to tasks and people. Zaleznik (1964), for example, devised a creative nine-cell matrix with which to classify approaches to management, that combined rows comprising people, fusion and task orientations, and columns made up of reactive, mediative and proactive work styles.

The second main evidential source is the pattern of successive waves of ascendancy through which management theories have progressed. Barley and Kunda (1992) typified this developmental movement as the rise and fall, and rise and fall again, of successive rational and normative ideologies. 'Rational' and 'normative' roughly parallel the previous tasks and persons distinction, so that if the battle for managerial control of the workplace could be reduced to a choice between winning the hearts of the workers or their minds, then normative theories privileging emotional needs, feelings and sentiments were symbolised by appeals to the 'heart' and 'soul' (see Mirvis, 2000). Barley and Kunda's concern was mainly with US management theories, but to the extent that global flows of knowledge have been dominated by US commentators, then their scheme describes a broad pattern of global, not merely US, discourse diffusion. The most notable theoretical exemplar of the focus on sentiments and emotions was the human relations movement that dominated managerial discourse for about three decades until the mid-1950s, during which leadership came to mean (Barley and Kunda, 1992, p. 375) 'leashing the power of normative systems to enhance a firm's integration': 'Since primary work groups were the ultimate point of integration, managers all the way down to first-line supervisors were said to require communication skills, sensitivity in interpersonal relations, methods for instilling if not inspiring motivation, and knowledge of how to mould the dynamics of a group.' While Barley and Kunda's thesis is broadly consistent with Bramel and Friènd's (1987) ideas about the prominence of particular industrial group formations (although they do not cite the latter study), the resurgence and decline of rational and normative approaches to management and leadership bear an even closer relationship to long wave economic developments. Thus, when economies expand, rational structures and procedures prove attractive to management, but with economic decline, theories about how best to utilise labour and maximise workforce commitment rise in popularity.

In light of Barley and Kunda's claim, the new phenomenon of designer-leadership reviewed in Chapter 1 suggests, perhaps, that following a recent period of improved Anglo-American economic performance and competitiveness after the market downturn and restructuring associated with the 1970s and 1980s, rational approaches to leadership may be about to surge once again. But while either of the rational and normative antinomies is in the ascendency, the other never disappears entirely (Barley and Kunda, 1992, p. 393). This latter tendency may partly explain the paradox referred to earlier that, for the foreseeable future, despite their obvious dissonance, distributed approaches to work practice and leadership by design are likely to coexist in uneasy tension. James and Vince (2001, p. 307) describe the void between standards and practice as 'the space occupied by the emotional dimension of leadership'. This space between these rational-normative antinomies of design and distribution may also be gendered. Thus, in the view of some commentators, self-managed schooling is increasingly 'steered' from a masculinised policy centre while the emotional consequences of work intensification are mainly borne by a female-dominated teaching service of 'rowers' at the periphery (Limerick and Anderson, 1999). On this point, Blackmore (1996, p. 345) notes the coincidence in Victoria that when women were being officially encouraged to assume leadership roles to 'oversee the decline in the "public" in public education and the "deprofessionalisation" of their profession', they were also being 'lauded for their superwoman capacities in doing the emotional management work in education in handling stress and low morale within the profession this has created'. Secondary women heads in the UK appear to have found this responsibility more dissatisfying than male heads, although they have been 'more resilient and better "copers" than their male counterparts' (Cooper and Kelly, 1993, p. 141).

The current normative theoretical resurgence (dating from *c.* 1980, according to Barley and Kunda) has seen a quickening of interest in emotions at work, so much so that Rafaeli and Sutton (1989, p. 36) suggested 'all leaders could benefit from knowledge about the influence of emotions expressed between members of the organizations that they manage'. This interest is evident in a host of diverse ways, and includes the growing publicity and attention âccorded such phenomena as emotional intelligence and 'change fatigue' and, at a less popular level, the preoccupation with stress, trust and OCB. The purpose of this chapter is to review the more prominent of these developments. I begin by clarifying the nature of feelings and emotions. This section is followed by a consideration of leaders as objects and embodiments of emotions, including both others' feelings about them and their own feelings of success and failure. Next, I examine some of the typical emotional knots to which organisations are susceptible, following which I discuss the importance of play and playfulness, especially the significance of humour and sense of humour for leader-managers.

Emotionality

The long-standing scholarly dichotomisation of the realms of rationality and emotions just adverted to, and the tendency to marginalise the latter at the expense of the former are understandable when considered in light of key historic developments. In the Netherlands, for example, the transition from weapons to words, so to speak, or the containment of the passions as part of the civilising process, saw a strong emphasis on emotional control emerge in early meetings of the Dutch Reformed Church. Here, the meeting chair became known as a moderator. And it was only as recently as 1656, in Groningen, that, in the case of weaponry, the decision was taken not to wear arms as part of state meeting apparel (Van Vree, 1999, p. 115). Another important and more general historical trend has been the growth of bureaucracy. Often cited as the quintessence of rational impersonality, bureaucratic principles and the reform of western public administration which they underwrote during the nineteenth century, were the heirs to deeply entrenched systems of personal patronage, preferential treatment, favours and nepotism. The reforms and new procedures ushered in by these and similar broad secular trends resulted in the creation of organisational roles and role systems designed to eradicate the preceding influence of personal factors.

In the most recent resurgence of interest accorded emotions in organisations, commentators are now highlighting the significance of the subjective realm. In doing so, they generally distinguish four key terms: feelings, emotions, emotion work and emotional labour. From the individual's point of view, feelings are subjectively experienced physiological and psychological sensations or states. Common examples include frustration or anger. These and similar feelings may be privately contained or expressed interpersonally, either spontaneously and unconsciously or deliberately. Feelings may be distinguished from emotions. Private feelings become emotions whenever they are expressed publicly. Such emotions take verbal and/or bodily forms. Thus, angry people may vent their feelings by shouting and gesticulating, and by becoming red-faced and tense. To onlookers, such behaviour signals an actor's internal state or frame of mind. Most societies generate grammars (or sets of rules and conventions) regarding the expression of feelings. For individuals, these define socially acceptable feelings and also which feelings are appropriate in which particular circumstances. Feeling rules can be recognised 'by inspecting how we assess our feelings, how other people assess our emotional display, and by sanctions issuing from ourselves and from them' (Hochschild, 1983, p. 57). In some instances, feeling rules become deeply institutionalised. In the case of grief, for example, where there are strong feeling and cultural display rules, the expression of feelings of sorrow may be legitimised through tearfulness at a funeral service or requiem for the deceased.

But while feeling rules legitimate grief as an appropriate response to severe personal loss, they generally preclude visible expressions of joy or exhilaration.

In the case of emotions, there are also rules and conventions about their interpretation and display. Such display rules are institution-wide and society-wide norms of admissibility and inadmissibility, i.e., 'about which emotions members of a social system ought to *express*' (Rafaeli and Sutton, 1989, p. 8, original emphasis). Awareness of such rules is acquired through socialisation. Display rules regulate the maintenance and loss of social face. The idea of a person's 'face' is the balance sheet of someone's social credit and debit or standing. Social face is closely linked to emotion work. Such 'emotion work' is a way of referring to the effort expended to sustain face, i.e., to ensure that 'private feelings are suppressed or re-presented to achieve the socially acceptable emotional face' (Fineman, 1999, p. 292). While for most people feelings, emotions and emotional work may tend to be associated with the private and domestic lives of individuals, the workplace, as will be evident shortly, is an important arena for their expression. The notion of emotional labour, on the other hand, contrasts with these three phenomena in that it is exclusively job- and workplace-related. Emotional labour means the calculated manipulation of individual feelings for the purposes of engineering desired displays of emotions, or 'the buying of an employee's emotional demeanour', as part of which the individual 'is being paid to "look nice", smile, be caring, be polite' (Fineman, 1999, p. 292). Emotional labour, therefore, is a role-related instrumental term which signals the commodification of feelings in the interests of task performance. As part of emotional labour, the socialisation norms peculiar to particular occupations demarcate sets of appropriate and inappropriate negative and positive emotions to be learned and utilised, with varying levels of intensity, in different sets of circumstances. Beatty's (2000, p. 355) five educational leader informants, for example, maintained 'strict emotional management' of themselves and others, and found it difficult to let go their control, and the behaviour of 'Mrs Wyatt', one of Barker's (2001, p. 71) sample of heads, 'complicated the emotions with which she had to deal'. Educational leaders, therefore, are no exception to the need for emotion management, but are there forms of emotional labour peculiar to educational leadership and, if so, what factors might account for that patterning?

Leaders as Emotional Objects

At some stage in their relations with their followers and colleagues, all leaders, be they in public life or working within particular organisational confines, become psychological containers for other people's emotions. On this point, James and Vince (2001, p. 312) note that 'like many managers', headteachers 'carry invisible rucksacks on their backs into which the various people around them deposit rocks', with these rocks or burdens being the weight of others' emotions, behaviour and expectations. Fineman (1993, p. 22) has also suggested how the circulation of gossip and stories about their bosses provides, 'in lightly coded form', a means 'of venting anger and frustration' for employees. On the other hand, the negative overtones in these instances should not detract from the reciprocal nature of emotional flow and the recognition that such flows can be positive. Wallace and Huckman (1999, p. 141), for example, cite the case of the Winton head who, on one occasion, was supported by her SMT after feeling 'mangled' by her involvement in a child-protection case.

As Fineman (1993, p. 10) notes, commentators have taken two broad, complementary approaches to emotions in organisations: the perspective of social constructionism, as evident in the above discussion of emotion work and labour, and a psycho-dynamic viewpoint. The latter framework has provided a rich vein of research on the emotional basis of leadership.

The Psycho-Social Dynamics of Leadership

Two of the most important full-length studies from within this perspective have been Hodgson, Levinson and Zaleznik's (1965) *Constellation* role study and Elizabeth Richardson's (1977) *The Teacher, the School and the Task of Management*.

A Freudian Perspective   In addition to the distributed division of leadership role labour created by the triumvirate of Drs Suprin, Cadman and Asche, there was an emotional division of labour. More than two years prior to Hodgson, Levinson and Zaleznik's fieldwork, Suprin had succeeded Dr Sherman, the previous psychiatric hospital superintendent. Leadership succession processes and crises invariably provide critical occasions for the venting of emotions (Gronn, 1999b, pp. 125–44). While Sherman had been much loved by the staff, initial reactions to Suprin had been mainly negative. One reason why leader-managers become targets for the emotions of their staff is because their superordinate role authority endows them with extensive power and influence, although the organisational authority structure is usually silent about the manner of the exercise of that authority. In assimilating Suprin, for example, the hospital staff had to 'find out when, where, and how to act dependent, and when, where, and how to act independent under the new superintendent' (Hodgson, Levinson and Zaleznik, 1965, p. 259). Would he be more authoritarian or liberal in approach than his predecessor? In the new emotional climate, Hodgson, Levinson and Zaleznik (1965, p. 260) found their informants better able to 'admit or express more aggression and less affection towards the superintendent than they had towards his predecessor.' Within the executive constellation itself, Cadman and Asche succeeded in re-negotiating their previously preferred joint role constancy with their new superior, which in their case comprised 'customary patterns of supportiveness and friendliness' (Hodgson, Levinson and Zaleznik, 1965, p. 277). These co-authors differentiated the triumvirate's psycho-emotional structure into the complementary and specialist internal relations of the traditional family archetype: paternal-assertive Suprin, maternal-nurturant Asche (his assistant superintendent) and fraternal-permissive Cadman (the clinical director).

An Object Relations Perspective   An alternative model of emotional containment to this Freudian imagery is evident in Richardson's (1977) depiction of Denys John, the head of Nailsea School. Here, Richardson developed a theoretical standpoint associated historically with the Tavistock Institute which emphasised the importance of 'sentient' systems. From sentient groups organisation members draw emotional strength through mutual commitment to one another and 'to something that can be shared as a valued object' (Richardson, 1977, p. 23). Part of the job of leaders, from this perspective, is to ensure that system sentience is harnessed to the completion of the core or primary task. With this initial imagery of group anchorage, Richardson developed her view of operational dynamics by drawing on theories of small group behaviour, in particular the work of Wilfred Bion (1961).

Bion proposed a three-fold set of assumptions about a work group's relations with its leaders and barriers to its learning: dependence, fight–flight and pairing. Operating under the basic assumption or culture of dependence, a group would behave as though it was incapable of self-learning and would wait to be nourished or fed with ideas by its nominal leader. Under circumstances of fight–flight, by contrast, a group's collective mindset would oscillate between standing and combating a presumed or actual hostile object or turning tail and running away. Finally, a pairing response denoted the likelihood that the group structure and consensus would fragment and that subgroups of at least two members might form and search proactively for creative solutions to collective problems. Each of these three possibilities represents a response to collectively experienced anxiety in uncertain work environments. Faced with these circumstances, leaders would exercise a 'holding' or 'containing' function (Richardson, 1977, p. 28) in which they became 'good objects' who assisted others to cope with their feelings and fears. Anxiety is heightened during organisational transition, precisely the circumstances in evidence at Nailsea which, during Richardson's research consultancy, was transforming itself from a grammar to comprehensive secondary school. Organisational transitions are anxiety-inducing because they threaten existing identities, loyalties and commitments. From this psycho-dynamic perspective, the characteristic emotional response of individuals to the likelihood of change is one of ambivalence, as they try to cling to the positives and discard the negatives amidst the continuities and discontinuities unleashed by change. In circumstances of institutional transition and identity change, leaders may find themselves to be objects of fantasies of love or hate, and hope or despair. Their challenge is to 'use dependency, fight/flight and pairing appropriately on different occasions, and thus free staff members to trust but not trust blindly, to fight but not fight unthinkingly, to pair but not to pair irresponsibly' (Richardson, 1977, p. 209). Johns's preferred mode of leadership during his school's transition was to foster a dependency-pairing culture in which staff worked with, rather than for, him.

Managing Anxiety

Arguably, more than writers from any other theoretical standpoint, psycho-dynamic theorists have provided powerful explanations of how and why organisation members devise elaborate patterns of defensive and resistant emotional behaviour. Reporting on his clinical work in industry, Jaques (1957, p. 478) was one of the earliest commentators to note 'how much institutions are used by their individual members to reinforce individual mechanisms of defence against anxiety', in particular the threat of 'early paranoid and depressive anxieties'.

Some of the more familiar emotionally defensive behaviour in the personal repertoire of individuals includes procrastination and equivocation, denial of reality and avoidance. Organisationally, these examples, along with stalling, buck-passing, playing safe, misrepresentation, fabrication etc., may be developed into calculated micro-political strategies designed to protect and further key sets of interests (Ashforth and Lee, 1990). For Jaques, there were three particularly important strategies in relation to leaders: introjection, projection and splitting.

Introjection   Introjection is a form of interpersonal attachment in which there is an overwhelming positive regard for a leader. So strong can the desire to identify be that individuals may even experience the urge to consume or devour the leader as a good object and, as it were, to absorb her or him as a part of themselves. Evidence of introjection is found in such common phenomena as idealisation, celebration, adulation, canonisation, praise or deference of a leader or leader-surrogate. Introjection occurs for all sorts of reasons, but especially because of the anticipated feelings of nurturance, warmth, security, protection or care.

Projection   Projection is the opposite impulse. Projection usually means displacement, expulsion or the removal of an unwanted or bad object or thing, perhaps by transferring it to someone else. The most common form of projection is scapegoating. The book of Leviticus (16:7–10, 18, 21–2) refers to two goats, the one chosen as a sin offering and the other to make atonement (i.e., at-one-ment) with the Lord. The second goat survives death and sacrifice but is cast into the wilderness – i.e., the escaping goat – bearing the sins and iniquities of the Hebrew people. That is, the community's bad deeds are projected onto it (Aaron 'shall put them upon the head of the goat') and the good deeds and impulses are retained or incorporated (i.e., introjected) through the spilt blood of the sin goat. Projection in form of scapegoating, therefore, is a powerful means of externalising or disowning unwanted feelings.

Splitting   Splitting lies at the heart of both introjection and projection, and it refers to the tendency to divide or segment personal feelings into two broad types: good or desired and bad or unwanted. Good, positive sensations are to be retained and the bad expelled. 'Good' carries an entire chain of emotional associations, including care, protection, warmth and purity, while 'bad' may encompass such meanings as anger, hurt, coldness and frustration.

Emotional Leadership

The significance of these kinds of emotional processes is heightened by educational leaders' work intensification as they mediate NPM policies in their school communities. Not only are there 'greedy institutions' (Coser, 1974), there are also greedy policies demanding high-level emotional engagement. There is no place for faceless bureaucratic ciphers under NPM. On the contrary, intensified work arises partly from the consequences of accountability which, in the case of principals, require that they identify strongly with 'their' schools. Citing the cases of three South Australian principals, Max, Alan and Dave, Thomson (2001, p. 18) noted that, 'in order to play the game of educational administration': 'these principals must not only take on responsibility for the school as an entity, but also identify with it. What happens to the school is something that happens to them. If the school is "successful" they are "successful" and vice versa. Principals are thus particularly vulnerable'. Carr (1994, p. 352) found that 'playing the game' in South Australia came at a severe emotional cost, for 35 of 94 school principals he surveyed were found to have higher than average anxiety and/or depression scores. Of the 35, 31 he interviewed cited heavy work demands, lack of employer (i.e., education department) support and a general lack of control of their work as the major contributors to their above average scores. These findings parallel those of Cooper and Kelly (1993, p. 141) in the UK where the two main job stressors for principals were found to be work overload and handling relationships with staff.

Two feelings to which leaders have been shown to be particularly susceptible throughout their careers are the fear of failure and the fear of success. According to Zaleznik (1990, p. 115), a fear of failure or inadequacy exists when an individual 'will not undertake or complete work because an overriding sense of guilt tells him [*sic*] he is not worthy and will (or should) fail'. This observation suggests the presence of self-punishment and an inability to secure the pleasures and rewards that go with genuine autonomy. Fear of success, or the paradoxical sense of disappointment which often accompanies individual achievement, on the other hand, relates to the harbouring of fantasised, grandiose ambitions in which the individual's desire is to dominate and control other people. In such circumstances, 'when the fruits of one's labor appear as only the simple pleasures, and not the pleasures envisioned in the secret fantasies', according to Zaleznik (1989, p. 116), then 'the reaction is likely to be rage'.

Feelings of Failure

Failure is both an individual feeling and a social emotion. An individual sense of failure or inadequacy may be internalised, harboured as part of one's innermost thoughts and need not be reinforced socially. It may be bred out of a low sense of self-esteem, in which an individual has internalised a view of unworthiness in the face of unrealistically high self-imposed standards or due to a punishing, crushing sense of being defeated and always losing. The discomfort of failure may be momentary or enduring. If a social knockback is experienced as severe, for example, an individual's entire course of life may change, resulting in sullenness, irritability, resentment and even a sense of suppressed fury. In such circumstances, the memory of past failures or indiscretions may be a powerful motivator in an individual's passion to succeed. Recovery from career failure entails finding new or substitute channels for psychologically reinvesting or rebuilding one's identity, such as discovering new goals or new objectives, but with the once-bitten, twice-shy wariness of Fineman's (1983) sacked and subsequently re-employed managers. It also entails knowing oneself, facing the pain of disappointment and working through the emotions associated with career or goal loss (Zaleznik, 1967, p. 70). For Winnicott (1986, p. 72) the experience of even mild depression or sadness may be helpful here because it is believed to contain within it 'the germ of recovery' or 'the built-in tendency to recover' which conduces to maturity and emotional health.

Where, on the other hand, failure is defined socially, as in the experience of public humiliation or embarrassment (e.g., when managers' contracts are not renewed or managers are 'downsized'), it carries a stigma entailing a painful redefinition of status. In addition to guilt, public failure may be accompanied by feelings of shame, disappointment and depression, and attendant bodily manifestations such as blushing, perspiration, palpitations and distorted locomotion. Despite these negative features, an apparatus of failure has been institutionalised under NPM as part of school accountability, in particular as a means of controlling school performance. A school's ranking in the national league tables now creates a system of winners and losers, and a negative outcome following an OFSTED inspection as part of a 'naming, blaming and shaming' culture serves to demonise a school. Jeffrey and Woods (1996, p. 335) found their primary teacher informants to be absolutely rattled, anxious and depressed at the prospect of an OFSTED inspection, with 'much talk of grieving' and the subversion of their professional values. For Barker (2001, p. 72), on the other hand, OFSTED's reports on 'Mr Wake', 'Mrs Wyatt', 'Mr Anderson' and 'Mr Southern', their fellow incompetent ilk and their schools were simply unproblematic, and provided four 'studies in [the] failure' of heads and powerful evidence of 'the pervasive influence of poor leaders and their impact'.

Feelings of Success

Definitions of success form part of the work ethic which originated during the English Reformation when the early Puritans interpreted their worldly success and business prosperity as a sign of salvation through God's grace. Economic success and the individual effort that produced it were underwritten by a religious world view. Later, this religious justification was transformed into a social and economic doctrine of individual striving, exemplified by a socially moral outlook in which profit, thrift, effort, industry and frugality became the kinds of standards by which one lived in life's 'competitive struggle' (Whyte, 1963, p. 9). More recently, these standards have been supplanted by egoistic striving for self-achievement and advancement (Whyte, 1963, p. 138).

But success has its price. The competitive pursuit of career advancement and success breeds a range of emotions. One is the need for mastery at all costs. This may result in a workaholic pattern of job performance. Such expansive type individuals 'whose burning ambition, extreme hard work, and aggressive style' may help cause their organisations to achieve, but 'at a considerable human cost' (Kaplan, 1990, p. 323). Another emotion is peer envy, an unpleasant feeling 'caused by the desire to possess what someone else has' which may give rise to 'frustration, anger, self-pity, greed, and vindictiveness' (Kets de Vries, 1992, pp. 45–6). Envy expresses itself in a number of ways. It may be repressed, by idealising the envied object (such as a leader's achievements), thereby putting the person above comparison and criticism. Alternatively, an envious individual may spoil or devalue an envied object by demeaning it or by stirring up rivalry in others. Finally, envious individuals may withdraw altogether from the competition for status and in this way devalue themselves as a means of nurturing their injured pride. The earlier phenomenon of leader disengagement may well lend itself to this interpretation. Ironically, the price of success may be failure. Some successful individuals have been known to self-destruct when their ambitions are fulfilled, as Freud's (1957 [1916]) tantalisingly worded essay title 'Those wrecked by success' acknowledged. The experience of 'being there', it would seem, is different from 'getting there'. On the former situation, Jackson (1977), for example, reflected on the loneliness of command: first, he encountered the unnerving experience of being the only person at the very top, and having to come to terms with that fact and, second, he had to acquire the ability to be alone without succumbing to a sense of abandonment and loneliness.

Emotional Organisational Knots

Not only are individuals, both within and beyond the workplace, consumed from time to time by feelings, but organisations and organisational subunits may also be captive of positive and negative patterns of emotions. The dynamics of a selection of the more intractable phenomena documented by commentators are considered in this section. The selection is: trouble, vicious circles, scapegoating, splitting and triangulation.

Trouble

Awareness of the existence of a trouble, that 'something is wrong' or that 'things are not as they should be', signals the first step in recognition of the onset of a problem. Troubles may be personal or shared. Personal troubles are often detectable in dimly perceived symptoms, such as 'parents see their daughter getting overly interested in boys, or their son starting to hang out with a tough gang of friends' (Emerson and Messenger, 1977, p. 122). Hard and fast distinctions between personal, interpersonal and organisational troubles, however, are often difficult to draw. How, for example, is the discovery of a colleague sobbing at work to be interpreted? As work induced, work exacerbated or work unrelated?

With the meaning of the symptoms yet to be firmly established, the initial perceptions may be met with either denial or an attempt at further clarification. From this point, the natural history of a particular trouble may be said to have commenced. But troubles have an emergent character. In fact, the life course of a particular trouble, personal or organisational, is analogous to the imperceptible spread of bruising or mould on a piece of fruit, so that unanticipated and unplanned circumstances and occurrences observe an imperative or momentum of their own making. Even at the outset, leader-managers may be reluctant to acknowledge that a trouble is in fact a trouble. In this response they may be driven by an instinct to protect the reputations of individuals and their organisations, and to avoid the need for public damage control by devising a solution that will 'nip the problem in the bud'. Confronted by student complaints of incompetent teaching, for example, university department heads and deans may well prefer 'in-house' solutions to the claim, counter-claim, negative publicity and hurt associated with the implementation of formal grievance procedures. Nevertheless, the avoidance of such channels and a failure to act still shapes a trouble or problem's subsequent trajectory, and constitutes complicity or culpability in its definition and regime of remediation. For reasons of these complexities and possibilities one is said to be caught 'between a rock and a hard place' or 'damned if one does and damned if one doesn't'. But not only may the rights and interests of the various parties to a trouble be contested, candidate solutions and remedies may also be disputed in ongoing tests of what is to count as wrong or as 'the' trouble and for whom. This is because 'claims about the existence or nature of a trouble, are embedded in and products of the troubled situation itself' (Emerson and Messenger, 1977, p. 125). If solutions do not work or are dismissed as illegitimate, then a trouble is defined anew. Likewise with strategies for intervention: troubleshooters, so-called, allegedly neutral third parties, may be invited to generate solutions, but their intervention can also be contested so that it too 'may fundamentally shape what the trouble will become' (Emerson and Messenger, 1977, p. 128). Similarly with the attribution of 'victim', 'complainant' and associated statuses and rights of the parties to a trouble: these may also be contested and become the subjects of negotiation. Depending on the severity and intractability of troubles, then, leader-managers are likely to be caught up in a quagmire of conflicting workplace emotions and passions.

Vicious Circles

A vicious circle is the opposite of a virtuous circle. The logic of a vicious circle is that 'by trying to avoid undesired outcomes, human actors actually create those very same outcomes' and that 'by continuing their activities, they continue to reproduce those undesired outcomes' (Masuch, 1985, p. 15). Mention of a 'circle' is a reference to the cybernetic representation of a cyclic model of action with a feedback loop completing the information cycle. A loop provides information in respect of the original starting point or point of reference for an action. The loop is positive if the information approaches, and thereby reinforces or strengthens, the original point and is negative if the information deviates from it. A circle is vicious if the consequences of an action are deviation-amplifying. That is, the consequences accentuate movement away from a reference point in an undesired, counter-productive direction. The original point of reference may be an actual, or a desired, state of affairs.

A good illustration of a vicious circle in education is declining school enrolments. The desired state of affairs for a school may be the maintenance of sufficient pupil enrolments to satisfy a system target and to warrant a continued educational presence on a school site. The actual state of affairs, however, may be a downturn in pupil numbers – a frequent experience for schools during the 1980s and 1990s with the contraction of the public sector. Should enrolments over a period of years at the critical intake level (e.g., Year 7 in secondary schools) continue to trend downwards, and be insufficient to counteract student attrition and exit rates at other levels, then a contracting spiral with the potential to close the school may have set in. As in the case of failing bank liquidity and imminent bankruptcy, where eroding trust and an absence of cash flow fuel depositor panic (Masuch, 1985, p. 18), school leaders may be unable to arrest the decline. In education, falling enrolment trends reduce a school's requirement for, and entitlement to, teaching staff numbers. Coupled with declining numbers of students, this diminution of appointments reduces a school's capacity to sustain a diverse set of curriculum offerings. In such circumstances, staff begin to seek transfers to greener pastures and replacement staff prove difficult to attract. With subject choice restricted, particularly at the post-compulsory levels, the school becomes less educationally attractive for the offspring of discerning parents. Last-ditch measures, such as pupil recruitment drives, appear to make little impression on the downward spiral. Then, with initiatives to arrest the slide exhausted, only two options remain: closure or merger. Somewhere in this pernicious cycle of deviation amplification the school has crossed a threshold point of no return, and it is also likely to have lost its ability to identify such a point. Decline induces the pooling amongst school community members of emotions such as pessimism, loss and grief.

In the late 1980s, the then Victorian Ministry of Education (MoE) tackled this problem of decline with a policy of school consolidation and merger known as 'District Provision and School Reorganisation'. Instead of itself forcing school closures or amalgamations, the MoE handed this responsibility to neighbouring schools. This initiative had the effect of transferring feelings of uncertainty and lack of hope for the future to a wider pool formed by a group of schools. With the requirement that a 'comprehensive curriculum' be available across a school district, school groups were required to devise a consensually based set of recommendations about curriculum provision. The effect of this process within delegates' meetings, where thriving schools were reluctant to participate and sought to stave off amalgamation, and declining schools were desperate to survive by securing institutional amalgamations as satellite campuses of larger secondary colleges, was to heighten differences over school traditions and identities, and feelings of frustration and resentment at having to do the MoE's 'dirty work' (Gronn, 1994, pp. 72–5).

Scapegoating

The 'blame game', or the apportioning of blame and culpability, provides another opportunity for heightened emotions in organisations. The mechanism of scapegoating distinguished earlier is central to blame apportionment. There are two main types of scapegoating: instrumental and expressive. Instrumental scapegoats are people who are incriminated through no fault of their own, but as a result of 'strategies employed by power-holders when they feel liable to be accused of being responsible for misdemeanours, the blame for which may legally accrue to them' (Bonazzi, 1983, p. 2). Expressive scapegoats, on the other hand, are those target individuals or groups subjected to sanctions 'as a consequence of widespread and spontaneous aggressiveness', rather than as a result of a superior's calculated behaviour.

Instrumental scapegoating is particularly evident in politics and government. It occurs whenever politicians or leader-managers try to shift the blame for their own misdeeds on to subordinates or victims who are then required to 'carry the can'. Here, the scapegoated parties are made an example of by being moved or removed (as when 'heads roll'). This form of scapegoating is prompted by need for those concerned to protect their interests by taking defensive action in response to allegations of misdemeanours or by going on the offensive in response to criticism. Thus, an official or an organisational role incumbent may be dismissed from office to preserve the dignity or prestige of a public figure, or those in charge act as they do to make the very point that it is they who are in charge. Where public outrage over misdeeds is strong, a head may have to be 'seen to roll', or a politician or leader-manager is able to save face by someone else accepting the blame on their behalf. Expressive scapegoating was evident in the school amalgamation case just cited. There, five secondary colleges in a school district maintained a united front against the MoE as the 'common enemy' in the face of the latter's pressures to rationalise curriculum provision. When one of the five, a small co-educational school ('New Co-ed'), entrapped in a vicious circle of enrolment decline, broke ranks in pursuit of its own interests, the remaining four secondary colleges expressed their wrath in a report to the MoE. They felt trapped in a distasteful process which required them to recommend on site closures and mergers, and forced them to endure 'the resultant pain, anger and losses' rather than being able to 'direct their fury at MoE officials' for not having consulted them (Gronn, 1994, p. 77). One of the four schools with which New Co-ed sought to amalgamate ('Old Co-ed') distanced itself 'totally and unreservedly' from any future association with New Co-ed (Gronn, 1994, p. 76) and another ('Old Girls') withdrew from the process in protest.

Splitting and Triangulation

The same kinds of emotional tensions inherent in accelerating troubles, and which may be triggered off by escalating vicious circles, are also evident during organisational conflicts. Smith (1989) spent six months investigating local school board politics in 'Ashgrove', a small New England community in the USA. In a pioneering study of the channelling of conflicts in communities and organisations, Smith found that emotional displacement was a significant conflict management strategy which was sustained by the mutually reinforcing processes of splitting and triangulation.

Smith proposed that two opposing parties (individuals or groups: A and B) are likely to manage the tensions in their differences and strengthen their positions vis-à-vis one another by drawing in third and fourth parties (C and D). The effect of this addition to the number of disputants is twofold: first, the conflict between opponents now becomes conflict between opposing coalitions; second, the possible avenues down which that conflict might be directed and conducted increases numerically, as does the number of parties through which conflict may be indirectly re-routed. One result is that conflict displacement may take a form analogous to an oedipal triangle, for example, similar to that in which only children are drawn into family disputes with their parental loyalties tested by being pushed and pulled emotionally in support of one or the other adult. These conflicting loyalties may be overlaid by the good/bad form of splitting touched on earlier, in which an ambivalent self vacillates between rival feelings and displaces them onto one or the other party (Smith, 1989, p. 8). For about five years, the Ashgrove community and its school board were evenly split between the supporters of the values of educational innovation and financial rectitude. Reluctant to prejudice the interests of his local business, the board chair refused to break the deadlock by exercising his casting vote. During a public forum, at which community members endorsed one or the other conflicting value, the board retained a united front and effectively displaced its own differences through this third party. A similar pattern of triangular conflict displacement occurred during the appointment of a second assistant principal. Then, when two assistants were appointed, resulting in a principal group of four, a similar factionalised pattern became evident amongst the four principal group members. In hierarchical terms, board differences appeared to have been rerouted downwards into horizontal splits, while horizontal differences were re-routed vertically back to the board. All of the splits within the ranks of the key Ashgrove groups were 'intense' and the struggle between the groups for dominance was 'endless' (Smith, 1989, p. 17).

The Play of Emotions

But the expression of feelings need not always be manifest in organisational conflicts and outbursts of emotion, for another significant vehicle for emotional display is humour. So-called black or 'gallows humour' in the face of impending tragedy or crisis, for example, is a well-known means of emotional displacement (Ashforth and Humphrey, 1995, p. 108).

Although leader-managers commonly employ humour, Hatch (1997, p. 276) notes that 'managerial humour has seldom been studied.' On the other hand, a number of commentators have noted how, during meetings and in committees, for example, organisation members often experience an attack of the sillies by playing the fool and horsing around. This phenomenon may represent tension release, a momentary retreat from serious business, the search for common interests or the expression of the 'we' feeling of group solidarity, in the same way that Burns (1955, p. 657) noted how in all societies 'the joke is the short cut to consensus.' A good illustration is to be found in Hochschild's (1997, p. 55) example of senior executives' use of humour as a means of coping with the intensive work ethic at 'Amerco', the site of her workplace ethnography:

Managers often started or ended meetings with workaholic jokes. A colleague quipped at an 8 A.M. meeting, 'How's the weather in Tokyo, Jim?' to a colleague who had arrived directly from the airport. 'When I get home from a trip, I never know if I'm kissing my wife hello or goodbye,' chimed in another to a round of rueful laughter.

Significance of Humour

Humour is expressed in a variety of forms. The judgement of what counts as humour or mirth depends entirely on the interpretation by an individual or a group of numerous cues such as utterances, thoughts, images, gestures, objects, printed expressions etc. Thus, stimuli that are intended to be mirthful may not be hilarious while other unintendedly witty stimuli may be interpreted as extremely funny. Laughter, ranging from the minimalist expressions of a thin smile and giggling on the one hand to prolonged raucousness on the other, is the socially accepted signal that a cue has been deemed humorous. Humour and laughter form part of a joking relationship, in which there may be humour without (much) laughter, but not usually laughter without humour. When joking, we 'play with meanings' so that 'all the possibilities of an unexpected change or alteration of meaning are tried out and exploited' (Zijderveld, 1983, pp. 6, 7). These institutionalised meanings are legitimated by social values, while the zone of tolerance for exploiting the incongruity and ambiguity associated with such meanings varies in different cultural contexts. The result is that acceptable targets for joking in one culture may be politically incorrect in another.

Purposes of Humour

The range of humorous stimuli is extensive and encompasses children's nonsense rhymes, riddles, spoonerisms, teasing, kidding, punning, banter and conundrums (e.g., 'Did you hear about the teacher who was cross-eyed? She couldn't control her pupils') through to more biting and aggressive instances of repartee, farce, sarcasm, caricature, parody, satire and irony, as in this ironic remark about national differences in humour (Davies, 1984, p. 148):

> In hierarchical and deferential England where overstatement or overt bragging would be 'bad form', personal and national assertions of superiority still occur but in the disguise of mock modesty, contrived coolness in the face of adversity, and in understatement. In any case, the English have an awful lot to be modest about.

Depending on the particular context, humour serves a dual purpose. It can be both socially subversive and integrative. In the former case, public figures may be mocked and ridiculed as incompetent or even foolish by cartoonists, for example, while in the latter, humour may lubricate social relations, repair breaches in the social order and affirm group solidarity.

Joking is a well-documented component of workplace culture, where it serves as 'a culturally creative response to social structural situations of conflict and anxiety' (Mechling and Mechling, 1985, p. 340). To cope with anxiety, groups invoke a variety of themes (including race, ethnicity and sexuality) to affirm their sense of collective identity, and to stereotype and scapegoat out groups. The masculinity themes in the humour of 250 English male lorry-making workers, for example, expressed resistance. The men's working-class distinctiveness from management and their white-collar colleagues was captured in a joke about supervisors displayed on a union noticeboard. This poster rehearsed the successive bodily functions of each of the limbs, with all of them pleading in the end for the anus to be the supervisor (Collinson, 1988, p. 187): 'And so it came to be. That all the other parts did their work and Bum simply Supervised and passed a load of CRAP ... MORAL: You don't have to be a Brain to be a Supervisor ... only a Bum'. Through such 'piss-taking' humour, these operatives displayed bravado about their sexual prowess and virility, and disciplined their potentially deviant members while testing their capacity to endure insults and ridicule. Likewise, Mealyea's (1989) group of overwhelmingly (although not exclusively) male mature-aged tradespersons who were returning to formal education used both sexist and racist humour, during class and socially, to cushion blows to their esteem and as a reaction to the rejection of their former occupational selves by the college's training programme. Recently, of course, those subcultural norms which have traditionally legitimated the expression of these kinds of aggression, hostility and obscenity have been under legal challenge or have been proscribed.

In other circumstances of danger or uncertainty, humour may take a more subdued form. Patients' joking in hospital wards, for example, helps alleviate their personal anxieties and their submission to a rigid ward authority structure and treatment routines. In one case of confusion resulting from the admission of two women bearing identical first and given names, each of them was misdiagnosed (Coser, 1959, p. 174): 'Well, finally they got her [the correct Mrs Brosemen]. She was raving mad and red as a beet. She came here for high blood-pressure in the first place. Well, it must have gone sky-high after that!' Nurses, as well as patients, also cope with anxiety displacement through humour:

> Two young student nurses in their first week on the wards heaved an elderly male patient up the bed into a sitting position via a 'shoulder lift'. The patient grinned contentedly. As they left the ward the first nurse said to the second: 'Next time, Jane, grab hold of my hand under the legs'. Jane: 'But I did'. They then blushed with embarrassment and amusement when they realized what they had done.[1]

Humour can, of course, observe a more decorous and refined pattern. In weekly meetings of the Sunbeam Club, a public speaking group, for example, in which speech-making and delivery were rehearsed, excessive behaviour and demonstrative, emotional outbursts were frowned upon by members. Here, wittiness was somewhat sedate and, rather than signalling time for play, speakers laced their rehearsed presentations with adroit expressions of mild and restrained 'safe' joking (Bjorkland, 1985).

Humour in Management

Some commentators have promoted humour as a tool for effective management. Thus, managers are often advised to abstain from 'put down' humour at colleagues' expense or, alternatively, to make light of their own errors with such self-mocking antics as 'I must be getting senile' or 'I'm having a senior's moment'. Pierson and Bredeson (1993), for example, highlighted the importance of principals' humour in bolstering school morale and creating a 'climate of connectedness'.

Consistent with Bailey's (1983) earlier findings on meeting play, Consalvo's (1989) two-year study of management group meetings showed that lapses into humour provided release from seriousness and that, while the initial incidence of committee laughter was low, it increased towards the point of decision. Likewise, in staff meetings in a mental hospital humour provided 'mutual reassurance' for work which was fraught with uncertainties, and group support 'for facing ambiguities in role performance' (Coser, 1960, p. 83). In this context, the downwards direction of humour towards those lacking in formal authority endorsed the hospital's status structure. 'Not once was a senior staff member present at a meeting a target of a junior member's humor', for example, and whenever senior staff did become the targets of juniors' joking, the targets were absent (Coser, 1960, p. 85, original emphasised). A similar pattern was evident in the safe haven of school staffrooms where teachers' 'real' selves could be let loose and management ridiculed. Woods (1979, p. 219) recounted a senior mistress, Gertrude Harmer, who was frequently lampooned in 'restorative staffroom chats' for such legendary school assembly howlers as, 'Paul Entwhistle has been fudging in my drawers again. Next time I'll put a mousetrap in it' and 'Now, somebody's been trampling my flowers. You must understand that the playing areas of the field are public. But these gardens are mine. They are my private parts, and the only person allowed in there is the gardener'. Such levity points to the significance of the need for a sense of humour in the workplace.

Sense of Humour

For leader-managers, the capacity to make light of something and to be able to see the funny side, as in the Monty Python refrain at the Crucifixion scene in *The Life of Brian*: 'Always look on the bright side of life ... ', may mean being able to not take oneself, or an otherwise grim organisational outlook, too seriously.

Yet, making light of things is not always easy. Thus, on the occasion of an impending OFSTED inspection, for example, Jeffrey and Woods (1996, p. 332) found that the incidence of humour as the 'teachers' usual main coping strategy' had dried up significantly. In addition, some people, such as fanatical and authoritarian personality types, may be utterly incapable of ever seeing the funny side. For true believers, for example (be they of the more traditional Marxist or more recent NPM varieties), ridicule is seen as harming the cause, so that 'humour and laughter are perhaps the only luxuries [such people] cannot afford' (Zijderveld, 1983, p. 10). What counts as funny, as suggested earlier, is culturally determined. The Australian tradition of egalitarianism, with its mateship, social levelling, the idea of 'Jack is as good as his master' and cutting down of tall poppies, for example, means that forms of humour such as satire, caricature, ridicule and parody figure prominently in public life. As a result, much Australian joking is earthy, sceptical, irreverent, crude, vulgar and aggressively masculine. Humorous American 'whoppers', by contrast, celebrate entrepreneurial values, and capture the bravado and boasting of individual success. The incidence of humour amongst leader-managers is an important indicator of the robustness of an organisation's culture, for the presence of humour says much about coping and stress levels. But joking may also backfire. When people fail to see the joke, particularly with painful subject matter, there may be a taboo on laughing. In a 'beyond a joke' incident in a hospital ward, for example, a medical student tried to make light of the plight of a 26-year-old unmarried woman. When the patient, who was making an unexpected recovery from the consequences of an illegal abortion, heard him say, innocently: 'You have a lot of teenage magazines around here. Are you a teenager?', she replied, sardonically: 'Evidently in spirit.' To the medical student's solemn inquiry, 'What do you mean by that?', the young woman then launched into a 'confessional discussion about how adolescent she sees herself in believing she can get away with doing what she wants regardless of what adults say' (Emerson, 1969, p. 173).

In light of the serious import of these aspects of humour, and the proneness of leader-managers to occasional egotistical follies and conceits which cause them to lose touch with reality, some commentators (e.g., Kets de Vries, 1990) have gone as far as canvassing the resurrection of the ancient idea of 'the fool'. Just as the verbal jousting between Shakespeare's Lear and his fool served to remind that particular monarch of 'the transience of power' (Kets de Vries, 1990, p. 757), then so too might institutionalised foolishness serve as an antidote or corrective to organisational pathology. This possibility is made real because the fool, as the official 'mad object', would be granted a licence to reveal uncomfortable realities, and to utter the unspeakable and the unforgivable. In the meantime, in the absence of such possible vehicles for the venting of one's feelings, the 'bottom line' of emotion management under conditions of intensified work for leader-managers, particularly women, as Sachs and Blackmore (1998) have suggested, continues to be the maintenance of at least the pretence of being able to cope. The 17 Queensland women principals Sachs and Blackmore (1998, p. 267) interviewed all told emotional stories of 'courage, pain, disappointment, dissatisfaction and even depression'. For these 17 women, the experience of leading restructured schools was proving to be qualitatively different in scope and intensity from anything their predecessors had ever encountered. Their disappointment 'at being let down by colleagues and the system' (Sachs and Blackmore, 1998, p. 275), for example, was palpable and compounded these principals' feelings of professional isolation and loneliness. The example of their feelings is symptomatic of what it means to lead in the new work order. Self-managing, institutional level devolution in competitive, marketised policy environments, be they in schooling or higher education, calls for workers with a previously unheard of appetite to not only succeed but to win. As an implicit or explicit criterion of potential employee worth and value, the idea of having to be 'hungry enough' means being willing not merely to pay one's own way, but to keep on striving to take one's performance to 'the next level'. To perform way beyond expectations means to gives one's all for the improved productivity and growth of the organisation. If this dimension of sustained super-performance has become the reality of intensified work regimes, then it suggests the need for a new understanding of the commitments leaders are being required to make as part of their stewardship. Leaders' work has now become greedy work – greedy work performed on behalf of greedy organisations in the pursuit of voracious and stingy public policies. This level of sacrifice demanded of greedy occupations, which has been implicit in everything said so far about work intensification, is the subject matter of the next, concluding, chapter.

Note

1 An actual hospital ward incident recounted by a student nurse in a class assignment for the author.

8   Leadership as Greedy Work

I conclude this book by advancing the thesis just alluded to that the new work of educational leaders is being reconstructed as greedy work and that educational leadership is to be understood as an increasingly greedy occupation. This represents the core idea of what might be termed the grammar of the new educational leadership. Following Abbott (1997), I argued in the Introduction that a new trajectory of school and educational leadership is taking shape. Then, in the first part of the book, I outlined some of the key architectural features of this emerging trajectory. It is during such periods of social and institutional transition and transformation, suggests Lewis Coser (1974, p. 33), in his book *Greedy Institutions*, that 'reliable servants of power become especially useful', because: 'rulers want to wrest economic and political resources from dispersed power centers not under their control. At such historical junctures rulers become especially greedy. They then attempt to recruit to their staff men [*sic*] who will serve them totally'. As historical examples of the exploitation of segments of society by greedy institutions, Coser considered such disparate groups as the eunuchs and alien nationalities employed in courtly society, royal mistresses, celibate religious orders, domestic servants, housewives in male-dominated families and societies, and militant utopian and religious sects among others. My purpose in the discussion that follows is to build on Coser's concept of greediness to show that, far from being a historical aberration, and having disappeared as a result of the cessation of the exploitation of some of Coser's examples, greediness has recently colonised a range of new work practices, particularly amongst what were previously referred to as the autonomous or semi-autonomous professions.

I shall begin by distinguishing voluntary, greedy and total institutions. Then I develop the theme that the logic and ethos of work in the service sectors of increasingly service-based and knowledge-based economies, in particular the leadership of schools, represents a new form of servility. Here, in effect, I shall be inverting Hayek's (1994 [1944]) claim in *The Road to Serfdom* that the greater dependence of a civil society on the apparatus of government substitutes corrosive enslavement for liberty, by showing that, rather than diminishing servility, the marketised regulation of public sector agencies and the creation of an enterprise culture breed their own new and unique forms of exploitation and serfdom, which I term greedy work practices. Next I flesh out the idea of greedy work in respect of leadership roles, leadership identities and the claims that greedy policies make on leaders. Finally, I consider some of the consequences of this new mode of occupational servility.

Greed and Institutional Greediness

Coser (1974, p. 4) defined greedy institutions as those powerful groups and agencies which 'make total claims on their members' and 'attempt to encompass within their circle the whole personality'. Such institutions seek 'exclusive and undivided loyalty' by endeavouring to: 'reduce the claims of competing roles and status positions on those they wish to encompass within their boundaries. Their demands on the person are omnivorous'. Even though it may make substantial, undivided or total claims on its members, Coser is careful to distinguish a greedy institution from Goffman's (1961, p. 11) idea of a total institution, which was: 'a place of residence and work where a large number of like-situated individuals, cut off from the wider society for an appreciable period of time, together lead an enclosed, formally administered round of life'. Goffman's examples included prisons, barracks, mental asylums (as they were once known), boarding schools, convents, prisoner-of-war camps, concentration camps and all places and agencies where the membership comprises mostly extended, isolated and involuntary incarceration. While the line distinguishing these two forms of membership may be thinly drawn, both contrast with the membership of voluntary agencies. The latter, which are generally seen by social theorists as the core of the fabric that defines a civil society, include numerous interest groups: community associations, sporting bodies, churches, youth groups, service clubs (e.g., Rotary), and leisure and recreation societies. Unlike the two other institutional types, volunteerism comprises mostly unremunerated, part-time or spare-time work arising out of individuals' goodwill allegiances as citizens. Such is the nature of the voluntary ethic that citizens will often divide their loyalties between a number of institutions with claims on their personal energies and resources.

This implied continuum of voluntary–greedy–total forms of institutional membership is not meant to be definitive, but it is helpful for delineating the qualitative differences in the levels and types of work demands made on individuals. The key point is that wherever there exists evidence of work intensification, one should expect to find instances of greedy work. Thus, in public sector work settings, such as schools, hospitals, local and municipal governments, libraries, universities and welfare agencies, and in some broad areas of management, where there has been a significant diminution of a public agency's government-derived funding base, a downsizing of its staff, and an increased reliance of non-tenured and short-term contract staff, there is likely to be found evidence of the new greediness. Agencies faced with significant shortfalls in resources, but also corresponding increases in responsibilities (e.g., increased case loads, student enrolments, patient care needs), are imposing a significantly higher burden of work on fewer staff. In these circumstances, greedy work becomes a leitmotif for societies which, in accordance with increasingly pervasive 'greed is good' ideologies, function as vehicles for the realisation of self-interests and the pursuit of personal aggrandisement. In their greedy work environments, educational leaders in self-managing schools, for example, especially principals, work at the kind of relentless, full-on, treadmill pace expressed so graphically earlier on by NEWPRIN#4. They respond incessantly to the demands of their employers, but they are reluctant to call on senior officials for their advice or help because they fear that to do so may be interpreted as personal weakness and, consequently, as an indelible blot on their annual performance appraisals. After all, to self-manage a school means to be on one's own and to work it out all by oneself within one's own resources. Such is the way in which greedy rulers and policy-makers, in Coser's terms, secure total service from dispersed power centres, individuals and heads of operating units. From the perspective of overall NPM steerage capacity, then, the solution to the system's problem of alleged provider capture is the imposition of greedy work on its rowers. Greedy work is such that it demands one be constantly and 'fully there' (Kahn, 1992): always attentive, alert, absorbed in and utterly committed to the particular task as a totally functioning, fully available, non-stop cognitive and emotional presence in the workplace.

The New Servitude

There are four key features of the new grammar of servitude that is a product of greedy work which are worthy of comment. These are: changed understandings of the idea of service, reconfigured roles, reconstructed identities and new claims on leaders.

Service

Economic prosperity in the knowledge economy is claimed to depend less on the production of physical goods and increasingly on the outputs of the services sector. This sector covers institutions in both the public and private realms, and includes such diverse endeavours as insurance, banking, finance, computing, education, health care, tourism, the arts and media, and numerous emerging high-tech, knowledge-based 'sunrise' occupations. In the public sector, instrumentalities and agencies whose charters include service provision continue to deliver services directly themselves or, increasingly, indirectly through such mechanisms as outsourcing to a range of providers in accordance with the contractual provisions of 'service agreements'. In these and similar ways, the market economy puts a price on diverse commodified services, such as the provision of care and learning, for in this cosmology of marketisation, service, like everything else, is required to 'pay its way'.

This understanding of service, however, is a corruption of longstanding ideals of altruistic public duty and servanthood. Traditionally, service to society was legitimated in non-market terms as a vocation or calling. This sense of disinterested motivation, complete with its implicit religious overtones, was equally true of doctors, dentists, engineers, teachers, etc., regardless of whether they were employed on a salaried or a fee-for-service basis. In short, as an occupational neophyte one trained and then pursued a career in a chosen domain that permitted the free expression of one's inherent and acquired gifts, out of an implicit sense of duty and public spiritedness, and for the attainment of various ethical ends associated with the betterment of some aspect of the human condition. At least, that was roughly what was understood as the role of the professions in society. Status, power and other occupational perquisites formed part of this kind of idealist mindset, but (at least in theory) they were kept in check as by-products of more noble considerations such as duty, loyalty, devotion and trust. In the 1980s and 1990s, however, western liberal democratic governments, in particular, swallowed the Osborne and Gaebler (1993, p. 51) line that existing public bureau patterns of service provision undermined the confidence and competence of citizens and communities, and resulted in the iniquity of dependency or 'client-hood'. The antecedents of this reasoning go back as least as far as Hayek (1994 [1944], p. xxxix), for whom the principal evil of the incubus of government intervention in the life of a free society, in particular 'the blessings of a paternalistic welfare state', was 'a psychological change, an alteration in the character of the people'. The NPM antidote for this and other abuses, such as the alleged provider capture of taxpayer-funded resources (e.g., through so-called 'cushy' employment conditions and associated 'rorts') otherwise intended for service beneficiaries, was seen as citizen empowerment through competitive provision, which was designed to unlock 'bureaucratic gridlock' (Osborne and Gaebler, 1993, p. 79). But the adoption of competitive service provision has a number of implications. One significant implication is that service provision agreements create a strong incentive for the providers of services to think of their resources, including personnel, as potential costs. The reduction of resources, and a concomitant expansion of the expectations of the work to be performed within an existing quantum of resources, serve to intensify the performance of service work, thereby providing fertile ground for the seeds of greedy work.

Roles

In this kind of service provision environment, work becomes greedy when, as part of its intensification, as was seen particularly in Chapter 2, the role space occupied by a role incumbent expands. Role expansion increases to such an extent that an incumbent becomes responsible for an amount and quality of work output, and a depth of emotional and cognitive commitment and work engagement that might previously have been demanded of more than one person. Moreover, that same role incumbent's zone of discretion tends to be circumscribed and regulated, less by the need to obey the directives of a supervisory superior than by a framework of target-driven accountability requirements tied in turn to publicly audited performance-related and target-related levels of remuneration. An important factor here is enterprise-level wage bargaining. Typically, each successive round of negotiations between employer and employee interests for the purposes of achieving industrial agreements compounds these tendencies towards work intensification. This is because higher productivity targets and trade-offs related to working conditions are frequently invoked as preconditions for salary increases. In order to obtain salary increments under a new industrial award, then, employees are required (and they invariably agree) to work even harder (e.g., in what was once thought of as their own time and during weekends) for additional wage increments, which means, in effect, that salary increases amount to a form of overtime payment.

Distributed forms of workplace leadership have arisen for a number of reasons. One is organisation managers' recognition that effective leadership requires the support and participation of one's colleagues. Thus, distributed leadership is a response to the pressures of time, the scope and extent of the accountabilities to be fulfilled by a role incumbent, and the need to rely on pooled expertise and the collectivisation of risk assessment. These factors have led to the formation of working partnerships, teams and similar synergistic structures, with a view to achieving quality decisions and a sense of enhanced ownership. Distributed leadership is also a response to role expansion and intensification although, in some ways, distributed leadership compounds the difficulties associated with these trends because the consultation involved in the allocation of work tasks, information and responsibilities can lengthen the lead time required to complete complex tasks, and increases the number of potential veto points throughout the process. In addition, greater participation in decisions requires more time, energy and identification with colleagues. Despite this apparent symbiotic relationship between distribution and intensification, as self-managing unit-level leaders search for adaptive solutions to problems created by their contextualised role demands and constraints, customised service provision threatens to create even greedier leadership work. As we saw in Chapter 1, for example, recently introduced designer leadership standards and competencies have escalated beyond all previous recognition the expectations that are now intended to shape role performance. Curiously, the reward for individual competence has become ever more work overload and responsibility. As the evidence considered in Chapter 3 showed, however, a pattern of teacher resistance to being gobbled up by greedy policies has emerged in the form of a withdrawal from potential leadership roles, particularly principalships. The idea of co- or partner-principalships (in effect, an increase in the number of incumbents to occupy an expanded role space) may provide a temporary antidote to role overload (Court, 2001), although the appointment of two people instead of one is open to the criticism that it is an unduly generous concession to greedy demands.

Identity

The effect of greediness may be to narrow and concentrate the life commitments of school professionals, particularly at the expense of their engagement in domestic and voluntary institutional activities. Coser (1974, p. 7) notes how, historically, conflicting pressures on individuals from contradictory expectations and cross-cutting ties have been minimised by greedy institutions because 'outside role partners have, so to speak, been surgically removed or because their number has been sharply limited'. As suggested above, a feature of the work of voluntary institutions is that the membership's commitments, allegiances and ties are usually segmented and compete with one another. The effect is that an individual's identity is always an amalgam of a variety of affiliations. Such, however, is the level of work commitment currently demanded of school leaders, that the possibility of multiplex sources of identity formation has been significantly diminished.

Apposite to this point are the observations of historians of schooling who have noted that, particularly during the early era of nineteenth-century proprietor school heads in England and colonial Australia, long-serving bachelor and spinster school-owners were, to all intents and purposes, married to their enterprises. This was understandable, if only because in a number of cases these small preparatory schools were conducted in the owners' homes. At any event, the observation signalled the depth of the owners' body and soul identification with their vocational livelihoods. Without their schools, these owner-heads were, literally, nothing for the threat of penury waited them should they fail to attract pupils. The depth of the commitment of these early heads is analogous to that now required of current school leaders. This is Coser's point about omnivourousness. This phenomenon results in the kinds of time binds and personal conflicts identified by Hochschild (1997, p. xxi), in which the balance between the respective 'pulls' of family and work have been found to be shifting: 'The cultural world of paid work was growing stronger, while families and communities – the social worlds with which we associate our deepest bonds of empathy – were growing weaker.' But at the same time that greater levels of OCB are being demanded of leader-managers and their colleagues, contemporary career identities are displaying much more malleability and less predictability. This is the phenomenon which commentators refer to as career boundarylessness. Younger generations of teachers, as I pointed out in Chapter 3, have learned well the lessons promoted and modelled by their elders. The signs are that they may be less career committed in the vocational sense of service distinguished above and that, as part of the increasingly acceptable 'greed is good' social ethos, they seem willing to pursue their self-interests through role choices designed to keep their career options open, rather than locking themselves in, and to countenance leaving education altogether for other work sectors. This would seem to be a case of greediness coming back to bite the hands of those responsible for greedy policies.

Claims on Leaders

This last observation suggests that the notion of greediness is two-edged, in that while greedy work may be hugely draining and demanding on individual role incumbents, or even exploitative, it also, ironically, encourages the greedy pursuit of self-interestedness. But there is a third dimension to greediness. Workers in greedy occupations seem to be increasingly complicit in their own greediness. That is, by being willing to rise to the intensification challenges imposed by the new work order, as we saw was the case in Chapter 3 with NEWPRIN#4 when she exclaimed 'But I love it', employees are also signalling their own preparedness to be entrapped.

In this way, greedy work is addictive. The explanation for this curious phenomenon, which was likened in Chapter 3 to the fatal attraction of a moth to a flame, is not clear. Hochschild (1997, p. 34) queries why, in the case of working parent families, their newly intensified work demands are not prompting them to forge a 'culture of resistance'. Her speculation is that changes in work practices are giving rise to the phenomenon of 'reversals'. This notion means that the workplace is beginning to be seen as a respite or an escape route, where people are freed from their domestic emotional entanglements and where their identities as persons are affirmed, in some cases, in increasingly supportive workplace communities. Thus, the experience of some service sector managers and professionals has been that they (Hochschild, 1997, pp. 44–5): 'virtually marry their work, investing it with an emotional significance once reserved for family, while hesitating to trust loved ones at home'. Further, as one rises to meet the challenges created by work intensification, one may jettison or reduce a range of competing social attachments to make space for a greater commitment to work, which is perhaps made possible for the first time at that point in the career cycle when one's offspring leave the domestic nest. The effect is to so narrow the number and range of one's non-domestic and non-work attachments that work rhythms begin to shape lifestyle commitments, in which case (Hochschild, 1997, p. 45): 'The more attached we are to the world of work, the more its deadlines, its cycles, its pauses and interruptions shape our lives and the more family time is forced to accommodate to the pressures of work.' The hallmark of the emerging work servitude, as the fieldwork studies of teams in Chapter 6 revealed, is the preparedness of workers to submit themselves to self-disciplined control and sophisticated systems of surveillance.

No Laughing Matter

In greedy occupations, then, workaholicism is fast becoming the grammar or culturally accepted norm of the new work order. According to this norm, work has to become an end in itself, rather than a means to an end. Thus, when one signs up for or takes on a leadership role and joins the growing army of greedy workers, one is signing up for an implicit work contract, the terms of which are that 'One lives to work, rather than works to live'. That is, work becomes the overriding end of and for one's life. In consuming one's whole being, it does more than merely provide the physical and psychological wherewithal for a life. Because it becomes one's life, greedy work consumes one's life, so that work becomes the measure of what one is and not just what one does.

Greedy work is no laughing matter, for at least two reasons. From the point of view of individual role incumbents, for example, the potential for work stress is not funny. On the other hand, the strength and depth of the commitment across party political lines to NPM-style policies in many western countries is also no joke. In retrospect, the speed with which NPM became the new public policy orthodoxy during the 1980s was extraordinary. In fact, so strong has the current endorsement of NPM become that to question its assumptions or to countenance alternative possibilities to competitive service provision is to invite serious ridicule. While much of this political commitment exists for reasons of ideology, its support is also fuelled by political expediency. Governments everywhere see a huge potential for electoral success, provided they can appease the voters with promises of 'more bang for the buck' (Osborne and Gaebler, 1993, p. 80) in the form of budget savings with which to underwrite tax relief for middle- and high-income earners. Despite these personal and social costs of greedy work, those who espouse NPM-style policies take themselves very seriously. The zealous, true believer commitment to public sector reform and to greedy work as the price which has to be paid for it, calls to mind an anti-Marxist joke once intended by the former critics of communism to pillory its claims to human liberation: 'Under capitalism man exploits man. Under socialism it is precisely the other way around' (Davies, 1984, p. 144). Transposed to the current context of greedy work, a corresponding way of mocking the reinventing government agenda might be: 'Under welfare state bureaucratic service provision, service needs were met by greedy people; under state-sponsored, competitive service delivery it is exactly the same.'

What, then, is the grammar of leadership practice? In his preface to Lipman-Blumen and Leavitt's (1999, p. x, original emphasis) *Hot Groups*, the management guru Tom Peters suggests that what is missing in the appearance of rafts of books on the impact of the new technology is the work itself: 'What is it? (The *new* it.) How does it get done?' In respect of leadership in school and educational settings, this book has endeavoured to provide an answer to these what and how questions. The realm of leadership practice has been shown to be marked by the dynamism of processes and flows, a fluid world in a state of perpetual and almost seamless motion. In these circumstances, educational leaders are made as much as makers, and agents acted upon as much as initiating agents. Enmeshed in networks of interdependent workplace relations, they live a life increasingly on the edge: engulfed by wave upon wave of information, beset by incessant demands on their time, required to be constantly on the go and attentive, but made to feel unendingly world weary and devoid of energy. They have little time for considered judgement and reflective thought, nor for indulging in personal or domestic interests and pursuits. During the period in which they are engaged at work, and for most of the remaining time and space that is available to them outside their work, the extent of their emotional commitment is almost total. 'To be always at the highest pitch of involvement, commanding the entire span of attention', remarks Coser (1974, p. 134) of the demands traditionally imposed by greedy institutions, is to prevent the mind from 'running in other perpetual grooves'. Further, in addition to a policy environment populated by mandated performance targets and the need for audited outcomes – in short, a life controlled by numbers – the educational leader's scope for creative movement is further circumscribed by a bevy of designer-leadership standards.

What is to be Done?

In The Making of Educational Leaders (Gronn, 1996), my purpose was to develop the theme of leader formation. The aim was to provide aspiring and incumbent leaders with a conceptual template for understanding their own personal career trajectories. There, for the most part, I concentrated on a range of micro-level factors, such as personal socialisation and organisational succession processes, which I suggested provided vehicles for the expression leaders' professional agency. Subsequently (Gronn, 2002b), I developed a macro-level outline of leader formation processes from both a historical and a culturally comparative perspective. This was summarised in Chapter 1. Throughout the present discussion, I have said very little about the agency of leaders, other than when citing occasional research details that illustrate my core themes. Instead, the discussion has been skewed towards structural factors, such as the most recently emerging environmental imperatives that are beginning to shape the roles and role contexts of educational leaders, and organisational processes. Thus, although my notion of designer-leadership is predicated on the existence of a standards and assessment policy component nestled within an overarching accountability regime, I have not traversed the details of particular policies or policy contexts to any great extent.

There are a number of ways, in relation to the emerging 'new work' trajectory of design, distribution and disengagement, that future research might address the agency of leaders and build on the preceding analysis. First, there is a series of issues concerned with aspects of professional career and institutional role identities. Some of these arise out of the implementation of designer-leadership and were canvassed in Chapter 1. Leadership standards may be expected to 'bite' during practitioners' overall career development mainly at the time of their initial accreditation and during subsequent reassessment or reaccreditation of their role competence. But beyond those critical points of identity transition, what difference, if any, are standards and competencies likely to make to practitioners' day-to-day leadership practice? To what extent will principals and other school leaders pay mere lip-service to standards, and regard them as yet one more systemic hurdle to be negotiated and then forgotten until next time? Finally, what will be the impact of standards and competency frameworks on potential and aspiring educational leaders? Will an unintended consequence of the implementation of standards, as was foreshadowed earlier, be to confirm incumbents in their current roles and to dissuade them from pursuing career advancement? These questions connect with a wider set of issues being addressed by commentators in the field of career theory. Here, opinion is currently divided over whether career jobs and career ladders as traditionally understood are dead or slowly dying. Jacoby (1999, p. 124), for example, insists that employers have shifted more of the burden of employment risk sharing to their employees, but that this is a change 'of degree, not of kind' in welfare capitalism. Cappelli (1999, p. 148), by contrast, maintains that career jobs, understood as advancement prospects with the same employer, 'are in decline'.

The second main avenue for research concerns distributed leadership. The key to understanding the realities of practice, as has been suggested throughout, is for researchers to attend to changes in the division of leadership labour. I have also suggested that the commitment of the field to the hero paradigm of leadership might, finally, be wearing thin. Not merely in Sayles's (1964) pioneering work, but in a number of other research studies, the hints that some key theorists have recognised for some time the interdependence between leader-managers and their colleagues, rather than the dominance of the former over the latter, are palpable. The tenacious adherence of the majority of commentators to focused conceptions of leadership, despite Gibb's early iconoclasm, seems to be weakening, with increasing numbers of mentions of distributed leadership appearing in the literature.

That said, with the exception of those studies cited in Chapter 2, there are still remarkably few analyses of the dynamics of distributed practice. The discussion in Chapter 6 highlighted the current state of knowledge of teams, as versions of distributed practice but, unlike the burgeoning numbers of ethnographies in the interdisciplinary field of workplace studies, there are, as yet, no first-hand field investigations of the distributed leadership of schools. An activity theory template for such research was outlined in Chapter 4. Equally, there is a paucity of knowledge about schools as intelligent learning systems and the extent to which they encourage distributed practice as part of the development of school-wide leadership capability. Finally, with school leaders currently labouring under an intensified regime of greedy work, the question of the extent to which distributed forms of practice have been adopted with a view to easing the pain of the new servitude, or whether these patterns have emerged in local contexts quite independently of the constraints imposed by policy, still requires an answer.[1]

The work of educational leaders described in this book is analogous in its greedy demands to that undertaken by high profile CEOs. Over the last two decades or so, a number of these entrepreneurial types have been appointed by corporate boards, amidst massive media hype and fanfare, to head up ailing firms. Unlike their humbler school principal counterparts, however, these CEOs earn salaries running into millions of dollars, along with associated stock options and benefits. As good company men (invariably), they work punishingly long hours, give of themselves body and soul, and try to perform the miracles sought by dividend-hungry shareholders. Then, when their contracts expire, or if their efforts at market turnaround fail, their services are likely to be dispensed with, usually amidst the high public drama of threatened legal challenges or out of court financial settlements. When at last the dust settles, a new replacement 'white knight' may be welcomed on board with elaborate marketing hype and media billing. Television viewers have become accustomed to the solemnity of such rituals with their passing parade of such faces, each of them in their turn consumed by the onerousness of their shareholders' expectations. Every hapless CEO is ground down, chewed up, spat out and then replaced, often by a successor who is paid at an even higher level of remuneration and embodies equally or more demanding expectations of performance, by still hungrier boards of directors. While the profile and drama associated with the conduct of educational leadership may pale into insignificance by comparison, the greedy work expectations of educational policy-makers have brought about a very similar kind of work intensification narrative in education. Such is the new world order of greediness. In numerous ways, greedy work has become a powerful and pervasive metaphor for our times. The new educational leadership work ethic is the cult of salvation through greedy work.

Note

1 These and related aspects of distributed leadership are currently being investigated by the author and his colleague Dr Felicity Rawlings as part of a Monash University project funded by the Australian Research Council and entitled 'Patterns of Distributed Leadership in Australian Schools'.

References

Abbott, A. (1997) On the concept of turning point, in L. Mjøset, F. Engelstad, G. Brochmann, R. Kalleborg and A. Leira (eds), *Comparative Social Research*, vol. 16 (Greenwich, CT: JAI Press), pp. 85–105.

Acker, S. (1990) Managing the drama: the headteacher's work in an urban school, *Sociological Review*, 38(2): 247–71.

Aldag, R.J. and Fuller, S.R. (1993) Beyond fiasco: a reappraisal of the groupthink phenomenon and a new model of group decision processes, *Psychological Bulletin*, 113(3): 533–52.

Allcorn, S. (1997) Parallel virtual organizations: managing and working in the virtual workplace, *Administration and Society*, 29(4): 412–39.

Anderson, G. (2001) Disciplining leaders: a critical discourse analysis of the ISLLC national examination and performance standards in educational administration, *International Journal of Leadership in Education*, 4(3): 199–216.

Anderson, R.J., Hughes, J.A. and Sharrock, W.W. (1987) Executive problem-finding: some material and initial observations, *Social Psychology Quarterly*, 50(2): 143–59.

Annan, N. (1988) Gentlemen and players, *New York Review of Books*, 29 September.

Archdale, B. (1972) *Indiscretions of a Headmistress* (Sydney: Angus and Robertson).

Archer, M.S. (1995) *Realist Social Theory: The Morphogenetic Approach* (Cambridge: Cambridge University Press).

Argyris, C. (1998) Empowerment: the emperor's new clothes, *Harvard Business Review*, 76(3): 98–105.

Argyris, C. and Schon, D. (1978) *Organizational Learning: A Theory of Action Perspective* (Reading, MA: Addison-Wesley).

Armstrong, J.A. (1973) *The European Administrative Elite* (Princeton, NJ: Princeton University Press).

Arrow, H. and McGrath, J.E. (1995) Membership dynamics in groups at work, in L.L. Cummings and B.M. Staw (eds), *Research in Organizational Behavior*, vol. 17 (Greenwich, CT: JAI Press), pp. 373–411.

Ashforth, B.E. and Humphrey, R.H. (1995) Emotion in the workplace: a reappraisal, *Human Relations*, 48(2): 97–125.

Ashforth, B.E. and Lee, R.T. (1990) Defensive behavior in organizations: a preliminary model, *Human Relations*, 43(7): 621–48.

Attkinson, M.A., Cuff, E.C. and Lee, J.R.E. (1978) The recommencement of a meeting as a member's accomplishment, in J. Schenkein (ed.), *Studies in the Organisation of Conversational Interaction* (New York: Academic Press), pp. 133–53.

Baer, W.C. (1987) Expertise and professional standards, *Work and Occupations*, 13(4): 532–52.

Bailey, F.G. (1965) Decisions by consensus in councils and committees, in M. Banton, (ed.), *Political Systems and the Distribution of Power* (London: Tavistock Publications), pp. 1–20.

Bailey, F.G. (1970) *Stratagems and Spoils: A Social Anthropology of Politics* (Oxford: Basil Blackwell).

Bailey, F.G. (1977) *Morality and Expediency The Folklore of Academic Politics* (Oxford: Basil Blackwell).

Bailey, F.G. (1983) *The Tactical Uses of Passion: An Essay on Power, Reason and Rationality* (Ithaca, NY: Cornell University Press).

Ball, S.J. (1998) Labour, learning and the economy: a 'policy sociology' perspective, *Cambridge Journal of Education*, 29(2): 195–206.

Barber, J.D. (1974) Strategies for understanding politicians, *American Journal of Political Science*, 18(3): 443–67.

Barker, B. (2001) Do leaders matter?, *Educational Review*, 53(1): 65–76.

Barker, J.R. (1993) Tightening the iron cage: concertive control in self-managing teams, *Administrative Science Quarterly*, 38(3): 408–37.

Barker, J.R. (1999) *The Discipline of Teamwork: Participation and Concertive Control* (London: Sage).

Barley, S. and Kunda, G. (1992) Design and devotion: surges of rational and normative ideologies of control in managerial discourse, *Administrative Science Quarterly*, 37(3): 363–99.

Baum, H.S. (1991) Creating a family in the workplace, *Human Relations*, 44(1): 1137–59.

Beatty, B. (2000) The emotions of educational leadership: breaking the silence, *International Journal of Leadership in Education*, 3(4): 331–57.

Bensimon, E.M. (1991) How college presidents use their administrative groups: 'real' and 'illusory' teams, *Journal for Higher Education Management*, 7(1): 35–51.

Bernthal, P.R. and Insko, C.A. (1993) Cohesiveness without groupthink: the interactive effects of social and task cohesion, *Group and Organization Management*, 18(1): 66–87.

Bilmes, J. (1981) Proposition and confrontation in a legal discussion, *Semiotica*, 34(3/4): 251–75.

Bion, W.R. (1961) *Experiences in Groups, and Other Papers* (London: Tavistock).

Birnbaum, R. (1992) *How Academic Leadership Works: Understanding Success and Failure in the College Presidency* (San Francisco: Jossey-Bass).

Bjorkland, D. (1985), Dignified joking: humor and demeanour in a public speaking club, *Symbolic Interaction*, 8(1): 33–46.

Blackmore, J. (1996) Doing 'emotional labour' in the education market place: stories from the field of women in management, *Discourse*, 17(3): 337–49.

Blease, D. and Lever, D. (1992) What do primary headteachers really do?, *Educational Studies*, 18(2): 185–99.

Blount, J.M. (1998) *Destined to Rule the Schools: Women and the Superintendency, 1873–1995* (Albany, NY: SUNY Press).

Boden, D. (1995) Agendas and arrangements: everyday negotiations in meetings, in A. Firth (ed.), *The Discourse of Negotiation: Studies of Language in the Workplace* (Oxford: Pergamon), pp. 83–99.

Boisot, M. and Liang, X.G. (1992) The nature of managerial work in the Chinese enterprise reforms: a study of six directors, *Organization Studies*, 13(2): 161–84.

Bolam, R. (1997) Management development for headteachers: retrospect and prospect, *Educational Management and Administration*, 25(3): 265–83.

Bonazzi, G. (1983) Scapegoating in complex organizations: the results of a comparative study of symbolic blame-giving in Italian and French public administration, *Organization Studies*, 4(1): 1–18.

Bowker, G.C. and Star, S.L. (2000) Invisible mediators of action: classification and the ubiquity of standards, *Mind, Culture and Activity*, 7(1 & 2): 147–63.

Boyle, M. and Woods, P. (1996) The composite head: coping with changes in the primary headteachers' role, *British Educational Research Journal*, 22(5): 549–68.

Bradbury, M. (1975) *The History Man* (London: Secker & Warburg).

Bramel, D. and Friend, R. (1987) The work group and its vicissitudes in social and industrial psychology, *Journal of Applied Behavioral Science*, 23(2): 233–53.

Bredeson, P.V. (1996) New directions in the preparation of educational leaders, in K. Leithwood, J. Chapman, D. Corson, P. Hallinger and A. Hart (eds), *International Handbook of Educational Leadership and Administration*, part 1 (Dordrecht: Kluwer), pp. 251–77.

Brooks, A.K. (1994) Power and the production of knowledge: collective team learning in work organizations, *Human Resource Development Quarterly*, 5(3): 213–35.

Brown, M.H. (1989) Organizing activity in the women's movement: an example of distributed leadership, in B. Klandermans (ed.), *International Social Movement Research*, vol. 2 (Greenwich, CT: JAI Press), pp. 225–40.

Brown, M.H. and Hosking, D-M. (1986) Distributed leadership and skilled performance as successful organization in social movements, *Human Relations*, 39(1): 65–79.

Brundrett, M. (2001) The development of school leadership preparation programmes in England and the USA: a comparative analysis, *Educational Management and Administration*, 29(2): 229–45.

Bryman, A. (1996) Leadership in organizations, in S.R. Clegg, C. Hardy and W. Nord (eds), *Handbook of Organization Studies* (London: Sage), pp. 276–92.

Burnham, J. (1962) *The Managerial Revolution* (Harmondsworth: Penguin).

Burns, T. (1954) The directions of activity and communication in a departmental executive group, *Human Relations*, 7(1): 73–97.

Burns, T. (1955) The reference of conduct in small groups, *Human Relations*, 7(4): 467–86.

Burns, J.M. (1996) Empowerment for change: a conceptual working paper, The James MacGregor Burns Academy of Leadership, University of Maryland, http://www.academy.umd.edu/scholarship/casl/klspocs/jburn_p1.htm

Bush, T. (1998) The National Professional Qualification for Headship: the key to effective school leadership?, *School Leadership and Management*, 18(3): 321–33.

Bush, T. (1999) Crisis or crossroads? the discipline of educational management in the late 1990s, *Educational Management and Administration*, 27(3): 239–52.

Callahan, R.E. (1962) *Education and the Cult of Efficiency: A Study of the Social Forces that Have Shaped the Administration of the Public Schools* (Chicago: University of Chicago Press).

Cappelli, P. (1999) Career jobs *are* dead, *California Management Review*, 42(1): 146–67.

Cardno, C. (1998) Teams in New Zealand schools, *Leading and Managing*, 4(1): 47–60.

Carlson, S. (1951) *Executive Behaviour: A Study of the Work Load and Working Methods of Managing Directors* (Stockholm: Strombergs).

Carr, A. (1994) The 'emotional fallout' of the new efficiency movement in public administration in Australia: a case study, *Administration and Society*, 26(3): 344–58.

Carrroll, S.J. and Gillen, D.J. (1987) Are the classical management functions useful in describing managerial work?, *Academy of Management Review*, 12(1): 38–51.

Castells, M. (1996) *The Rise of the Network Society* (Oxford: Basil Blackwell).

Chitayat, G. (1985) Working relationships between the chairman of the boards of directors and the CEO, *Management International Review*, 25(3): 65–70.

Chung, K.A. and Miskel, C.G. (1989) A comparative study of principals' administrative behaviour, *Journal of Educational Administration*, 27(1): 45–57.

Clarke, J. and Newman, J. (1997) *The Managerial State: Power, Politics and Ideology in the Remaking of Social Welfare* (London: Sage).

Cohen, S.G. (1993) New approaches to teams and teamwork, in J.R. Galbraith, E.E. Lawler and Associates, *Organizing for the Future: The New Logic for Managing Complex Organizations* (San Francisco: Jossey-Bass), pp. 194–26.

Coleman, J.S. (1990) *Foundations of Social Theory* (Cambridge, MA: Harvard University Press).

Collinson, D.L. (1988) 'Engineering humour': masculinity, joking and conflict in shop-floor relations, *Organization Studies*, 9(2): 181–99.

Committee on Human Factors (1990) *Distributed Decision Making: Report of a Workshop* (Washington, DC: National Academy Press).

Consalvo, C.M. (1989) Humor in management: no laughing matter, *Humor*, 2(3): 285–97.

Cooley, V.E. and Shen, J. (2000) Factors influencing applying for urban principalship, *Education and Urban Society*, 32(4): 443–54.

Cooper, B. and Boyd, W.L. (1987) The evolution of training for school administrators, in J. Murphy and P. Hallinger (eds), *Approaches to Administrative Training* (Albany, NY: SUNY Press), pp. 3–27.

Cooper, C.L. and Kelly. M. (1993) Occupational stress in head teachers: a national UK study, *British Journal of Educational Psychology*, 63: 130–43.

Cornford, F.M. (1973 [1908]) *Microcosmographia Academia* (London: Bowes and Bowes).

Coser, L.A. (1974) *Greedy Institutions: Patterns of Undivided Commitment* (New York: Free Press).

Coser, R.L. (1959) Some social functions of laughter, *Human Relations*, 12(2): 171–81.

Coser, R.L. (1960) Laughter among colleagues: a study of the social functions of humour among the staff of a mental hospital, *Psychiatry*, 23(1): 141–57.

Council of Chief State School Officers (2000) Leadership for learning in the 21st century: leadership for student achievement, responsibility and respect, http://www.ccsso.org/ projects/projects.html

Court, M. (2001) Collaborative or managerial? Reviewing studies of co-principalships and shared teacher initiatives. Paper presented to the annual conference of the British Educational Research Association (Leeds).

Cuff, E.C. and Sharrock, W.W. (1985) Meetings, in T.A. Van Dijk (ed.), *Handbook of Discourse Analysis*, vol. 3 (New York: Academic Press), pp. 149–59.

Culbertson, J.A. (1988) A century's quest for a knowledge base, in N. Boyan (ed.), *Handbook of Research on Educational Administration* (New York: Longman), pp. 3–26.

Cullingford, C. and Swift, H. (2001) Beleaguered by information? the reactions of head-teachers to school effectiveness initiatives, *Educational Review*, 53(3): 271–83.

Cunningham, K.S. and Radford, W.C. (1963) *Training the Administrator: A Study with Special Reference to Education* (Melbourne: Australian Council for Educational Research).

Csikszentmihaly, M. (1991) *Flow: The Psychology of Optimal Experience* (New York: HarperCollins).

Dann, D.T. (1991) Strategy and managerial work in hotels, *International Journal of Contemporary Hospitality Management*, 3(2): 23–5.

Davies, C. (1984) Commentary on Anton C. Zijderveld's trend report on 'The sociology of laughter and humour', *Current Sociology*, 32(1): 142–57.

Davies, P. (1999) What is evidence-based education?, *British Journal of Educational Studies*, 47(2): 108–21.

Denis, J-L., Lamothe, L. and Langley, A. (2001) The dynamics of collective leadership and strategic change in pluralistic organizations, *Academy of Management Journal*, 44(4): 809–37.

Denis, J-L., Langley, A. and Cazale, L. (1996) Leadership and strategic change under ambiguity, *Organization Studies*, 17(4): 673–99.

Donnellon, A. (1996) *Team Talk: The Power of Language in Team Dynamics* (Boston, MA: Harvard Business School Press).

Doyle, M. and Myers, V. (1999) Co-principalship: a different approach to school leader-ship, *Learning Matters*, 4(2): 33–5.

Draper, J. and McMichael, P. (2000) Secondary school identities and career decision making, *Scottish Educational Studies*, 32(2), pp. 155–67.

Dubin, R. (1979) Metaphors of leadership: an overview, in J.G. Hunt and L.L. Larson (eds), *Crosscurrents in Leadership* (Carbondale, IL: Southern Illinois University Press), pp. 225–38.

Duerst-Lahti, G. (1990) But women can play the game too: communicative control and influence in administrative decision-making, *Administration and Society*, 22(2): 185–205.

Duignan, P. (1980) Administrative behaviour of school superintendents: a descriptive study, *Journal of Educational Administration*, 18(1): 5–26.

Dunford, R. (1999) 'If you want loyalty get a dog!': loyalty, trust and the new employment contract, in S.R. Clegg, E. Ibarra-Colado and E. Bueno-Rodriquez (eds), *Global Management: Universal Theories and Local Realities* (London: Sage), pp. 68–82.

Dunphy, D. and Bryant, B. (1996) Teams: panaceas or prescriptions for improved performance, *Human Relations*, 49(5): 677–99.

Edelsky, C. (1981) Who's got the floor?, *Language in Society*, 10: 383–421.

Elmore, R.F. (2000) *Building a New Structure for School Leadership* (Washington, DC: The Albert Shanker Institute).

Emerson, J.P. (1969) Negotiating the serious import of humour, *Sociometry*, 32(2): 169–81.

Emerson, R.M. and Messenger, S.L. (1977) The micro-politics of trouble, *Social Problems*, 25(1): 121–34.

Emirbayer, M. and Mische, A. (1998) What is agency?, *American Journal of Sociology*, 103(4): 962–1023.

Engeström, Y. (1999) Expansive visibilization of work: an activity-theoretical perspective, *Computer Supported Cooperative Work*, 8(1), pp. 63–93.

Engeström, Y. and Middleton, D. (eds) (1998) *Cognition and Communication at Work* (Cambridge: Cambridge University Press).

English, F.W. (2000) Pssssst! What does one call a set of non-empirical beliefs required to be accepted on faith and enforced by authority? [Answer: a religion, aka the ISLLC standards], *International Journal of Leadership in Education*, 3(2): 159–67.

Evans, L. (1998) The effects of senior management teams on teacher morale and job satisfaction, *Educational Management and Administration*, 26(4): 417–28.

Ezzamel, M. and Willmott, H. (1998) Accounting for teamwork: a critical study of group-based systems of organizational control, *Administrative Science Quarterly*, 43(2): 358–96.

Fineman, S. (1983) Work meanings, non-work, and the taken-for-granted, *Journal of Management Studies*, 20: 143–57.

Fineman, S. (1993) Organizations as emotional arenas, in S. Fineman (ed.), *Emotion in Organizations* (London: Sage), pp. 9–35.

Fineman, S. (1999) Emotion and organizing, in S.R. Clegg and C. Hardy (eds), *Studying Organization: Theory and Method* (London: Sage), pp. 288–30.

Finholt, T. and Sproull, L.S. (1990) Electronic groups at work, *Organization Science*, 1(1): 41–64.

Follett, M.P. (1973) *Dynamic Administration: The Collected Papers of Mary Parker Follett*, Eds. E.M. Fox and L. Urwick (London: Pitman and Sons).

Fondas, N. and Stewart, R. (1994) Enactment in managerial jobs: a role analysis, *Journal of Management Studies*, 31(1): 83–103.

Francis, D.W. (1986) Some structures of negotiation talk, *Language in Society*, 15: 53–80.

Freud, S. (1957 [1916]) Those wrecked by success, in *Standard Edition of the Collected Works of Sigmund Freud*, vol. 13 (London: Hogarth Press), pp. 316–31.

Gabarro, J.J. (1978) The development of trust, influence, and expectations, in A.G. Athos and J.J. Gabarro (eds), *Interpersonal Behavior: Communication and Understanding in Relationships* (Englewood Cliffs, NJ: Prentice-Hall), pp. 290–303.

Galbraith, J.K. (1963) *The Great Crash 1929* (Harmondsworth: Penguin).

Galbraith, J.K. (1992) *The Culture of Contentment* (Boston, MA: Houghton Mifflin).

George, A.L. and George, J.L. (1964) *Woodrow Wilson and Colonel House: A Personality Study* (New York: Dover Publications).

Gersick, C.J.G. (1988) Time and transition in work teams: towards a new model of group development, *Academy of Management Journal*, 31(1): 9–41.

Gibb, C.A. (1954) Leadership, in G. Lindzey (ed.), *Handbook of Social Psychology*, vol. 2 (Reading, MA: Addison-Wesley), pp. 877–917.

Gibb, C.A. (1969) Leadership, in G. Lindzey and E. Aronson (eds), *The Handbook of Social Psychology*, vol. 4, 2nd Edn (Reading, MA: Addison-Wesley), pp. 205–83.

Goffman, E. (1961) *Asylums: Essays on the Social Situation of Mental Patients and Other Inmates* (Harmondsworth: Penguin).

Goffman, E. (1976a) *Frame Analysis: An Essay on the Organization of Experience* (Harmondsworth: Penguin).

Goffman, E. (1976b) *The Presentation of Self in Everyday Life* (repr. edn, Harmondsworth: Penguin).

Golding, J. (1986) Some problems in the concept of secretary, *International Studies of Management and Organization*, 18(1): 94–111.

Grace, G. (1995) *School Leadership: Beyond Education Management – an Essay in Policy Scholarship* (London: Falmer).

Grant, M. (1960) The technology of advisory committees, *Public Policy*, 10: 92–108.

Greenleaf (1977) *Servant Leadership: A Journey into the Nature of Legitimate Power and Greatness* (New York: Paulist Press).

Griffiths, L. (1997) Accomplishing team: teamwork and categorisation in two community mental health teams, *Sociological Review*, 45(1): 59–78.

Gronn, P. (1982) Neo-Taylorism in educational administration?, *Educational Administration Quarterly*, 18(4): 17–35.

Gronn, P. (1983) Talk as the work: the accomplishment of school administration, *Administrative Science Quarterly*, 28(1): 1–21.

Gronn, P. (1984a) 'I have a solution … ' : administrative power in a school meeting, *Educational Administration Quarterly*, 20(2): 65–93.

Gronn, P. (1984b) On studying administrators at work, *Educational Administration Quarterly*, 20(1): 115–29.

Gronn, P. (1985) Committee talk: negotiating 'personnel development' at a training college, *Journal of Management Studies*, 22(3): 245–68.

Gronn, P. (1986) Choosing a deputy head: the rhetoric and reality of administrative selection, *Australian Journal of Education*, 30(1), pp. 1–22.

Gronn, P. (1987) Obituary for structured observation, *Educational Administration Quarterly*, 23(2): 78–81.

Gronn, P. (1994) Labor pains: implementing the Australian Labor Party's policy of 'district provision and school reorganisation' in Victoria, 1989–1992, *School Organisation*, 14(1): 63–80.

Gronn, P. (1998) 'Our playmates': the culture of teaming in a human resource development unit, *Leading and Managing*, 4(4): 294–318.

Gronn, P. (1999a) Substituting for leadership: the neglected role of the leadership couple, *Leadership Quarterly*, 10(1): 41–62.

Gronn, P. (1999b) *The Making of Educational Leaders* (London: Cassell).

Gronn, P. (2000) Distributed properties: a new architecture for leadership, *Educational Management and Administration*, 28(3): 317–38.

Gronn, P. (2002a) Designer-leadership: the emerging global adoption of preparation standards, *Journal of School Leadership*, 12(5): 552–578.

Gronn, P. (2002b) Distributed leadership, in K. Leithwood, P. Hallinger, G. Furman, P. Gronn, J. MacBeath, W. Mulford and K. Riley (eds), *Second International Handbook of Educational Leadership and Administration* (Dordrecht: Kluwer). (In press)

Gronn, P. (2002c) Leader formation, in K. Leithwood, P. Hallinger, G. Furman, P. Gronn, J. Macbeath, W. Mulford and K. Riley (eds), *Second International Handbook of Educational Leadership and Administration* (Dordrecht: Kluwer). (In press)

Gronn, P. (2002d) Without leadership?, in B. Davies, and J. West-Burnham (eds), *Handbook of Educational Leadership and Management: The Ultimate Guide for Every School Leader and Manager – Key Ideas in Education Leadership and Management* (London: Pearson Education). (In press)

Gunter, H. (1999) Contracting headteachers as leaders: an analysis of the NPQH, *Cambridge Journal of Education*, 29(2): 251–64.

Gurr, D. (2000) The impact of information and communication technology on the work of school principals, *Leading and Managing*, 6(1): 63–76.

Hales, C.P. (1986) What do managers do?: a critical review of the evidence, *Journal of Management Studies*, 23(1): 88–115.

Hales, C.P. (1987) The manager's work in context: a pilot investigation of the relationship between managerial roles demands and role performance, *Personnel Review*, 16(5): 26–33.

Hales, C.P. (1989) Management processes, managerial divisions of labour and management work: towards a synthesis, *International Journal of Sociology and Social Policy*, 9(5–6): 9–38.

Hales, C. and Tamangani, Z. (1996) An investigation of the relationship between organizational structure, managerial role expectations and managers' work activities, *Journal of Management Studies*, 33(6): 731–56.

Hall, V. (1997) Leadership and team learning, *School Leadership and Management*, 17(3): 327–9.

Hall, V. (2001) Management teams in education: an unequal music, *School Leadership and Management*, 21(3): 327–41.

Hall, V. and Southworth, G. (1997) Headship, *School Leadership and Management*, 17(2): 151–70.

Hall, V. and Wallace, M. (1996) Let the team take the strain: lessons from research into senior management teams in secondary schools, *School Organisation*, 16(3): 297–308.

Hambrick, D.C. (1994) Top management groups: a conceptual integration and reconsideration of the 'team' label, in B.M. Staw and L.L. Cumming (eds), *Research in Organizational Behavior*, vol. 16 (Greenwich, CT: JAI Press), pp. 171–213.

Hambrick, D.C. (1995) Fragmentation and the other problems CEOs have with their top management teams, *California Management Review*, 37(3): 110–27.

Hambrick, D.C. and Mason, P.A. (1984) Upper echelons: the organization as a reflection of its top managers, *Academy of Management Review*, 9(2): 193–206.

Hanak, I. (1998) Chairing meetings: turn and topic control in development communication in rural Zanzibar, *Discourse and Society*, 9(1): 35–56.

't Hart, P. (1991) Irving L. Janis' *Victims of Groupthink, Political Psychology*, 12(2): 247–78.

Hatch, M.J. (1997) Irony and the social construction of contradiction in the humor of a management team, *Organization Science*, 8(3): 275–88.

Hay Group (2000) *Excellence in School Leadership: Creating a First Class Learning Environment – a Report on a Study of the Characteristics of Outstanding School Leaders in Victorian Schools* (Melbourne: Department of Education, Employment and Training).

Hayek, F.A. (1945) The use of knowledge in society, *American Economic Review*, 35(4): 519–30.

Hayek, F.A. (1994 [1944]) *The Road to Serfdom* (Chicago: University of Chicago Press).

Heenan, D.A. and Bennis, W. (1999) *Co-Leaders: The Power of Great Partnerships* (New York: John Wiley and Sons).

Heller, M.F. and Firestone, W.A. (1995) Who's in charge here?: sources of leadership for change in eight schools, *Elementary School Journal*, 96(1): 65–86.

Hewitt, J.P. and Stokes, R. (1975) Disclaimers, *American Sociological Review*, 40(1): 1–11.

Hochschild, A.R. (1983) *The Managed Heart: Commercialization of Human Feeling* (Berkeley, CA: University of Los Angeles Press).

Hochschild, A.R. (1997) *The Time Bind: When Work Becomes Home and Home Becomes Work* (New York: H. Holt and Co.).

Hodgson, R.C., Levinson, D.J. and Zaleznik, A. (1965) *The Executive Role Constellation: An Analysis of Personality and Role Relations in Management* (Boston, MA: Harvard University, Graduate School of Business Administration).

Hood, C. (1995) The 'new public management' in the 1980s: variations on a theme, *Accounting, Organizations and Society*, 20(2/3): 93–109.

Horne, J.M. and Lupton, T. (1965) The work activities of middle managers: an exploratory study, *Journal of Management Studies*, 2(1): 14–33.

Hosking, D.-M. (1988) Organizing, leadership and skilful process, *Journal of Management Studies*, 25(2): 147–66.

Hultman, G. (2001) Leading cultures: a study of 'acting in concert' and the creation of meaning in school leaders' work activities, *International Journal of Leadership in Education*, 4(2): 137–48.

Hunt, J.G. (1991) *Leadership: A New Synthesis* (Newbury Park, CA: Sage).

Hunt, J.G. and Dodge, G.E. (2001) Leadership déjà vu all over again, *Leadership Quarterly*, 11(4): 435–58.

Hutchins, E. (1996) *Cognition in the Wild* (Cambridge, MA: MIT Press).

Ilgen, D.R., Major, D.A., Hollenbeck, J.R. and Sego, D.J. (1993) Team research in the 1990s, in M.M. Chemers and R.A. Ayman (eds), *Leadership Theory and Research: Perspectives and Directions* (San Diego, CA: Academic Press), pp. 245–32.

Interstate School Leaders Licensure Consortium (1996) *Standards for School Leaders* (Council of Chief State School Officers) hhtp://www.ccsso.org/isllc.html

Jackson, P.W. (1977) Loneliness at the top, *School Review*, 85(3): 425–32.

Jacobsson, B. (2000) Standardization and expert knowledge, in N. Brunsson, B. Jacobsson and associates, *A World of Standards* (Oxford: Oxford University Press), pp. 40–9.

Jacoby, S.M. (1999) Are career jobs headed for extinction?, *California Management Review*, 42(1): 123–45.

James, C. and Vince, R. (2001) Developing the leadership capabilities of headteachers, *Educational Management and Administration*, 29(3): 307–17.

Janis, I. (1982) *Groupthink: Psychological Studies of Policy Decisions and Fiascoes*, 2nd edn (Boston, MA: Houghton Mifflin).

Jaques, E. (1957) Social systems as a defence against persecutory and depressive anxiety, in M. Klein, P. Heimann and R.E. Money-Kyrle (eds), *New Directions in Psycho-Analysis* (New York: Basic Books), pp. 478–98.

Jaques, E. (1970) *Work, Creativity and Social Justice* (London: Tavistock).

Jeffrey, B. and Woods, P. (1996) Feeling deprofessionalised: the social construction of emotions during an OFSTED inspection, *Cambridge Journal of Education*, 26(3): 325–43.

Jenkins, A. (1994) Teams: from 'ideology' to analysis, *Organization Studies*, 15(6): 849–60.

Jones, N. (1999) The real world management preoccupations of primary school heads, *School Leadership and Management*, 19(4): 483–95.

Jones, N. and Connolly, M. (2001) Construing systems of management among primary teachers: moving forward from work activity studies, *Educational Management and Administration*, 29(3): 319–32.

Kahn, W.A. (1992) To be fully there: psychological presence at work, *Human Relations*, 45(4): 321–49.

Kanter, R.M. (1989) The new managerial work, *Harvard Business Review*, 67(6): 85–92.

Kaplan, R.E. (1990) The expansive executive: how the drive to mastery helps and hinders organizations, *Human Resource Management*, 24(1): 307–26.

Kasl, E., Marsick, V.J. and Dechant, K. (1997) Teams as learners: a research-based model of team learning, *Journal of Applied Behavioral Science* 33(2): 227–46.

Katzenbach, J.R. (1997) The myth of the top management team, *Harvard Business Review*, 75(6): 83–91.

Keller, E. (1981) Gambits: Conversational strategy signals, in F. Coulmas (ed.), *Conversational Routine* (Hague: Mouton), pp. 93–113.

Kerr, S. and Jermier, J. (1978) Substitutes for leadership: their meaning and measurement, *Organization and Human Performance*, 22: 374–403.

Kets de Vries, M.F.R. (1990) The organizational fool: balancing a leader's hubris, *Human Relations*, 43(8): 751–70.

Kets de Vries, M.F.R. (1992) The motivating role of envy: a forgotten factor in management theory, *Administration and Society*, 24(1): 41–60.

Kotter, J. (1982) *The General Managers* (New York: Free Press).

Krantz, J. (1989) The managerial couple: superior-subordinate relationships as a unit of analysis, *Human Resource Management*, 28: 161–75.

Kruse, S.D. and Louis, K.S. (1997) Teacher teaming in middle schools: dilemmas for a schoolwide community, *Educational Administration Quarterly*, 33(2): 261–89.

Kurke, L.B. and Aldrich, H. (1983) Mintzberg was right! A replication and extension of *The Nature of Managerial Work*, *Management Science*, 29(8): 975–84.

Langley, J. and Pruitt, D.G. (1980) Groupthink: a critique of Janis's theory, *Review of Personality and Social Psychology*, 1(1): 74–93.

Larson, L.L., Burssom, R.S., Vicars, W. and Jauch, L. (1986) Proactive *versus* reactive manager: is the dichotomy realistic?, *Journal of Management Studies*, 23(4): 385–400.

Latham, A.S. and Pearlman, M.A. (1999) From standards to licensure: developing an authentic assessment for school principals, *Journal of Personnel Evaluation in Education*, 13(3): 245–62.

Laws, J.F. and Dennison, W.F. (1990) Researching the role of the primary school head: a limited base for promoting managerial self-development, *Educational Studies*, 16(3): 269–80.

Leithwood, K., Steinbach, R. and Ryan, S. (1997) Leadership and team learning in secondary schools, *School Leadership and Management*, 17(3): 303–25.

Lembke, S. and Wilson, M.G. (1998) Putting the 'team' into teamwork: alternative theoretical contributions for contemporary management practice, *Human Relations*, 51(7): 927–44.

Leont'ev, A.N. (1978) *Activity, Consciousness and Personality*, transl. M.J. Hall (Englewood Cliffs, NJ: Prentice-Hall).

Leont'ev, A.N. (1981) *Problems of the Development of the Mind* (Moscow: Progress Publishers).

Levačić, R. and Glatter, R. (2001) 'Really good ideas?': developing evidence-informed policy and practice in educational leadership and management, *Educational Management and Administration*, 29(1): 5–25.

Limerick, B. and Anderson, C. (1999) Female administrators and school-based management, *Educational Management and Administration*, 27(4): 401–14.

Lipman-Blumen, J. and H.J. Leavitt (1999) *Hot Groups: Seeding Them, Feeding Them, and Using Them to Ignite your Organization* (New York: Oxford University Press).

Locke, R.R. (1984) *The End of the Practical Man: Entrepreneurship and Higher Education in Germany, France and Great Britain, 1880–1940* (Greenwich, CT: JAI Press).

Louden, W. and Wildy, H. (1999a) 'Circumstance and proper timing': Context and the construction of a standards framework for school principals' performance, *Educational Administration Quarterly*, 35(3): 397–422.

Louden, W. and Wildy, H. (1999b) Short shrift to long lists: an alternative approach to the development of performance standards for school principals, *Journal of Educational Administration*, 37(2): 99–121.

Luthans, F., Rosenkrantz, S.A. and Heennessey, H.W. (1985) What do successful managers really do? An observation study of managerial activities, *Journal of Applied Behavioral Science*, 21(3): 255–270.

Luthans, F., Welsh, D.H.B. and Rosenkrantz, S.A. (1993) What do Russian managers really do? An observational study with comparisons to US managers, *Journal of International Business Studies*, 24(4): 741–61.

Maguire, M., Ball, S.J. and Macrae, S. (2001) 'In all our interests': internal marketing at Northwark Park School, *British Journal of Sociology of Education*, 22(1): 35–50.

Malone, T.W. and Crowston, K. (1994) The interdisciplinary study of coordination, *ACM Computing Surveys*, 26(1): 87–119.

Manz, C.C. (1986) Self-leadership: toward an expanded theory of self-influence processes in organizations, *Academy of Management Review*, 11(3): 585–600.

Manz, C.C. and Sims, H.P. (1980) Self-management as a substitute for leadership: a social learning theory perspective, *Academy of Management Review*, 5(3): 361–7.

Manz, C.C. and Sims, H.P. (1984) Searching for the 'unleader': organizational member views on leading self-managed groups, *Human Relations*, 37(5): 409–24.

Manz, C.C. and Sims, H.P. (1987) Leading workers to lead themselves: the external leadership of self-managing work teams, *Administrative Science Quarterly*, 32(1): 106–28.

Manz, C.C. and Sims, H.P. (1992), Self-leading work teams: moving beyond self-management myths, *Human Relations*, 45(11): 1119–40.

Manz, C.C., Mossholder, K.W. and Luthans, F. (1987) An integrated perspective of self-control in organizations, *Administration and Society*, 19(1): 3–24.

March, J.G. (1984) How we talk and how we act: administrative theory and administrative life, in T.J. Sergiovanni and J.E. Corbally (eds), *Leadership and Organizational Culture: New Perspectives on Administrative Theory and Practice* (Chicago: University of Illinois Press), pp. 18–35.

March, J.G. and Simon, H.A. (1958) *Organizations* (New York: John Wiley and Sons).

Markham, S.E. and Markham, I.S. (1995) Self-management and self-leadership re-examined: a levels-of-analysis perspective, *Leadership Quarterly*, 6(3): 343–59.

Martin, W.J. and Willower, D.J. (1981) The managerial behavior of high school principals, *Education Administration Quarterly*, 17(1): 69–90.

Martinko, M.J. and Gardner, W.L. (1985) Beyond structured observation: Methodological issues and new directions, *Academy of Management Review*, 10(4): 676–95.

Martinko, M.J. and Gardner, W.L. (1990) Structured observation of managerial work: A replication and synthesis, *Journal of Management Studies*, 27(3): 329–57.

Masuch, M. (1985) Vicious circles in organizations, *Administrative Science Quarterly*, 30(1): 14–33.

McCarthy, M.M. (1998) The evolution of educational leadership preparation programs, in J. Murphy and K. Seashore Louis (eds), *Handbook of Research on Educational Administration*, 2nd edn (San Francisco: Jossey-Bass), pp. 119–39.

McCulloch, G. (1991) *Philosophers and Kings: Education for Leadership in Modern England* (Cambridge: Cambridge University Press).

McLeod, G.T. (1984) The work of school board chief executive officers, *Canadian Journal of Education*, 9(2): 171–90.

Mealyea, R. (1989) Humour as a coping strategy in the transition from tradesperson to teacher, *British Journal of Sociology of Education*, 10(3): 311–33.

Mechling, E.W. and Mechling, J. (1985) Shock talk: from consensual to contractual joking relationships in the bureaucratic workplace, *Human Organization*, 44(4): 339–43.

Miller, E.J. (1998) The leader with the vision: is time running out?, in E.B. Klein, F. Gabelnick and P. Herr (eds), *The Psychodynamics of Leadership* (Madison, CT: Psychosocial Press), pp. 3–25.

Mintzberg, H. (1973) *The Nature of Managerial Work* (New York: Harper and Row).

Mirvis, P.M. (2000) 'Soul work' in organizations, in P.J. Frost, A.Y. Lewin and R.L. Daft (eds), *Talking about Organization Science: Debates and Dialogue from Crossroads* (Thousand Oaks, CA: Sage), pp. 267–91.

Mohamed, A.A. and Wiebe, F.A. (1996) Towards a process theory of groupthink, *Small Group Behavior*, 27(3): 416–30.

Moorhead, G., Ference, R. and Neck, C.P. (1991) Group decision fiascoes continue: space shuttle Challenger and a revised groupthink framework, *Human Relations*, 44(6): 539–50.

Morgenthaler, L. (1990) A study of group process: who's got WHAT floor?, *Journal of Pragmatics*, 14(6): 537–57.

Morrill, C. (1991) Conflict management, honor, and organizational change, *American Journal of Sociology*, 97(3): 585–621.

Mouzelis, N.P. (1991) *Back to Sociological Theory: The Construction of Social Orders* (New York: St. Martin's Press).

Moyle, C.R.J. and Andrews, K.C. (1987) The Institute of Educational Administration in Australia, in J. Murphy and P. Hallinger (eds), *Approaches to Administrative Training* (Albany, NY: Suny Press), pp. 164–81.

Murnighan, J.K. and Conlon, D. (1991) The dynamics of intense work groups: a study of British string quartets, *Administrative Science Quarterly*, 36(2): 165–86.

Murphy, J. (1990) Preparing school administrators for the twenty-first century: the reform agenda, in B. Mitchell and L.L Cunningham (eds), *Educational Leadership and Changing Contexts of Families, Communities and Schools* (Chicago: University of Chicago Press), pp. 232–51.

Murphy, J. (1998) Preparation for the school principalship: the United States' story, *School Leadership and Management*, 18(3): 359–72.

Murphy, J. (2000) A response to English, *International Journal of Leadership in Education*, 3(4): 411–14.

Murphy, J. and Shipman, N. (1999) The Interstate School Leaders Licensure Consortium: a standards-based approach to strengthening educational leadership, *Journal of Personnel Evaluation in Education*, 13(3): 205–24.

Murphy, J., Yff, J. and Shipman, N. (2000) Implementation of the Interstate School Leaders Licensure Consortium standards, *International Journal of Leadership in Education*, 3(1): 17–39.

Myers, F.R. (1986) Reflections on a meeting: structure, language, and the policy in a small-scale society, *American Ethnologist*, 13(3): 430–47.

Neck, C.P. and Manz, C.C. (1994) From groupthink to teamthink: towards the creation of constructive thought patterns in self-managing work teams, *Human Relations*, 47(8): 929–52.

Neck, C.P. and Moorhead, G. (1992) Jury deliberations in the trial of U.S. v. John DeLorean: a case analysis of groupthink avoidance and an enhanced framework, *Human Relations*, 45(10): 1077–91.

Neck, C.P. and Moorhead, G. (1995) Groupthink remodeled: the importance of leadership, time pressure, and methodical decision-making procedures, *Human Relations*, 48(5): 537–57.

Neumann, A. (1991) The thinking team: toward a cognitive model of administrative team-work in higher education, *Journal of Higher Education*, 62(5): 485–13.

Newton, P.M. and Levinson, D.J. (1973) The work group within the organization: a sociopsychological approach, *Psychiatry*, 36: 115–42.

Noordegraaf, M. and Stewart, R. (2000) Managerial behaviour research in private and public sectors: distinctiveness, disputes and directions, *Journal of Management Studies*, 37(3): 427–43.

O'Donnell, K. (1990) Difference and dominance: how labor and management talk conflict, in A.D. Grimshaw (ed.), *Conflict Talk: Sociolinguistic Investigations of Arguments in Conversations* (Cambridge: Cambridge University Press), pp. 210–40.

Organ, D.W. (1990) The motivational basis of organizational citizenship behavior, in B.M. Staw and L.L. Cummings (eds), *Research in Organizational Behavior*, vol. 12 (Greenwich, CT: JAI Press), pp. 43–72.

Osborne, D. and Gaebler, T. (1993) *Reinventing Government: How the Entrepreneurial Spirit is Transforming the Public Sector* (Harmondsworth: Plume).

Owens, D.A. and Sutton, R. (2001) Status contests in meetings: negotiating the informal order, in M.E. Turner (ed.), *Groups at Work: Theory and Research* (Mahwah, NJ: Lawrence Erlbaum Associates), pp. 299–316.

Paap, W.R. and Hanson, B. (1982) Unobtrusive power: interaction between health providers and consumers at council meetings, *Urban Life*, 10(4): 409–31.

Perkin, H. (1990) *The Rise of Professional Society: England since 1880* (London: Routledge).

Peterson, K.D. (1978) The principal's tasks, *Administrator's Notebook*, 26(8): 1–4.

Pettigrew, A.M. (1992) On studying managerial elites, *Strategic Management Journal*, 13 (special): 163–82.

Pierson, P.R. and Bredeson, P.V. (1993) It's not just a laughing matter: school principals' use of humor in interpersonal communications with teachers, *Journal of School Leadership*, 3(5): 522–33.

Pirrie, A. (2001) Evidence-based practice in education: the best medicine?, *British Journal of Educational Studies*, 49(2): 124–36.

Pounder, D.G. and Merrill, R.J. (2001) Job desirability of the high school principalship: a job choice theory perspective, *Educational Administration Quarterly*, 37(1): 27–57.

Powell, M. (1997) The Whitlam labor government: Barnard and Whitlam: a significant historical dyad, *Australian Journal of Politics and History*, 43: 183–99.

Power, M. (2001) *The Audit Society: Rituals of Verification* (Oxford: Oxford University Press).

Rafaeli, A. and Sutton, R.I. (1989) The expression of emotion in organizational life, in L.L. Cummings and B.M. Staw (eds), *Research in Organizational Behavior*, vol. 11 (Greenwich, CT: JAI Press), pp. 1–42.

Reich, R.B. (1987) Entrepreneurship reconsidered: the team as hero, *Harvard Business Review*, 65(3): 77–83.

Richardson, E. (1977) *The Teacher, the School and the Task of Management* (London: Heinemann).

Riehl, C. (1998) We gather together: work, discourse, and constitutive social action in elementary school faculty meetings, *Educational Administration Quarterly*, 34(1): 91–125.

Riseborough, G. (1993) Primary headship, state policy and the challenge of the 1990s: an exceptional story that disproves total hegemonic rule, *Journal of Educational Policy*, 8(2): 155–73.

Rost, J.C. (1993) *Leadership for the Twenty-First Century* (Westport, CT: Praeger).

Sachs, J. and Blackmore, J. (1998) You never show you can't cope: women in school leadership roles managing their emotions, *Gender and Education*, 10(3): 265–79.

Salem, M., Lazarus, H. and Cullen, J. (1992) Developing self-managing teams: structure and performance, *Academy of Management Review*, 11(3): 24–32.

Sandelands, L. and St. Clair, L. (1993) Towards an empirical concept of group, *Journal for the Theory of Social Behavior*, 23(4): 423–58.

Sayer, A. (1992) *Method in Social Science: A Realist Approach*, 2nd edn (London: Routledge).

Sayer, A. (2000) *Realism and Social Science* (London: Sage).

Sayer, A. and Walker, R. (1992) *The New Social Economy: Reworking the Division of Labor* (London: Blackwell).

Sayles, L.R. (1964) *Managerial Behavior: Administration in Complex Organizations* (New York: McGraw-Hill).

Schwartzman, H.B. (1986) The meeting as a neglected social form in organizational studies, in B.M. Staw and L.L. Cummings (eds), *Research in Organizational Behavior*, vol. 8 (Greenwich CT: JAI Press), pp. 233–58.

Schwartzman, H.B. (1987) The significance of meetings in an American mental health center, *American Ethnologist*, 14(2): 271–94.

Schwartzman, H.B. (1989) *The Meeting: Gatherings in Organizations and Communities* (New York: Plenum Press).

Scott, A. (2000) Exploitation or exploration? Secondary school administrative team learning, in K. Leithwood (ed.), *Understanding Schools as Intelligent Systems* (Stamford, CT: JAI Press), pp. 75–95.

Scott, M.B. and Lyman, S.M. (1968) Accounts, *American Sociological Review*, 33(1): 46–62.

Senge, P. (1993) *The Fifth Discipline: The Art and Practice of the Learning Organization* (Sydney: Random House).

Sennett, R. (1998) *The Corrosion of Character: The Personal Consequences of Work in the New Capitalism* (New York: W.W. Norton).

Sennett, R. (2002) A short, flat community of broken eggs, *Australian Financial Review*, 4 January.

Sergiovanni, T.J. (1984) Leadership and excellence in schooling: excellent schools need freedom within boundaries, *Educational Leadership*, 41(5): 4–14.

Sewell, G. (1998) The discipline of teams: the control of team-based industrial work through electronic and peer surveillance, *Administrative Science Quarterly*, 43(2): 397–428.

Shapin, S. (1989) The invisible technician, *American Scientist*, 77(6): 554–63.

Shenkar, O., Ronen, S., Shefy, E. and Chow, I.H-S. (1998) The role structure of Chinese managers, *Human Relations*, 51(1): 51–72.

Simon, H.A. (1976 [1945]) *Administrative Behavior: A Study of Decision-Making Processes in Administrative Organization* (New York: Free Press).

Simon, H.A. (1991) Organizations and markets, *Journal of Economic Perspectives*, 5(2): 25–44.

Sinclair, A. (1995) The seduction of the self-managed team and the reinvention of the team-as-group, *Leading and Managing*, 1(1): 44–62.

Sinclair, A. Baird, J. and Alford, J. (1993) What do chief administrators do? Findings from Victoria, *Australian Journal of Public Administration*, 52(1): 12–24.

Siskin, L. (1994) *Realms of Knowledge: Academic Departments in Secondary School* (London: Falmer).

Smith, K.K. (1989) The movement of conflict in organisations: the joint dynamics of splitting and triangulation, *Administrative Science Quarterly*, 34(1): 1–20.

Smith, V. (1997) New forms of work organisation, *Annual Review of Sociology*, 23: 315–29.

Spillane, J.P., Halverson, R. and Diamond, J.B. (2000a) Investigating school leadership practice: a distributed perspective, *Educational Researcher*, 30(3): 23–8.

Spillane, J.P., Halverson, R. and Diamond, J.B. (2000b) Towards a theory of leadership practice: a distributed perspective, Working Paper, Institute for Policy Research, Northwestern University.

Sproull, L.S. (1981) Managing educational programs: a micro-behavioral analysis, *Human Organization*, 40(2): 113–22.

Stewart, R. (1982) A model for understanding managerial jobs and behaviour, *Academy of Management Review*, 7(1): 7–13.

Stewart, R. (1988) *Managers and their Jobs: A Study of the Similarities and Differences in the Ways Managers Spend their Time*, 2nd edn (London: Macmillan).

Stewart, R. (1989) Studies of managerial jobs and behaviour: the ways forward, *Journal of Management Studies*, 26(1): 1–10.

Stewart, R. (1991a) Chairmen and chief executives: an exploration of their relationship, *Journal of Management Studies*, 28(5): 511–27.

Stewart, R. (1991b) Role sharing at the top: a neglected aspect of studies of managerial behaviour, in S. Carlson, *Executive Behaviour (reprinted with contributions from Henry Mintzberg and Rosemary Stewart)* (Uppsala: Studia Oeconomiae Negotiorum), pp. 120–36.

Strauss, A.L. (1985) Work and the division of labor, *Sociological Quarterly*, 26(1): 1–19.

Strauss, A.L. (1988) The articulation of project work: an organizational process, *Sociological Quarterly*, 29(2): 163–78.

Street, M.D. (1997) Groupthink: an examination of theoretical issues, implications, and future research suggestions, *Small Group Research*, 28(1), pp. 72–93.

Suchman, L. (1995) Making work visible, *Communications of the ACM*, 38(9): 56–64.

Tannenbaum, R.J. (1999) Laying the groundwork for a licensure agreement, *Journal of Personnel Evaluation in Education*, 13(3): 225–44.

Task Group on Training and Development of School Heads (1999) *Leadership Training program for Principals: Consultation Paper*, http://www.info.gov.hk/ed/english/resources/consultation_paper/leadership_training.htm

Teacher Training Agency (1998) *National Standards for Headteachers* (London: Teacher Training Agency).

Thomas, A.R., Willis, Q. and Phillips, D. (1981) Observational studies of Australian school administrators: methodological issues, *Australian Journal of Education*, 25(1): 55–72.

Thomson, P. (2001) How principals lose 'face': a disciplinary tale of educational administration and modern managerialism, *Discourse*, 22(1): 5–22.

Thompson, J.D. (1967) *Organizations in Action: Social Science Bases of Administrative Theory* (New York: McGraw-Hill).

Thompson, S.D. (1999) Causing change: The National Policy Board for Educational Administration, in J. Murphy and P.B. Forsyth (eds), *Educational Administration: A Decade of Reform* (Thousand Oaks, CA: Corwin Press), pp. 93–114.

Tomer, J.F. (1998) Organizational capital and joining-up: linking the individual to the organization and society, *Human Relations*, 51(6): 825–46.

Townsend, A.M., DeMarie, S.M. and Hendrickson, A.R. (1998) Virtual teams: technology and the workplace of the future, *Academy of Management Executive*, 12(3): 17–29.

Tsoukas, H. (1996) The firm as a distributed knowledge system: a constructionist approach, *Strategic Management Journal*, 17 (Winter special issue): 11–25.

Tyack, D. and Hansot, E. (1982) *Managers of Virtue: Public School Leadership in America, 1820–1980* (New York: Basic Books).

Van Vree, W. (1999) *Meetings, Manners and Civilization: The Development of Modern Meeting Behaviour* (Leicester: Leicester University Press).

Vanderslice, V.J. (1988) Separating leadership from followers: an assessment of the effect of leader and follower roles in organizations, *Human Relations*, 41(9): 677–96.

Vicinus, M. (1985) *Independent Women: Work and Community for Single Women, 1850–1920* (London: Virago).

Vygotsky, L.S. (1978) *Mind in Society: The Development of Higher Psychological Processes*, eds. M. Cole, V. John-Steiner, S. Scribner and E. Souberman (Cambridge, MA: Harvard University Press).

Wajcman, J. and Martin, B. (2001) My company or my career: managerial achievement and loyalty, *British Journal of Sociology*, 52(4): 559–78.

Walker, B. (1998) Meetings without communication: a study of parents' evenings in secondary schools, *British Educational Research Journal*, 24(2): 163–78.

Wallace, M. (1998) A counter-policy to subvert education reform: collaboration among schools and colleges in a competitive climate, *British Educational Research Journal*, 24(2): 195–215.

Wallace, M. (2001a) 'Really good ideas?': developing evidence-informed policy and practice in educational leadership and management: a 'rejoinder' to Rosalind Levačić and Ron Glatter, *Educational Management and Administration*, 29(1): 27–34.

Wallace, M. (2001b) Sharing leadership of schools through teamwork: a justifiable risk?, *Educational Management and Administration*, 29(2): 153–67.

Wallace, M. and Hall, V. (1994) *Inside the SMT: Teamwork in Secondary School Management* (London: Paul Chapman Publishing).

Wallace, M. and Huckman, L. (1996) Senior management teams in large primary schools: a headteacher's solution to the complexities of post-reform management?, *School Organisation*, 16(3): 309–23.

Wallace, M. and Huckman, L. (1999) *Senior Management Teams in Primary Schools: The Quest for Synergy* (London: Routledge).

Watkins, P. (1993) Finding time: temporal considerations in the operation of school committees, *British Journal of Sociology of Education*, 14(2): 131–46.

Webb, R. and Vulliamy, G. (1996) A deluge of directives: conflict between collegiality and managerialism in the post-ERA primary school, *British Educational Research Journal*, 22(4): 441–58.

Weick, K. (1982) Managerial thought in the context of action, in S. Srivastva and associates (eds), *The Executive Mind* (San Francisco: Jossey-Bass), pp. 221–42.

Weick, K.E. (1974) Review of *The Nature of Managerial Work*, *Administrative Science Quarterly*, 19: 111–18.

Weick, K.E. and Roberts, K.H. (1995) Collective mind in organizations: heedful interrelating on flight decks, *Administrative Science Quarterly*, 38(3): 357–81.

Wenger, E. (1999) *Communities of Practice: Learning, Meaning, and Identity* (Cambridge: Cambridge University Press).

Wenger, E. (2000) Communities of practice and social learning systems, *Organization*, 7(2): 225–46.

Whitley, R. (1989) On the nature of managerial tasks and skills: their distinguishing characteristics and organization, *Journal of Management Studies*, 26(3): 209–24.

Whyte, G. (1989) Groupthink reconsidered, *Academy of Management Review*, 14(1): 40–56.

Whyte, W.H. (1963) *The Organization Man* (Harmondsworth: Penguin).

Williams, R. (1995) Teamwork and group maintenance: collusion and collaboration in the team-that-builds-itself, *Leading and Managing*, 1(3): 226–37.

Williams, T.R. (2001) *Unrecognized Exodus, Unaccepted Accountability: The Looming Shortage of Principals and Vice Principals in Ontario Public School Boards*, Working Paper 24, School of Policy Studies, Queens University, Toronto.

Willis, Q. (1980) The work activity of school principals: an observational study, *Journal of Educational Administration*, 18(1): 27–54.

Willmott, H. (1987) Studying managerial work: a critique and a proposal, *Journal of Management Studies*, 24(3): 249–70.

Willmott, H. (1984) Images and ideals of managerial work: a critical examination of conceptual and empirical accounts, *Journal of Management Studies*, 21: 349–68.

Winnicott, D.W. (1986) The value of depression, in C. Winnicott, R. Shepherd and M. Davis (eds), *Home is Where We Start From: Essays by a Psychoanalyst* (Harmondsworth: Penguin), pp. 71–9.

Wood, A.H. (1976) Methodist Ladies' College, Melbourne, 1939–1966: A personal memoir, in S. Murray-Smith (ed.), *Melbourne Studies in Education, 1976* (Melbourne: Melbourne University Press), pp. 255–76.

Woods, P. (1979) *The Divided School* (London: Routledge and Kegan Paul).

Young, M.D. and McLeod, S. (2001) Flukes, opportunities, and planned interventions: factors affecting women's decisions to become school administrators, *Educational Administration Quarterly*, 37(4): 462–502.

Yukl, G. (1999) An evaluation of conceptual weaknesses in transformational and charismatic leadership theories, *Leadership Quarterly*, 10(2), pp. 285–305.

Zainu'ddin, A.T. (1981) The career of a colonial schoolmaster: Frank Wheen esq. B.A. (1857–1933), in S. Murray-Smith (ed.), *Melbourne Studies in Education 1981* (Melbourne: Melbourne University Press), pp. 60–97.

Zaleznik, A. (1964) Managerial behavior and interpersonal competence, *Behavioral Science*, 9(2): 155–66.

Zaleznik, A. (1967) The management of disappointment, *Harvard Business Review*, 45(6): 59–70.

Zaleznik, A. (1989) The mythological structure of organizations and its impact, *Human Resource Management*, 28(2): 267–77.

Zaleznik, A. (1990) *Executive's Guide to Motivating People: How Freudian Theory can Turn Good Executives into Better Leaders* (Chicago: Bonus Books).

Zijderveld, A.C. (1983) The sociology of humour and laughter, *Current Sociology*, 31(3): 1–100.

Index